SOLDIERS OF SONG

SOLDIERS OF SONG
The Dumbells and Other Canadian Concert Parties of the First World War

Jason Wilson

WILFRID LAURIER
UNIVERSITY PRESS

This book has been published with the help of a grant from the Canadian Federation for the Humanities and Social Sciences, through the Aid to Scholarly Publications Program, using funds provided by the Social Sciences and Humanities Research Council of Canada. Wilfrid Laurier University Press acknowledges the financial support of the Government of Canada through the Canada Book Fund for its publishing activities.

Library and Archives Canada Cataloguing in Publication

Wilson, Jason, 1970–
      Soldiers of song : the Dumbells and other Canadian concert parties of the First World War / Jason Wilson.

Includes bibliographical references and index.
Also available in electronic formats.
ISBN 978-1-55458-844-2

      1. Dumbells (Musical group). 2. Revues—20th century—History and criticism. 3. World War, 1914–1918—Music and the war. 4. Popular music—Canada—1911–1920. 5. Popular music—Canada—1921–1930. I. Title.

ML3484.W749 2012   792.70904   C2012-904283-8

————

Electronic monograph in PDF and EPUB formats.
Also available in print format.
ISBN 978-1-55458-882-4 (PDF).—ISBN 978-1-55458-883-1 (EPUB)

      1. Dumbells (Musical group). 2. World War, 1914–1918—Music and the war. 3. Revues—20th century—History and criticism. 4. Popular music—Canada—1911–1920. 5. Popular music—Canada—1921–1930. I. Title.

ML3484.W749 2012   792.70904   C2012-904284-6

Cover design by Martyn Schmoll. Front-cover image of the Dumbells onstage courtesy of John McLaren. Text design by Angela Booth Malleau.

© 2012 Wilfrid Laurier University Press
Waterloo, Ontario, Canada
www.wlupress.wlu.ca

RECYCLED
Paper made from
recycled material
FSC   FSC® C103567

This book is printed on FSC recycled paper and is certified Ecologo. It is made from 100% post-consumer fibre, processed chlorine free, and manufactured using biogas energy.

Printed in Canada

Contents

List of Figures vii

I   Introduction 1
II   The Music Hall and Beyond 9
III   In the Interest of Morale: The Dumbells and the Development
    of the Canadian Concert Party 35
IV   Only a Soldier Knows: The War and Humour 75
V   The Canadian Concert-Party Experience 95
VI   The Dumbells in Peace 131

Note on Sources and Acknowledgements 153

Appendices
A   *Dramatis Personae*: CEF Concert-Party Entertainers of WWI ... 157
B   Notable Concert Parties of the CEF and BEF 161
C   Important Casts of the CEF Concert Parties 163
D   Postwar Concert Party Revues 165
E   North American Tour Itineraries 167
F   Catalogue of Dumbells Sheet Music 173
G   Catalogue of Dumbells-Related Music 177
H   Miscellaneous Songs 179
I   Important British Music-Hall Revues 181

Notes 183
Bibliography 211
Index 231

List of Figures

1   Jack Ayre holding court   3
2   Jack Grace and Bell Allen in *Carry On*, c. 1922   12
3   Sheet-music cover of "Oh! It's a Lovely War"   14
4   Five players, c. 1920   21
5   Bill Tennent in *H.M.S. Pinafore*, c. 1920   31
6   Al Plunkett, crooner   34
7   Jack Holland, 1920   39
8   Jack McLaren, c. 1915   42
9   Captain Merton Plunkett   48
10 The "Y" hut, 1916   49
11 Charlie McLean as female impersonator   53
12 Alan Murray, c. 1920   55
13 Dumbells in uniform   57
14 Bill Cunningham   59
15 Al Plunkett and Ross Hamilton, c. 1918   61
16 Jack McLaren and T.J. Lilly in performance, 1918   64
17 Pianist N. Nicholson and Bill Filson, 1918   65
18 Soldiers await a Dumbells performance, 1918   66
19 Leonard Young, Al Plunkett, Bill Tennant, Jerry Brayford, 1921   68
20 The Dumbells in *H.M.S. Pinafore*, 1920   71
21 Bertram Langley in *H.M.S. Pinafore*, 1920   72
22 Ted Charter delivers his "Kit Inspection"   87
23 The Dumbells in "The Duchess Entertains"   101
24 Leonard Young as the Duchess   102
25 T.J. Lilly   115

26 Sheet-music cover of Jack Ayre's "Dumbell Rag," c. 1920   116
27 Ross Hamilton as Majorie, with suitors   117
28 Alan Murray as Marie, c. 1919   123
29 Ross Hamilton as Marjorie, c. 1919   123
30 The Dumbells on Broadway, 1921   133
31 The Dumbells onstage in Toronto, 1919   134
32 Pat Rafferty before he joined the Dumbells   138
33 Morley Plunkett   139
34 Core members of the splinter group, the Originals   140
35 Captain Plunkett at the Royal Alex, Toronto, 1926   141
36 The Dumbells' curtain call   142
37 Jack McLaren's *Let's All Hate Toronto*   148
38 Jack McLaren, c. 1966   150
39 Al Plunkett on sheet-music cover, 1923   176

1 Introduction

In light of its lack of preparation and the questionable quality of its officers, the Canadian army was viewed, by some Canadians, as the "Comedian Contingent" at the outset of the First World War.[1] By war's end, however, the Canadian Corps—who were later dubbed the "shock troops"—would mature into one of the premier fighting formations on the Western Front.[2] Still, concert parties of the Canadian Corps would ensure that at least some of that "comedian" quotient would be retained.

The seeds of black humour that inspired the likes of *Monty Python*, *Saturday Night Live* and *SCTV* were sown in the trenches of the Great War and Canadian concert parties were among the pioneers of this brand of comedy. To optimize the fighting potential of Canadian soldiers in the First World War, organized "concert parties"' satisfied the official Canadian Expeditionary Force (CEF; the administrative branch of the Canadian Corps) mandate of raising and maintaining the morale of Canadian soldiers. Ironically, concert-party performers were able to achieve this aim by mocking the military system and its high-ranking officers. Though many officers were aware of the subversive material in the concert-parties' performances, they chose to ignore it because of its positive effect on troop morale; the soldier-entertainers were not merely following the impersonal objective of bolstering the morale of the army at large, in order for them to *win* the war but rather, more intimately, the performers sought to reach the individual soldier, in the interest of helping him *survive* the war.

The Canadian Corps' concert parties helped soldiers enjoy a respite from the war while remaining literally and emotionally in the middle of it. The sonic assault of artillery bursts, alongside the prevalence of death and its unmistakable stench, always complemented the makeshift stages erected along the front lines; where troops watched one of their own channel a popular song from the music hall, act out a humorous and topical skit, or enjoy the most cherished component of the concert-party's repertoire—the female impersonators. Over the course of the war, the comedic material of both Canadian and British concert parties transformed from the light fare offered in the British music hall to a darker humour that was "exclusive" to front-line soldiers. And while some topics (such as killing and dying) would remain largely taboo and were avoided by the concert parties, this exclusive brand of soldier humour, relevant primarily (and sometimes only) to the Canadian Forces, forged an enduring and vital bond between the soldier-entertainers and their audiences who survived the war.

Although they were not the first concert party formed at the Front, the Dumbells would become, over time, *the* Canadian concert party of the First World War. By war's end, the Dumbells had adopted performers from several other Canadian Concert Parties, most notably the Princess Patricia's Canadian Light Infantry's Comedy Company (PPCLI CC). As such, this study necessarily reviews all of the Canadian Corps' concert parties more generally than concentrating exclusively on the Dumbells during the war. Leading up to the Armistice and in the years following the war, however, the study squarely spotlights that morphed entity that most Canadians living in this time period would come to know as the Dumbells.

Back in Canada, civilian audiences were introduced to the Dumbells and their satirical interpretation of the Great War through those soldiers who had seen the concert party perform in France. Among the pioneers of sketch comedy, the Dumbells are as important to the history of Canadian theatre as they are to the country's social and cultural history. If nationhood was won on the crest of Vimy Ridge, it was the Dumbells who provided the country with its earliest soundtrack.

Two years after the First World War had begun, military officials in the CEF felt that troop morale was in need of repair. One remedy suggested was the organization of concert parties. As the war dragged on, professional entertainers had become prohibitively expensive for the Canadian military. The hope was that concert parties could entertain Canadian soldiers for free and, more importantly, raise the spirit of the soldiers, which had been in a tailspin due to the increasing horrors of the front lines. As early as 1916, various battalions within the Canadian Corps followed the example of their counterparts in the British Expeditionary Force (BEF) and formed their own entertainment groups. These concert parties comprised talented soldiers from within the battalions themselves who may have possessed a penchant for singing, performing, or acting.

The musical and comedic content that made up most of the performances of the Canadian concert parties had their origins in the tradition of the British music hall. Borrowing from comedic themes and songs that were popular on the stages in London's West End, Canadian soldier-entertainers appropriated British

Figure 1 Jack Ayre holding court on piano during the war. Captain Plunkett discovered Ayre at one of the former's "Y" Hut "smokers." (Courtesy Stephen Plunkett)

themes into a Canadian context. Whether it was in the adaptations of popular music-hall songs, or works they had created themselves, Canadian concert-party performers targeted many contentious issues that affected the Canadian soldier. By parodying real soldiers' issues in their show—ranging from the inadequacies of the Ross Rifle to the popular subject of rum rations—the concert parties of the Canadian Corps were able to directly relate to the common soldier.

The surreal landscape of the war, the loss of life, and the misery of trench warfare had a profound effect on the content used by the singers and the comedians of the concert parties. And while there was a semblance of the innocence of the British music hall within the shows, soldier humour had, over the course of the war, become more coded and exclusive, and more faithfully reflected the atrocities of the Western Front and its unprecedented carnage. As far as the soldiers in the audience were concerned, their comrades on stage were telling it like it was.

That the entertainers were soldiers themselves further strengthened the bond between those both on and off the stage. Canadian soldiers embraced the concert parties with the knowledge that all of the entertainers had seen active duty. They were, in effect, seeing themselves on stage. Many entertainers returned to front-line service during the war, a fact that kept those who remained in the concert parties extremely aware of the war around them. Performers such as W.I. Cunningham and Norman "Nobby" Clarke of the PPCLI CC were taken out of the concert party and returned to active duty for the remainder of the war.[3] Long before he was a Dumbell, Al Plunkett caught some shrapnel shortly after he and the rest of the 9th Brigade were being relieved at Sanctuary Wood in

June 1916.[4] Others, like Stanley Morrison and Leonard Young, also of the PPCLI CC, were seriously wounded, but continued as best they could.[5] Cyril "Biddy" Biddulph left the Comedy Company and was killed at Monchy in August 1918. So when a regular private from the Canadian Corps saw the one-legged Young or the previously gassed Red Newman or Gitz Rice perform, he saw performers with a commitment not only to entertaining the troops but also those who had, with their wounds, endured a rite of passage. These were soldiers who *knew*.

Civilian audiences were not, at least initially, able to make sense of this new black comedy, for they had not seen the Western Front. And although the Dumbells and the PPCLI CC played command performances in London's major theatres, it was the concerts on makeshift stages at the Front that soldiers would remember. This very hands-on approach by the entertainers ensured the continued success of the concert party at the Front, and, in the case of the Dumbells, after the war too.

John Babcock was the last surviving Canadian soldier of the First World War before he passed away in February 2010 at the age of 109. Given the increasing distance between the present and the Great War, there were no surviving members of the Dumbells nor any of the other Canadian concert-party performers to consult for this work. As such, the author relied on existing radio and television interviews, newspapers, periodicals, recordings, and various personal memoirs of concert-party members and other soldiers to shape this study. The author was also privileged to interview surviving family members of some key soldier-entertainers, including Merton Plunkett's daughter, Annie O'Brien, and Jack McLaren's son, John D. McLaren, whose personal recollections proved extremely useful.

One of the main challenges throughout the research was finding a way to penetrate the exclusive language of the Front. Witness this excerpt from an article written by concert-party sketch writer Jack McLaren, in which he aptly demonstrated the highly coded quality of soldier slang:

> And so to those stout lads who from 1914 to 1918, or any part time thereof, did:
> volunteer to become a target or …
> eat "Mulligan" for 208 consecutive weeks or …
> wrestle with "A" frames down miles of narrow trenches or …
> play crown and anchor and win or …
> pray for a cushy Blighty or …
> get left in some saphead by some saphead of a relief party or …
> blow fish out of Zillebeck Lake with Mills bombs or …
> say "Hoot Mon" when a Chinese labour battalion passed by or …
> get all the soap off at the bath house or …
> eat Bully Beef and hard tack or …

wear the Balaclava and mitts knitted by some ladies' aid society or [*] ...
refuse a job in the London pay office or ...
dream of capturing the Kaiser or ...
sway the metal on sick parade.
To those stout lads I take off my hat, but:
To the hearty who sang A SONG IN A DUGOUT
I salute and dedicate these articles to you.[6]

While the written word does not always convey the fullest meaning or intent of its author, several hours of audiotape and even a little film was available to help this author get a better sense of it for the study. Admittedly, much is lost when reading Great War soldier songs through a 21st-century lens. As historian Peter Hawkins explained, the full meaning of the song cannot be known to scholars who are not able to hear "the inflexion of the voice that sings them, the melody line and the orchestration, not to mention the public image of the singer."[7] Thusly, the complete texts of these songs are unfortunately less accessible to modern historians. Yet, while much of the Dumbells' material holds up well even today, the real benefit of hearing the actual voices of these special entertainers lies in solving the code. On playback we uncover that exaggerated rolling "r" of the Harry Lauder variety; that obnoxious bellow of the regimental sergeant major; that class-defining banter of the WC rifleman and its antithesis: the "never drop a 'g' speak" of the pompous officer. And then there is that vital pause in the delivery of a given punchline that, *inter alia*, helped to define these pioneers and which, through text alone, would have certainly been missed. Living with several hours of audiotapes of soldier interviews, not to mention the dozens of musical recordings that individual concert-party performers released following the war, helped to make the formidable task of translating "soldier talk'" much easier.

While there are only a few reels of film that capture members of Canada's concert parties following the war (as well as footage that presents the performers at reunions and such), there does exist a very brief snippet of a front-line performance by a Canadian concert party that dramatically uncovers the grandness of their performances. By this I mean that, with the sheer size of the soldier-audience and given that microphone amplification was generally not available at this time, performances had to be larger than life, hugely physical in the tradition of ancient Greek tragicomedies where performers had to shout to be heard. With a few hundred possibly hostile soldiers stuffed into a small canteen or perhaps in an open field, resting under the thunder and lightning of war, the Canadian soldier-entertainer was no stranger to shouting.

This book intersects with various dominions of Canadian history and I hoped that in some small way this book positively reflects those watershed studies in Canadian military, social, and cultural history that have come before.

Militarily, J.L. Granatstein, Desmond Morton, and, more recently, Geoffrey Hayes, Ted Barris, and Tim Cook have produced some of the most informative studies about Canada and its role in the First World War.[8] And while my work is not military history in the strictest sense, it is military history after a fashion and I owe much of my understanding of Canada's Great War experience to these authors. With *Tapestry of War*, the late Sandra Gwyn may have written the most compelling cultural review of Canadian participants, male and female, in the First World War and, while I freely declare that mine is no match for Gwyn's poetic narrative, I hope that this book retains at least a little of the spirit of her *Tapestry* and that it will be appealing to those interested in the Canadian-centric war experience and the nationalistic spirit that emerged followed the war. Finally, I salute those many other scholars, such as Peter Bailey with his work on the British music hall, who held the lamplight high for me when the road was long and dark.

While the study is loosely chronological, the emphasis is on thematic arrange-ment. In Chapter II, for example, we will consider the influence of the British music hall, first on Canadian theatre and later on Canadian soldiers both fight-ing in France and on leave in London during the war. We will also identify the use of popular music-hall songs and various other sentimental touchstones that Canadian soldier-entertainers relied on during their front-line performances. In the age of imperialism, it was often very difficult to isolate the Canadian experi-ence from the British one: Canada was virtually a satellite of Britain. As such, in the years leading up to the First World War and indeed during the first part of the war, the concert parties of the Canadian Corps naturally borrowed heavily from the British music hall to entertain the Canadian soldiers.

In Chapter III, we will review the organization of the Canadian Corps' con-cert parties, the two most recognizable being the Dumbells of the 3rd Division and the PPCLI CC. Both groups performed up and down the front line and later in some of the premier vaudeville theatres in London. At war's end, the two comedy troupes merged, retained the name "Dumbells," and performed for soldiers of various armies in the months following the Armistice, including shows on their passage home to Canada in March 1919. Throughout Chapter III we will also examine the prevalence of anti-officer sentiment and irreverent material that could be found within the concert-parties' performances right from the start. Indeed, Canadian concert parties were able to satisfy the CEF's mandate of cheering up the troops by mocking the officers, trench life, and, on some occasions, even the senselessness of the war itself. Most officials chose to look the other way with the rationale that concert parties were playing some role in recharging the soldiers' will to fight.

We will examine more closely the mechanics of front-line humour in Chapter IV. Specifically, we will investigate the concert-parties' departure from the light fare of the music hall into a darker style of comedy that better reflected the war experience. By extension, Chapter V will discuss the Canadian-specific experience and how Canadian concert parties—armed with this new brand of humour—tailored their shows to appeal to Canadian soldiers.

Finally, Chapter VI will review the postwar legacy of the Dumbells and the role they played in the unprecedented rise of Canadian nationalism that ensued. A Dumbell revue entitled *Biff, Bing, Bang* was the first Canadian show to have a hit on Broadway. There were also 12 cross-Canadian tours over the course of a 14-year postwar career. Various members of the group recorded over 40 songs for the record label His Master's Voice (HMV). Given the size of the Canadian market at the time, these records and related sheet-music copies sold remarkably well. Ultimately, the Dumbells were able to rise from the mud of Flanders and attract a civilian audience interested in what their lads had experienced overseas. Capitalizing on their wartime legacy, the Dumbells embodied all of the Canadian concert parties and, in short order, became a household name in Canada.

II The Music Hall and Beyond

In the age of Imperialism, Canada was, in every sense, a satellite of Great Britain. Even long after Confederation, the British influence in Canada was still paramount and that which "was in vogue in the mother country was steadfastly followed in the Dominion."[1] Canadians continued to emulate British sensibilities in their education system, sports, fashion and literature. During special cultural events such as Dominion Day, the Union Jack, Canada's official flag, was prominently displayed in shopkeepers' windows and liberally waved by children and adults alike. As an institution, the British music-hall tradition had a profound influence on Canadian Theatre and consequently, the material, sentimental and otherwise, used in the Canadian Corps' concert parties of the First World War.

The British-styled music hall suffered very little by way of competition in Canada; especially as indigenous theatre companies modelled their own productions after their British counterparts. Although American productions managed to infiltrate Canadian theatre through touring companies and agencies, they were always at a disadvantage in pre-war Canada, a country where all things British were preferred.[2] The link between British music-hall performances and performers with Canada was further fortified during the war when Canadian soldiers spent a good time of their leave taking in the shows in London's Theatre District. Certainly, other sources influenced those in charge of putting together the performance material for the concert parties of the Canadian Corps, but even these sources were almost always filtered through the music hall; a medium that prescribed the necessary dosages of sentimentality, farce, and titillation.

Music Halls began to rise in Britain during the 1850s, meeting a growing demand for affordable entertainment for a working class with a modest disposable income. Music-halls' popularity soared, creating a competitive market, especially in London, where a "battle of the Music Halls" was waged.[3] The music halls emphasized variety entertainment, including sketch comedy, music, stunts, and sometimes dance. This mixture was foreign to the more "legitimate'" model of theatre, but prospered in the music-hall setting.

The music hall was not only the *choice* of the people but also their *mirror*. Beyond any given song or skit, there existed important messages in the performances on the music-hall stages that demanded from the crowd a sort of complicity or knowingness. Part of the unwritten contract between those on and off the stage required the audience to actively participate in the show so that the fullest meaning of a song or skit could be transmitted. In his crucial work on the British music hall, historian Peter Bailey highlighted the resulting discourse that emerged between the stage performers and the audience in London: "The Music Hall performer could count on the active engagement of an audience well practised not only in being hailed but in hailing back, for the language of the street and market-place that informed the exchanges with the audience was very much one of give as well as take."[4]

Here existed a coded dialogue that could be engaged only in by those in the know. This form, signified by such an exclusive brand of humour, would later emerge, albeit in a slightly darker tone, during the performances of the Canadian Corps' concert parties.

Graduating from Britain's bawdy Singing Saloons onto the stages of London's theatres, music-hall productions borrowed the form of various genres, largely from vaudeville, the French revues, and, most importantly, minstrels. The synthesis was a form of variety theatre that would soon be familiar to most Canadians living in the latter part of the 19th century. By the turn of the 20th century, variety theatre began to not only rival "legitimate" theatre in Canada, but also surpass it in popularity. The spectacle of vaudeville theatres in Canada at this time was irresistible to most. Conversely, if legitimate theatre produced something of a hit, its content, or a parody thereof, would soon be reinterpreted for a broader audience on the vaudeville stage.[5]

With theatrical pieces that featured light satirical songs, Toronto's four vaudeville theatres had a combined weekly capacity of 150,000—equal to a third of the city's population—compared to the combined capacity of 35,000 available at the city's three theatres dedicated to classic works and highbrow contemporary productions. Theatres designed specifically for vaudeville entertainment sprouted up all over Canada, especially in Ontario, where they tried to imitate the appearance of West London's lavish music halls.[6]

The French revue also contributed topical comedic and musical material later featured in British music-hall productions. Jack McLaren outlined the notable features of the revue, which was "composed of songs, dances and sketches. A revue dealt mostly with the topics of the day. Those shows supplied a gap in the national history and had a great deal to do with the national life, and current social and political happenings."[7]

There were two distinct branches of the revue. One, the "spectacular revue," was introduced to America by Florenz Ziegfeld. His popular Ziegfeld Follies captured the imagination of American theatregoers with numbers such as "Would You Rather Be a Colonel with an Eagle on Your Shoulder, or a Private with a Chicken on Your Knee?" A second, more intimate style of revue was introduced to London by Albert de Courville and refined by Charles Cochrane, also known as the British Ziegfeld. It was Cochrane's version that most resembled the concert-party revues developed by the Canadian Corps, where relevant political matters were often incorporated into the satirical quotient of the performance material.[8]

The minstrel was another predecessor of the music hall and was a key contributor to the way in which the latter's entertainment was presented. Thomas D. Rice, a white American actor who had developed several "blackface" characters based on highly racist caricatures of black slaves, was an extremely important influence on the evolution of the music hall after touring and performing in Britain in 1836.[9] With respect to racist traditions in Canadian theatre, Robertson Davies candidly offered that

> Our forebears had no squeamishness about what is now called racism. Every nation had its genially derogatory description: Scots were stingy, Irish wrong-headed, Dutch stupid, Jews crafty, French women-chasers, Yankees boastful, and even the English had their caricature figure in Lord Dundreay. Negroes were unfailingly funny because of their supposed ignorant simplicity, which tumbled into a kind of wit. Minstrel shows were to be seen right through the century, and their form changed little.[10]

As unpalatable as the minstrel show may appear to us today, it nevertheless provided popular theatre with an enduring form by which to facilitate the "variety" in variety entertainment.

American minstrel shows wielded a large influence on indigenous Canadian musical culture and music makers in the immediate post-Confederation period. Minstrel shows were common at venues such as Toronto's Shaftesbury Hall, Montreal's St. Patrick's Hall, and London's Music Hall. And Canada had its own minstrel impresarios. Quebec's Séraphin Vachon, for example, led the LaRue Minstrels in Montreal in the 1860s. The group enjoyed some successes

Figure 2 Jack Grace and Ben Allen in blackface for the Dumbells' *Carry On*, c. 1921–23. Allen wrote some of the Dumbells' early skits while he was with the 16th Battalion. (Courtesy Stephen Plunkett)

in both the United States and Canada before Vachon settled in Baltimore in 1872, where he became a musical conductor at a variety theatre.[11] Likewise, Canadian Tommy O'Connor joined the popular American minstrel group Lew Dockstader's Minstrels and toured North America with the group in the 1880s.[12] Between 1900 and 1930, Stratford, Ontario's Theatre Albert staged several well-received musicals by the local GTR Minstrels. And while vaudeville variety shows would challenge the form, the minstrelsy tradition in Canada remained intact well past the First World War.[13] Jack McLaren conceded that his famous wartime comedy sketch *The Duchess Entertains* was patterned on the old minstrel show days, with two funny characters flanking a "serious" or "straight" man. Indeed, minstrel troupes were pivotal in popularizing variety entertainment and moving it into the theatre, where future Canadian soldier-entertainers were most likely to see it.[14]

Black Americans would also unwittingly carve their own mark in the music of the concert parties. The ragtime element had firmly established itself in the revues of the British music hall by the outbreak of the war, but had not evolved into jazz proper.[15] In the many musical genres to be found in the war, the left-hand "stride" piano method began to slowly creep into and fuse with the more traditional military marches. No better evidence of this can be found than in Jack Ayre's own "Dumbell Rag," where the first and second accents still suggest a military march, but Ayre's left-hand stride and decorative right-hand piano work is much more Joplin than it is Sousa.

This hodgepodge of artistic influences from various cultures produced the prevailing form and content found in the British music hall. Its popularity in the years leading up to the war can hardly be overstated. In an age that predated television, radio and of course, the "talkies," a night at the music hall was the preferred choice of the people.[16] With two shows nightly, the music hall became the trendsetter, defining popular music for the public.

America's Tin Pan Alley, a group of New York City–based songwriters and music publishers, also profoundly shaped the trajectory of popular Canadian musical tastes in the years leading up to the First World War. Much to the joy of many songwriters, copyright protection laws had, by the end of the 19th century, become much more effective.[17] By the mid-1880s, lyricists, composers, and publishers (hitherto mired in antagonistic relationships) began working in concert for the mutual benefit of all parties. Tin Pan Alley's golden age had arrived. Concentrated chiefly on West 28th Street (between Fifth and Sixth Avenue in Manhattan), Tin Pan Alley songwriters and publishers churned out the early modern world's most popular music.

These significant developments in copyright law occurred at a time when pianos became, at least for some, affordable.[18] And with the popularity of the British music hall, the public demand for sheet music grew exponentially in the first decade of the 20th century. Music-hall hits, minstrel songs, brass band arrangements, parlour songs, and even ragtime numbers were now able to compete with the standard classical fare in the sheet music market.[19]

In 1909, some 25,000 songs were copyrighted in the United States alone. In 1910, sheet music sales totalled 30 million copies.[20] One of the biggest selling sheet music songs had a Canadian connection. The melancholic wartime ballad "Till We Meet Again," written by Richard Whiting and Ontario-born Raymond Egan, sold more than three and a half million copies for its Detroit-based publisher Jerome H. Remick & Co. in 1918.[21]

In terms of recorded music, many Canadian singers and songwriters mimicked the Tin Pan Alley style in the first two decades of the 20th century. Chatham, Ontario's Geoffrey O'Hara wrote "K-K-K-Katy (the Stammering

Figure 3 The sheet music for Red Newman's wildly popular and stirring version of "Oh! It's a Lovely War." (Courtesy Stephen Plunkett)

Song)," which became immensely popular via American tenor Billy Murray's 1918 rendition. Sheet music sales for "K-K-K-Katy'" were in excess of one million, though O'Hara received a royalty of only one cent per copy.[22] Similarly, prolific recording artist Henry Burr from St. Stephen, New Brunswick, sang in the Tin Pan Alley vein and recorded a significant body of work in both the United States and Canada.[23] Then there was Canadian Alfred Bryan who composed "Peg o' My Heart" (made famous by Burr) and the anti-war song "I Didn't Raise My Boy to Be a Soldier" in 1915:

> *Ten million soldiers to the war have gone,*
> *Who may never return again.*
> *Ten million mothers' hearts must break,*
> *For the ones who died in vain.*

Head bowed down in sorrow in her lonely years,
I heard a mother murmur thro' her tears:

I didn't raise my boy to be a soldier,
I brought him up to be my pride and joy,
Who dares to put a musket on his shoulder,
To shoot some other mother's darling boy?[24]

While Burr's target audience were Americans who were still unsure about their involvement in the war, his sentiment resonated with like-minded pacifists in Canada.[25] Regardless, the Tin Pan Alley form of the song was one that was readily understood by both Americans and Canadians, though such overtly anti-war sentiments were not sung in the concert parties.

It was the work of a Scottish singer, however, that was most referenced and copied by the English-speaking concert parties along the Western Front. Sir Harry Lauder gave tirelessly to the war effort and was also a fixture in recruitment drives on the North American side of the Atlantic, where he preached the cause of the Empire in Canada with great success.[26] At the invitation of the American YMCA, he returned to the United States during the middle years of the war to encourage American participation in the Allied effort.[27] The War Office recognized Lauder's efforts and successes in boosting morale. By playing up his "meanness," Lauder was also at the forefront of a food campaign that stressed the importance of conservation and saving bread.[28] The singer also lost his only son John, who was killed in action somewhere between Pozières and Courcelette on 28 December 1916, and Lauder intended to enlist in the army to avenge his son's death. The War Office, however, felt Lauder's morale-boosting efforts and recruiting initiatives were far more important.[29] Therefore, Lauder threw himself even deeper into the war effort and took his act to the front lines, where morale boosting was most needed.[30]

It was Lauder's success with non-Scottish populations that made him a national icon in Scotland and the highest paid music-hall artist of all time.[31] While this process had begun in the years leading up to the First World War, it was during it that Lauder galvanized his fame.[32] His success was accelerated not only by virtue of the hundreds of thousands of people who saw him perform live—either at the music hall or on the front line—but also because of revolutions in audio technology. Beginning in 1902 when the recording industry was in its infancy, Lauder recorded for Pathé, Edison, G&T, Zonophone, HMV, and Victor and was one of the first artists in the world to sell over a million records.[33]

The Highland character, or Scotch comic made so famous by Lauder appears at first to be a country bumpkin. The spirit of this persona was much like the Negro role in the minstrel.[34] Like the Negro, the Highlander often ended up looking the wiser at the performance's end, emerging, as historian Paul Maloney confirmed, "as the canny victors of city folks."[35] Lauder's Scotch comic character, though, was a composite of the exaggerated elements of the Highlands *and* the Lowlands. It was a caricature. Still, Lauder was capable of evoking a wide range of emotions from the audience.[36] H.V. Morton, the famous author and journalist for the *Daily Express*, witnessed one of Lauder's many onstage metamorphoses:

> Watch how he will concentrate his effect on one good laugh, quickly followed with another, funny but with a serious side to it; and then, suddenly, startlingly, and with a simplicity and a sincerity impossible to question, he is telling some story of the war. There is not a sound in the theatre. The little Scotsman stands in the full flare of the floodlights speaking words which come straight from his heart. Every word rings true. In two minutes he has carried hundreds of men and women of different types and mentalities to the opposite pole of emotion.[37]

And so Scotland's pawky caricature, stopping on a shilling, took his audience down a completely different road, only to rescue them soon afterward with another laugh. These comedic aesthetics profoundly influenced the concert parties of the First World War. Tacitly, the entertainers of the Canadian Corps knew that they needed to include Lauder's trademark character in their shows.

The Scotsman become so popular among Canadian soldiers that the 91st Battalion's concert party was nicknamed the "Harry Lauders."[38] And the PPCLI CC and the Dumbells boasted their own requisite "Scotty." This feat was rendered much easier given that Jack McLaren, Bill Tennent, John McCormick, Jock Holland, and Bill Redpath, to name a few, were all Scottish-born Canadian soldiers performing with the Canadian Corps. From those first roughshod shows on the makeshift stages along the front lines to the Royal Command performances in London's West End, Canada's concert parties incorporated material from every aspect of the British music hall. Many popular British productions toured Canada prior to the war. Musicals and farce comedies such as *East Lynne* and *The Old Homestead* were all the rage in Ontario's theatres.[39] Canadian concert-party performers would have seen, in various venues, this specific branch of British theatre. These productions would shape the future soldier-entertainers' style; they would arrive in Europe with a definite idea of what variety theatre meant even before they knew that their military career would be spent mostly onstage.

As soldiers, these Canadian men could now see the real thing while on leave in London. With each cycle of leave, men at the Front were constantly updated on the most current hits of the music hall. Indeed, those men returning from leave were entrusted by others in their unit to bring back new songs, jokes and even gramophone records from their visit to London.[40]

By all accounts, Canadian soldiers frequented the music halls of London often, as journalist Margaret Bell reported in *Maclean's*, "The officers were Canadians, and wore kilts. There were many of them in the audience, that night; and are a great many every night."[41] Music-hall star Gladys Cooper singled out soldiers from the Canadian Corps:

> I simply love playing to soldiers … and I get hundreds of letters from them, after they go back to the trenches, a great percentage of them being from Canadians. Nice, friendly letters, not the silly, sentimental kind one reads about.[42]

One revue actually added a Canadian theme to please its clientele, as Bell disclosed:

> Old Drury Lane—may the shades of Russian opera forgive it!—is wallowing in the most ostentatious display of Revue ever seen in London. The dignified home of music, as it once was, has become the rendevous of superficial superlatives. The most dazzling scenery, the most gorgeous dresses, the slimmest ankles, the shortest skirts, the most elaborate coiffures, the giddiest dancing, the most spectacular spectacles, including as the *pièce de résistance* a scene of Canadian skaters on real artificial ice.[43]

In her article, Bell offers samples to several of the revues running during this part of the 1916 season. There were an impressive number of revues documented in her piece, and Bell made no apologies for the amount of detail she gave, "I MUST go on talking about Revues, for they are the chief attraction to our soldiers. Hence there are more of them than any other kind of amusement."[44]

The Dumbells happily stole, and stole often from the music hall, supplementing their own material with well-known hits, as Max Braithwaite illustrated: "Except for the "Dumbell Rag," written by Jack Ayre, they lifted their musical numbers whenever the lifting was good—mostly from English music-hall hits like *Zig Zag* and *Yes, Uncle*."

Ayre himself concurred, "Most often songs were picked from revues that were in London."[45] It is with this in mind that a summary of songs and revues, popular with both Canadian soldiers and civilians during the war, will demonstrate how the British music hall predominantly figured in the material used by the concert parties of the Canadian Corps. Although concert parties could not possibly emulate the environment of a West London theatre, they were at least able to perform musical and comedic material that was familiar to their soldier-audiences who had seen the real thing, and who, with a short leap, could imagine themselves at the Alhambra.

Sentimental Songs

Of all the music-hall songs that were made popular during the "singing war," those connecting the soldier and home were among the most famous and were almost required material for Canada's concert parties.[46] Various numbers became popular when soldiers sang them on the march, in the huts, and behind the lines. Songs that were initially very popular among the early recruits included "In the Shadows," "Sister Susie's Sewing Shirts for Soldiers," "Here We Are Again," "Hitchy Koo" and perhaps most famous of all, Jack Judge and Harry Williams' "It's a Long Way to Tipperary." These songs, especially "Tipperary," remained well liked among civilian audiences because they had been popular with the soldiers but, over time, their popularity would wane with soldiers who, tired of war, were less likely to sing such positive refrains with any degree of sincerity.

There were exceptions, of course. And the odd sentimental choice was very nearly as important to the soldier as satirical numbers were. There was, after all, plenty of room left for artful subversiveness in the soldiers' repertoire.[47] Music-hall hits like Stoddard King and Alonzo "Zo" Elliot's unforgettable "The Long Trail" were as popular among soldiers as they had been among civilians in 1915:

> There's a long, long trail a-winding, into the land of my dreams,
> where the nightingales are singing and a white moon beams.
> There's a long, long night of waiting, until my dreams all come true,
> Till the day when I'll be going down that long, long trail with you.[48]

There were others too. Caddigan and Brennan's "The Rose of No Man's Land" was one that may have enjoyed a longer shelf life with civilian audiences, but was nevertheless popular among soldiers:

> There's a rose that grows on no man's land
> And it's wonderful to see;
> Though its place is there it will live for me
> in my garden of memories.
> It's the one red rose the soldier knows
> It's the work of the Master's hand,
> It's the sweet word from the Red Cross nurse,
> She's the rose of no man's land.[49]

Canadian singer Henry Burr styled a version of this song in 1918, demonstrating the appeal that most British music-hall hits had among the Colonials.

Another "Rose," Frederick E. Weatherley and Haydn Wood's "Roses of Picardy," was also a hit in 1916. Weartherly was an officer in the British army and his song remains one of the most memorable melodies of the war. "Roses of Picardy' was also incorporated into the Canadian concert-party's material, yet the two most popular versions among civilians were Ernest Pike's in 1916 and John McCormack's in 1919.[50] These sorts of songs connected the soldier with home and vice versa.

One of the many persuasive techniques that the Dumbells and various other Canadian concert parties employed was to use these choice, sentimental refrains to soothe their soldier audiences. Dumbell Al Plunkett remembered one "Y" Hut "smoker" where the PPCLI's Sergeant Silas Pickle pacified the crowd with the bass song "Asleep in the Deep" which, according to Plunkett "made a tremendous hit."[51] Written by Arthur J. Lamb and Henry W. Petrie in 1897, "Asleep in the Deep" was first popularized by bass vocalist J. Rodgers and was later recorded in 1913 by Wilfred Glenn for the Victor Talking Machine Company and was well known long before the outbreak of war.[52]

No single song better epitomized the homesick soldier, however, than Ivor Novello and Lena Ford's 1914 classic, "Keep the Home Fires Burning," which was sung in various concert parties of the Canadian Corps:

> Keep the home fires burning, while your hearts are yearning,
> Though your lads are far away they dream of home.
> There's a silver lining through the dark clouds shining,
> Turn the dark cloud inside out 'til the boys come home.[53]

"Keep the Home Fires Burning" is perhaps the most powerful of all the war's sentimental songs; Novello's music is as moving as it is indelible. Yet Ford's lyrics are equally as important. What might be dismissed by the 21st-century sensibilities of modern readers of the song as cheap sentimentality, these lyrics carried great weight with most soldiers. Life at the Front was extremely hard on the body, mind, and spirit of the soldiers, and as Brophy and Partridge explained, "The most ordinary details of normal life were longed for more intensely than saints on earth have desired the benefits of their paradise."[54] Songs like "Keep the Home Fires Burning" were the soldier's touchstones for those absent ideals: comfort, home, love, and peace.

Sentimental songs not related to the war, or written before its outbreak, were also commonly sung by both soldiers and civilians. Albert Chevalier, noted for his role as the cockney "Coster's Laureate" in the British music hall, wrote, along with his brother-in-law Charles Ingle, "My Old Dutch." Dumbell Red Newman, also famed for his cockney accent, made "My Old Dutch" his own, to the extent that he recorded it for Berliner's Gram-O-Phone label after the war:

> We've been together now for forty years, and it don't seem a day too much.
> Well, there ain't a lady living in the land, what I'd swap for my dear old
>   Dutch,
> there ain't a lady living in the land, what I'd swap for my dear old Dutch.[55]

Newman retained much of the sentiment of the original British version, which Chevalier had written for his wife, and somehow fused the ridiculous and exaggerated cockney with universal emotion, appealing to both soldiers and civilians.

British music-hall singers became so well known that every sentimental song they performed was likely to end up a hit and be recreated by the concert parties on the front lines. Mark Sheridan's versions of "Here We Are Again," "Tipperary," and "I Do Like to Be Beside the Seaside" were both extremely popular, yet the famous tenor John McCormack's "Tipperary" was equally as well known. Florrie Forde weighed in with her own version of "Tipperary," but more memorable may have been her version of George Asaf and Felix Powell's hit of 1915, "Pack Up Your Troubles in Your Old Kit Bag."[56]

Popular love songs would often be speedily incorporated into both the British and Canadian concert-parties' repertoire. Fritz Kreisler, a professional entertainer, enjoyed tremendous success with a rendition of Sir Julius Benedict's haunting "Lily of Killarney."[57] The song was soon worked into the Dumbells' repertoire by the "immaculate Scotsman" Bill Tennent, and Bertram Langley.[58] Likewise, Ross Hamilton, as the lovely "Marjorie," speedily worked the acclaimed "Someday I'll Make You Love Me" into the Dumbell show. That is not to say that the Canadian Corps' concert parties did not exercise discretion when choosing material; concert party performers were keenly aware of what the soldiers might like to hear. It was easy: they were soldiers themselves.

Perhaps the real sentimental favourite toward war's end was Egan and Whiting's "Till We Meet Again":

> *Wedding bells will ring so merrily*
> *Every tear will be a memory*
> *So wait and pray each night for me*
> *Till we meet again.*

The song was recorded several times by various British artists including Vernon Dalhart and Gladys Price, Albert Campbell, and Canada's own Henry Burr. Although the soldier's taste for humour would experience a metamorphosis during the war, as we will soon examine, the tremendous popularity of "Till We Meet Again" among the troops proves that there was always room in the soldier's heart for the odd tender refrain.

If songs were popular with the soldiers, even for a short while, they were certain to be embraced by civilian listeners. Mills, Godfrey, and Scott's "Take Me Back to Dear Old Blighty" was a raucous but universal lament that spoke to the homesickness most soldiers experienced at one point or another during the war. As a universal lament, "Blighty," or England, became for Dominion soldiers Canada, Australia, or South Africa, as the case may be. London, Liverpool,

Figure 4 Bertram Langley, Al Plunkett, Bill Tennent, C. Hall, and Ross Hamilton (seated) as "Marjorie," c. 1920. (Courtesy Stephen Plunkett)

Leeds, and Birmingham could be interchangeable with Toronto, Melbourne, and Capetown:

> *Take me back to dear old Blighty!*
> *Put me on the train for London town!*
> *Take me over there,*
> *Drop me ANYWHERE,*
> *Liverpool, Leeds, or Birmingham, well, I don't care![59]*

As "Tipperary" had done two years earlier, "Take Me Back to Dear Old Blighty," particularly Florrie Forde's version of 1917, had expressed the prevailing wish among most soldiers; namely, that they wanted to be anywhere else in the world but France and Belgium. Civilians could faithfully sing along with these songs, thinking of their lads "over there."

Whether commemorating or commiserating that which was left behind, life in peacetime was never far from the soldiers' mind. Communication with the larger world was essential and letters from home were coveted; despite the growing distance between the soldier's reality and the understanding of the war by those at home.

Used by both the BEF and the CEF, the Field Postcard was a form letter designed by the army for those soldiers actually engaged in fighting at the Front. Though it allowed for quick communication with home, its very nature bled out any real emotion. Jack Humphries, a star in the British music hall famous for his portrayal of Barinsfather's "Old Bill," delighted the crowds at London's Comedy Theatre. In a 1916 revue, Humphries, as "Old Bill," sang an ode lamenting the inadequacies of the Field Postcard. The card itself had various boxes that the soldier might check, yet no other comments were allowed to be written on the card or it would be destroyed by the official censors:

I am quite well.

I have been admitted into hospital

$\begin{cases} sick \\ wounded \end{cases}$ *and am going on well.*
and hope to be discharged soon.

I am being sent down to the base.

I had received your $\begin{cases} \text{letter dated} \underline{\hspace{2cm}} \\ \text{telegram ,, } \underline{\hspace{2cm}} \\ \text{postcard ,, } \underline{\hspace{2cm}} \end{cases}$

Letter follows at first opportunity.

I have received no letter from you

$\begin{cases} lately \\ for\ a\ long\ time \end{cases}$

Signature $\Big\}$
only.

Date $\underline{\hspace{5cm}}$ [60]

The song of the same name, as sung by the Dumbells, illustrates the soldier's difficulty in communicating any meaningful message to loved ones at home given his choices:

I can't write and tell 'er that I'm wounded,
because the bloody censor knows I'm not.
I can't say as how I got the DCM,
when 14 days CB was all I got.[61]
I just wants to say I'm kinda lonely,
and I'd like to hold her hand and 'ave a chat,
I only wants to say, "I love yous still,"
but I can't find the space for that.[62]

Apart from the obvious humour in "The Field Postcard," there was also sincere emotion, an element that could be found in many trench tunes. Songs could therapeutically restore that loving human touch, missing from the soldier's day-to-day army life.

Still, civilians in Britain and Canada continued to sing patriotic and quixotic anthems about the war, when such songs had lost meaning with the common soldier. "It's a Long Way to Tipperary" for example, was a soldier's song for only a brief time. A hit in 1913, "Tipperary" was sung by British soldiers who marched to Mons during the war's first months. This fact had caught the public's imagination and immortalized the song.[63] As Brophy and Partridge concluded: "To sing, to hum, or to whistle *It's a Long Way to Tipperary* was the patriotic and cheerful thing to do … although civilians retained their affection for it, the New Armies were nauseated. Attempts to start it were often howled and whistled down."[64]

First World War veteran F.T. Nettleingham agreed, stating that "Tipperary" was, "never Tommy's song … never greatly sung, yet it was often mentioned and frequently parodied."[65]

Similarly, a recruiting song such as Arthur Wimperis and Herman Finck's "I'll Make a Man of You" was another number that held little water with the service-hardened soldier:

The Army and the Navy need attention,
The outlook isn't healthy you'll admit,
But I've got a perfect dream of a new recruiting scheme,
Which I think is absolutely it.
If only other girls would do as I do I believe that we could manage it alone,
For I turn all suitors from me but the sailor and the Tommy,
I've an army and a navy of my own.
On Sunday I walk out with a Soldier,
On Monday I'm taken by a Tar,
On Tuesday I'm out with a baby Boy Scout,
On Wednesday a Hussar;
On Thursday a gang oot wi' a Scottie,
On Friday, the Captain of the crew;

> *But on Saturday I'm willing, if you'll only take the shilling,*
> *To make a man of any one of you.*[66]

Effectively parodied in Richard Attenborough's 1969 film based on the Joan
Littlewood play *Oh! What a Lovely War*, "I'll Make a Man of You," as sung by
temptress recruiter Vanessa Redgrave, represented the war myth; the sexy, patriotic touchstone may have raised the morale of civilians and gullible would-be
soldiers, but, given its cheerfulness, would have been too much to endure for
those who knew the reality of trench warfare and might have regretted the day
they first surrendered to the war's imagined charm every time they heard that
insufferable lyric.[67]

Some soldiers felt resentment toward those civilians who lived their daily
life not in constant peril but, rather, shamefully unaware of the horrors of the
front line. Witness the playful sarcasm found in the song (not to be confused
with the movie of the same name): "Oh! It's a Lovely War.... Don't we pity the
poor civilians, sitting beside the fire?" Less playfulness was afforded those able-
bodied men who had chosen to stay at home and not fight. Soldiers' opinion
of these objectors became more acerbic as the war progressed. Alfred Lester's
"A Conscientious Objector" from the 1915 music-hall revue *Around the Map*,
retains a great deal of humour in tackling a subject that grew increasingly more
delicate:

> *Send out the Army and the Navy, send out the rank and file.*
> *Send out the brave old "Territorials" they'll face the danger with a smile.*
> *Where are the boys of the "Old Brigade" who made olde England free?*
> *You can send out your mother, your sister and your brother,*
> *but for God's sake don't send me!*[68]

Certainly, McLaren introduced "A Conscientious Objector" with the caveat that
it was for those slackers who just didn't want to do their bit. These men, as
McLaren warned, should not be compared with those sincere objectors, who
genuinely did want to take another man's life.[69] At the same time, the song was
heartily sung by the lads in uniform, as it lent itself to a raucous singalong;
the last line in particular could be fairly belted out.[70] One gets the impression,
however, that after months of service, many of the lads were in full agreement
with the lyrics.

Ordinary soldiers did not always need prompting from their respective concert parties to proudly belt out tunes of irreverence. Songs like, "Skiboo," "We're
Here Because We're Here," "I've Lost My Rifle," and "Send Out the Army and
the Navy" were commonly sung by regular troops of the Canadian Corps. And
as Will Bird recalled, Canadian soldiers heartily crooned "I Want to Go Home"
before any big action on the Front.[71]

Home was at the root of most of these songs; a subject that was almost always foremost in the soldier's mind. Removed from the comforts of home as they were, soldiers constantly laboured over their precious recollections of family, friends, and neighbours and were understandably resentful of those men who had stayed home. Still, the soldier's taste for military songs had been redefined by the war and was explicitly distinct from that which appealed to the civilian.

Overt patriotic sentiment may have had currency among the recruits, but not for long, and as the war dragged on, both British and Canadian soldiers' preference for music increasingly tore away from civilian tastes. Canadian soldier Charles Henry Savage took some pleasure in asking volunteers why they enlisted:

> Probably the only answer that you will not get is that he did it out of patriotism. One seldom hears a soldier use that word. King and country, the Old Flag, the mighty British Empire are phrases that slip so readily from some people's lips that one is inclined to think that they come from no great depth—certainly not from as far down as the heart. The average man may feel deeply about these matters but he does not like to hear them shouted from the housetop. Generally he despises the shouters: he is embarrassed for them: they make him slightly sick.[72]

This goes some way in explaining the dearth of patriotic pap in the soldier-singer's setlist.

Patriotism was uncomfortable for those who had really seen the war, and was of little relevance to a soldier's day-to-day routine.[73] Philip Gibbs, an British journalist during the war, noted the distaste for all things patriotic among the common British soldiers, "Any allusion to 'the Empire' left [the troops] stone-cold unless they confused it with the Empire music hall, when their hearts warmed to the name."[74] A journalist writing in *Maclean's* in 1915 reported that: "In the trenches patriotic airs are not nearly so popular as music-hall ditties. People at home are inspired by national anthems on the march. The soldier prefers *Tipperary*, and more recently other songs perhaps more musical but less talked about."[75]

Though we know now that "Tipperary" had about run its course with the soldiers by 1915, the journalist's main sentiment was nevertheless on the mark. Great War veteran J.B. Priestley concurred: "The First World War, unlike the Second, produced two distinct crops of songs: one for patriotic civilians ... the other, not composed and copyrighted by anybody, genuine folk song, for the sardonic front-line troops."[76]

Although written in 1915—early enough in the war from a Canadian perspective—Morris Manley's "Good Luck to the Boys of the Allies" (as sung by Little Miss Mildred Manley: Canada's "greatest child vocalist" no less) was another example that demonstrated the experiential divide between Canadian soldiers on the Western Front with those at home:

> It's jolly good luck to Johnnie`Canuck,
> And all the Allie [sic] soldiers,
> They're fighting day by day, in trenches far away,
> They'll all march back with the union jack,
> In history they'll gain fame.
> Just give them a cheer and banish the tear,
> For they'll return again.[77]

Marching gloriously back home with the Union Jack simply didn't occur to Johnnie Canuck who was far more concerned with avoiding lice, trench foot, rats, and bullets.

Popular British music-hall songs had been hijacked by the concert parties, and were stripped of any perceptible "ebullient jingoism."[78] So too were songs from the military tradition; bugle calls, regimental songs, and hymns, had all been, at one time or another, personalized by the soldiers for a laugh. When contrasting those sardonic front-line songs with those songs sung on the home front, one is able to see just how different the popular perception of the war was among civilians, compared with the perception of the soldiers who did the actual fighting.

The "Other"

Part of the coded and exclusive experience of the music hall was that the material depended, or perhaps assumed, that the audience was legion, its members part of an extended, English-speaking culture. Even French Canadian soldiers, like the 22nd Battalion (a.k.a. the Van Doos), sang English songs, as well as their own self-styled Québécois folk songs. But the latter element was only a small, albeit significant subculture operating within the larger hegemony of Canada's soldier fraternity.[79]

The fraternity, of course, was also white. Canadian soldier Jack Napier, for example, thought his camp to be "very cosmopolitan," replete with "Canucks, British, French, + some Indians ... playing cards + singing all the latest choruses."[80] Perhaps Napier's camp was, given the age, cosmopolitan. Generally speaking though, the war for Canada remained the preserve of those white-skinned Canadians, who were mostly of British descent. Concert-party material pandered to that majority.

In the years leading up to the Great War, however, Canada had begun to absorb new immigrants from a variety of countries that had previously not figured prominently in Canada's ethnic mosaic. These non-traditional immigrant groups were largely viewed with suspicion and derision. In short: they were a dilemma to be solved.[81] They were also, for some, the source of comedic material, and entertainers, including the concert parties of the Canadian Corps, were able to draw on popular opinion regarding some ethnic groups to produce laughs.

The Canadian Government began to conduct studies on future immigrant groups as early as the 1880s. Mistrusted from the outset, Asian immigrants were at the centre of these early investigations. On the recommendations of a Royal Commission, the Chinese Immigration Act of 1885 was introduced. More commonly referred to as the Chinese Head Tax and Exclusion Act, the legislation was established to discourage Chinese immigrants (specifically those who sought to work on the CPR) from coming to Canada through the implementation of a $50 head tax.[82] A combination of xenophobic attitudes, economic factors, and big-business interests contributed to Canada's and specifically British Columbia's overtly racist policies toward Asians.[83] However, ultimately, such racist legislation only reflected popular sentiment. Riots in Vancouver in 1887 and later in 1907 reflected the anti-Asian sentiment that existed in British Columbia, a sentiment that pervaded the entire nation. In 1914, the Supreme Court of Canada reviewed a piece of provincial legislation in Saskatchewan in Quong Wing v. The King (1914).[84] The legislation specifically prohibited Chinese restaurant owners from hiring white women as employees for fear that they might lure them into a life of prostitution. Such powerful racist mythology remained an obstacle for all Asian-Canadians.

Still, while many new "hyphenated Canadians" held fast to the traditions of their homeland, many also began to explore the emerging abstraction of "Canada." Compelled perhaps by a need to demonstrate their respective communities' honour, non-whites in Canada enlisted voluntarily in the CEF. First Nations soldiers, for instance, wanted to gain respect and possibly had the goal of full enfranchisement after the war. Similarly, Japanese-Canadians wanted the franchise, as well as the opportunity to demonstrate their martial prowess.[85] Black Canadians, who also wanted the franchise, were discouraged from enlisting on the strength of a variety of ridiculous arguments. These included one which posited that blacks lacked valour, discipline and the necessary intelligence for modern warfare.[86] It must also be remembered that black Canadians had to campaign in order to simply enlist in the CEF. Over the course of the war, however, black Canadians were able to stretch the elasticity of a policy that was once set at "absolutely not," to—by the middle of 1916 when recruits were so desperately needed—"maybe."

Officials believed that whites would not want to fight side-by-side with "coloured" soldiers. General Willoughby Gwatkin, for one, believed the "civilized negro" to be:

vain and imitative; in Canada he is not being impelled to enlist by a high
sense of duty; in the trenches he is not likely to make a good fighter; and
the average white man will not associate with him on terms of equality.
Not a single commanding officer in Military District No.2 is willing to
accept a coloured platoon as part of his battalion; and it would be humili-
ating to the coloured men themselves to serve in a battalion where they
were not wanted.[87]

However, blacks and whites did fight together—and did so largely without incident. Individual blacks who had managed to slip through the cracks fought with
white compatriots. Likewise, when the 106th (a battalion that had some black
soldiers in it) was broken up, its remnants were sent to the Royal Canadian
Regiment. In this instance, the black reinforcements were welcomed.[88] Sadly,
this *esprit de corps*, not to mention the commitment demonstrated by Canada's
visible minorities, did not transcend into wide-scale gains for these communities
following the war. Indeed, Canada became even more entrenched in xenophobia
in the years following the armistice and leading up to the Second World War.[89]
And the minstrel tradition was in no danger of becoming obsolete within the
concert parties of the Canadian Corps.

Many Canadian concert parties boasted their own "blackfaces." Dumbell Bill
Tennent was well known for his blackface role in "A Wandering Minstrel," as was
fellow Dumbell Al Plunkett, whose character was known simply as "The Coon."[90]
Yet blacks were not the only race impersonated by the Canadian concert parties.
Montreal's Tom Lilly was lauded for his portrayal as a "Chinaman" while performing with the PPCLI CC; a show that was once performed in front of some
workers from the British Chinese Labour Corps (CLC).[91] While the number of
Chinese-Canadians who enlisted in the CEF would have been extremely low, it
is unlikely that either these soldiers or the workers from the British CLC would
have been thrilled with Lilly's "tribute."[92]

While the exaggerated portrayal of non-whites had been part of Canada's
pre-war theatrical tradition, its use in the First World War paralleled an extant
racism that became sharpened throughout the conflict. While some moderate
white voices expressed their discomfort with anti-Asian sentiment and legislation, xenophobic attitudes actually increased following the war and found
expression in the Anti-Chinese Riots in Lindsay, Ontario, in 1919.[93] Although
unpleasant to modern tastes, such xenophobia was a regular feature of variety
entertainment and rare was the concert-party revue that did not give some
expression, however "playful" to these common perceptions.

The Morally Ambiguous

By 1915, songs of a more risqué variety found their way onto the lips of those Canadian soldiers who had heard them while on leave in London. The nature of these sorts of songs stood in stark contrast to those that had been crafted in the morally inflexible age of Victoria. More Canadian soldiers were going to London and seeing the revues firsthand, and productions like *The Passing Show of 1915* and *Around the Map* contributed songs that would later be incorporated into the concert-parties' repertoire. The same can be said for *Chu Chin Chow*, a revue from 1916, a watershed year for revues.[94] Based on the book *Ali Baba and the Forty Thieves*, *Chu Chin Chow* was especially successful and was performed a staggering 2,238 times. Its immense popularity was described by Barbara Jones and Bill Howell in their *Popular Arts of the First World War*: "Chu Chin Chow at the Haymarket Theatre in London was a lavish oriental extravaganza with all the pop ingredients of paradise—songs and dance, slave-girls and jewels; going to see Chu was part of everyone's dream of Blighty."[95]

Frank Cousins was one Canadian soldier who was made a believer of the show during his leave in London. Cousins said as much in a letter home to mother: "yesterday afternoon we went to see a musical comedy "Chu Chin Chou" [*sic*] which was, I think, the finest thing of it's [*sic*] kind I've ever seen."[96] The show provided the Dumbells with "The Cobbler's Song," a cornerstone in that concert-party's repertoire that was sung by Bill Tennent.[97]

Another music-hall show that was wildly successful with Canadians was *The Bing Boys Are Here*.[98] The success of *The Bing Boys Are Here* among Canadian soldiers manifested in 1916 when Canadian soldiers adopted the nickname "Byng Boys"—a double entendre that simultaneously honoured the music-hall hit and was also a tip of the hat to the Corps Commander Julian Byng.[99] The show spawned a series of similar revues in later years including *The Bing Girls Are There* (1917), *The Bing Boys Are There*, and *The Bing Boys on Broadway* (1918). It may have been the single most influential revue during the war in terms of the number of songs it committed to the soldier's memory but was, of course, much loved by civilian audiences as well.

Very few people in Britain and Canada during the 1910s would not have heard the two most famous numbers from the *Bing Boys*, those being "Another Little Drink" and the more popular still Clifford Grey and Nat Ayre's "If You Were the Only Girl in the World":

If you were the only girl in the world, and I was the only boy,
nothing else would matter in the world today,
we would go on loving in the same old way.

> A "Garden of Eden" just made for two, with nothing to mar our joy.
> There would be such wonderful things to do,
> I would say such wonderful things to you,
> if you were the only girl in the world, and I was the only boy.

Originally sung by Violet Lorraine and George Robey on the British music-hall stage, the song was incorporated by the Dumbells into their own show. The vocalists in the Dumbells certainly were strong, and the difficult, pendular melodies, like "If You Were the Only Girl in the World," did not dissuade them from choosing the more ambitious numbers from London, if there was a chance to score big with their soldier audiences.

The Bing Boys series was also significant because it illustrated the new-found tolerance for morally ambiguous themes that began to emerge in some of the wartime music-hall songs. "The Clock Song" from The Bing Boys Are Here is a prime example of the emerging playful and risqué music-hall number:

> At 1 and 2, I'm with Maude and Lou,
> 3 and 4, two girls more,
> 5 and 6, with such dears I fix,
> 7 and 8, it's Clara and Caroline,
> 9 and 10, I'm at work again,
> 11 it's Kate, gee she's great,
> but the girl I meet at 12, oh I say,
> what a life, not a word to the wife, sssh!
> Tick, tock, wind up the clock,
> and I start my day over again.[100]

This moral ambiguity would seep into the Dumbells own material. Witness Al Plunkett's "Everybody Slips a Little":[101]

> Everybody slips a little, now and then.
> Everybody slips a little, now and again.
> Come on you teachers and preachers,
> you've surely got to admit,
> there's a stumbling step in the best of us,
> that should keep us from blaming the rest of us.
> It's so easy just to falter from the path,
> so be very, very careful when you condemn.
> So your wife's name is Rose and you love her a heap,
> there'll come a time you'll call her Maudie in your sleep,
> Everybody slips a little now and then.

The relaxation of strict Victorian values and the nature and subsequent acceptability of various strains of musical comedy was a by-product of a miserably
long war.

Two other popular revues were *Yes, Uncle* and *Zig Zag*, both from 1917.[102]
The latter gave Dumbell Hamilton as "Marjorie," one of "her" most memorable
concert-party pieces entitled "Hello My Dearie."[103] Fellow Dumbell Bill Tennent,
a soldier "somewhere in France," was the male voice in this duet singing to his
sweetheart (Hamilton) back in Britain. The Dumbells were able to manipulate
the mood of the piece ingeniously. Making full use of what little props they
were able to secure, the concert party was able to portray the distance between
the two singers, by having Marjorie sing her part through a circular hole in the
black curtain. As Marjorie was only partially visible, the mystery surrounding her was intensified; many soldiers were unsure whether they were seeing a

Figure 5 Scottish-born tenor Bill Tennent as Ralph Rackstraw in the
Dumbells' rendition of *H.M.S. Pinafore*, c. 1920. (Courtesy John McLaren)

real woman, an uncertainty that further solidified one of the Dumbells' most important attractions. Nearly every soldier could relate to that girl he had left behind, and to how precious contact with those at home had become in the dolour of trench warfare.

The British music hall contributed more than just songs to the concert parties of the Canadian Corps: catchphrases and comedic skits from the various revues were also incorporated into the soldier-entertainers' repertoire. Responsible for the still widely used "how's your father?," a cockney euphemism for sex, Harry Tate was revered by theatregoers as the premier comedian of the music hall.[104] From Tate's signature valediction "Good-bye-ee" sprang Florrie Forde's musical number of the same name. A multi-purpose composition, "Good-bye-ee!' was, as Brophy and Partridge demonstrated: "a quaint half-breed. Ostensibly it was a skit, a parody, a satire on home-sick and leave-taking songs, but often the melancholy it was intended to whip out of existence would creep quietly back into the singing voices."[105]

These multi-purpose songs were the preferred type of selection for the concert-party performers—mood-setting skits, flexible enough to operate as straight musical performances—and capable of simultaneously engineering both chuckles and melancholy in the audience.

While many popular numbers would be reworked to fit the sensibilities of soldier life, often by way of an irreverent parody of the original, many of the familiar pieces were carefully reproduced, retaining the integrity and quality of the original songs. While the lyrics of Harry Lauder's "Roamin' in the Gloamin'" would be completely reworked into a scathing satire on the inefficiency of the Ross Rifle, Novello's "Keep the Home Fires Burning" and its sacrosanct message was untouched and so retained its author's melancholic intention. Seemingly, the Canadian concert parties instinctively knew which musical standards were available for parody and which numbers were sacred cows. While soldiers might have wilfully laughed at their own woeful circumstances, their failing equipment, their desperate life in the trenches, and the questionable wisdom of those who made the decisions on their behalf, few were willing to have the very fact that they were still at war, away from home, and, most especially, away from loved ones tampered with. The concert parties were well aware of these soldier values and took great care in the pace and treatment of music-hall standards. Dumbell pianist Jack Ayre spoke to the parties' faithful rendering of many music-hall standards, "Many of the boys thought they were sitting in the west end of London when we did our first show."[106] Indeed, both the PPCLI CC and the Dumbells would pass the real litmus test, enjoying successful runs at London's premier music halls.

Outside Influences

Other influences shaped the performance material of the Canadian concert parties. And soldiers certainly brought their own individual musical tastes to the theatre of war.[107] Al Plunkett, the Dumbells' matinee idol (he was 16 when he enlisted) wooed the young Canadian girls with the American number, "Those Wild, Wild Women Are Making a Wild Man of Me," a song he had honed during the concert-party's performances at the Front.[108] American marching songs were also popular among British and Canadian troops including "Down Where That Swanee River Flows," "Texas Way," and "Tennessee":

> I'll see my sweetheart Flo,
> And friends I used to know.
> They'll be right there to meet me,
> Just imagine how they'll greet me,
> When I get back,
> When I get back,
> To my home in Tennessee.[109]

Just as "Tipperary" and "Take Me Back to Dear Old Blighty" had done, these American marching songs ironically came to represent home for many soldiers who had no idea where the Swanee River was.

Celtic and traditional folk songs from Scotland and Ireland that were distinct from the standard music-hall fare were also commonly heard at the Front. "Annie Laurie," originally written by William Douglas of Finland in the 1690s, was later improved by Alicia Anne Spottiswoode in the 19th century.[110] It may have been the song most often sung by soldiers of the First World War, a fact that historian and veteran of that war F.T. Nettleingham confirmed in *Tommy's Tunes*: "I have heard 'Annie Laurie' in peace and war; at home and abroad; in camp and on the march; in a big dining hall with 300 men and no dinner … The only other tune that approaches it in popularity … is the harmonised version of 'Home Sweet Home.'"[111]

There were other popular non-British songs. The Aussies sang "Australia Will Be There!," the Irish, "Sure a Little Bit of Heaven," and so forth. Prior to their armistice celebration show in Mons on 12 November 1918, Jack Ayre recalled that all who had jammed into the packed theatre in which the Dumbells performed were on their feet for over ten minutes to observe the singing of "God Save the King," "La Marseillaise," "O Canada," and "La Brabançonne." How appropriate that these four national anthems were followed by a rousing, and spontaneous version of "It's a Long Way to Tipperary," a song rightfully returned from exile at war's end.[112]

Figure 6 Though wounded at Sanctuary Wood, Al Plunkett enjoyed a significant postwar career as the Dumbells' central crooner. (Courtesy Stephen Plunkett)

Perhaps the biggest influence on the music of the trenches was the war itself. Much different from the war according to the civilians was the war according to the soldiers; soldier songs written by non-soldiers were painfully inauthentic to those at the Front and civilian-sung war anthems soon procured a disconnect with the fighting men. If songs of the British music hall had connected soldiers and civilians, the war experience polarized them, a fact born out in a substantial portion of the Canadian concert-parties' material. This material would forever change the face of sketch comedy.

III   In the Interest of Morale

The Dumbells and the Development of the Canadian Concert Party

Guns are alike to water pistols in the hands of fighting men
whose morale is deprived of sensation.

—Merton Plunkett

Napoleon said of morale that it "makes up three-quarters of the game; the relative balance of manpower accounts only for the remaining quarter."[1] Along with courage, fear, cohesion, disintegration, and the importance of primary groups, morale has been widely recognized as an important hallmark in the psychology of war, as it has been in military literature.[2] In the interest of preserving morale, military leaders came, perhaps grudgingly throughout the ages, to acknowledge the various elements that either contributed to, or impeded, the spirit of the troops. The First World War in particular, demanded that more attention be paid to the morale of the soldiers given the sheer size of the various militaries and their operations. Military officials on all sides were forced to consider the psychological realm of their own combatants as this war, unlike any other prior to it, was being fought by massive bodies of men with no previous military experience.[3]

Concert parties were a more official form of what soldiers had been doing at the Front for months: disabling the nightmare of the war through song and humour. Laughter could therapeutically reduce the gargantuan task of surviving the misery of war, neutralizing fear, making it manageable, and giving the soldier a much-needed escape from drudgery. One British soldier said of concert-party humour, "Had we been students of psychology I feel sure we should have seen this entertainment as an excellent means to releasing those tensions by which we are all inevitably troubled."[4] Another soldier recalled, "Concert party night was one of the highlights of our rest periods. The troupe did a wonderful job. Their work was of immeasurable value in raising morale, and one could almost

forget that the few days of safety would soon be over."[5] "Humour," according
to one British officer, "made a mockery of life and scoffed at our own frailty …
touched everything with ridicule and [took] the bite out of the last thing: death.
It was a working philosophy that carried us through the day."[6] And there were
many days to work through, many surreal moments to relive and much death.
Yet humour helped troops endure and accept the inevitable, discharge dangerous
tensions and achieve a distance from these threatening experiences.[7] As such,
humour and morale were inextricably linked and fed off each other.[8]

Only a few viewed the concert-party humour with any degree of derision.
Referring to the parties of the British Army, war poet Edmund Blunden depicted
war as theatre in his poem "Concert Party: Busseboum," comparing the hilarity
of the official concert parties with the chaos of war:

> We hear another matinée,
> We heard the maniac blast
> Of barrage south by Saint Eloi,
> And the red lights flaming there
> Called madness: Come, my bonny boy,
> And dance to the latest air.
>
> To this new concert, white we stood;
> Cold certainty held our breath;
> While men in the tunnels below Larch Wood
> Were kicking men to death.[9]

Ironically, over the course of the war, concert parties developed a darker brand
of humour, employing a sarcasm that might have appealed to Blunden.

Still, the concert parties had a wide appeal. Even those who possessed middle-class tastes were able to recognize this, as soldier Ralf Sheldon-Williams
testified: "To us there was more of the 'pep' we needed in one 'rag-time' or sickly
sentimental lyric than in ninety-and-nine fugues and symphonies. The concert
parties, permanent and itinerant, knew this and catered wisely to our needs.
Their bill of fare was strictly topical, and cheap old 'gags' and hoary 'patter songs,'
so be it they had a bearing on our lives, were never wearisome."[10]

This standard fare, the meat of the concert-party performance, was welcome
and familiar to men of all ranks and classes seeking a temporary anaesthetic to
the dreadful procedure at hand.

Deeply aware of the importance of humour and its effect on the soldiers'
morale, Canadian officials were, in many respects, pioneers among the world's
armies when it came to the organization of concert parties and entertainment. As
far as the Overseas Military Force in Canada was concerned, it was the Canadians
who led the way in recreational programs that proved so potent a factor in the

matter of soldier morale.[11] British officials took the first steps in standardizing recreational initiatives for soldiers of not only the British, but also the Dominion Armies. Yet, the issue of concert parties and entertainment for Canadian soldiers would soon fall squarely on the shoulders of Canadian officials.

Concert parties had existed in the BEF before the Canadian Divisions began their own, but Canadians would, in many ways, perfect the concept of the concert party, organizing nearly 30 permanent groups at a school in Mons specifically designed for the instruction of new parties. Still, entertaining Canadians troops initially came under the charge of the British military and British charitable organizations, including the YMCA, the Salvation Army, the Red Cross, and the Knights of Columbus. This changed when the costs of putting on entertainment events began to rise. By 1915, Canadian charitable organizations that had relied on their British counterparts were now responsible for financing their own entertainment.[12] When the cost of the war continued to rise, the British cut the apron strings, thus presenting a dilemma for the Canadians: professional entertainers raised the troops' morale, but cost money. The Canadian YMCA, by example, had been hiring English entertainers to appear at Canadian camps in England to the tune of $9,000 per month.[13] Still, a few professional entertainers continued to lift spirits at little or no cost.

Sir Harry Lauder was certainly the most famous of this exclusive network. And while other professionals wished to get only so close to the Front, Lauder was not nearly as shy. With the help of influential friends at the War Office, Lauder implored military authorities to allow him to perform at the Front: not at bases safely behind the lines, but actually on the front lines. Following weeks of debate, the War Office finally capitulated and Harry Lauder became the first professional entertainer to perform for troops at the actual front. Lauder sang at field hospitals and for units in the dugouts, chateaus, and pillaged barns of the front lines. Distributing cigarettes wherever he went, Lauder sang at the various YMCA huts—including those frequented by Canadians—and sometimes even at the side of the road to soldiers who could scarcely believe that the world's most famous Scotsman was, perhaps unceremoniously, giving them a song. He did so under extremely dangerous circumstances and often while the enemy's "whiz bangs" sailed perilously close overhead.[14] Lauder wanted to be close enough that the Germans "could hear [him], if they cared to listen."[15] He sang for the Aussies outside Albert's famous church.[16] And he sang for the Canadians in a crater near Vimy.[17] For his trouble, Lauder found a place in the hearts of the soldiers throughout the BEF and the Dominion Armies; a point we will return to later on.

The war, however, boasted few Harry Lauders. While many independently civilian-raised amateur concert performers did their bit, the great majority of professional entertainers required payment for their services; however, these salaries were prohibitively expensive for the Canadian military's entertainment budget.[18] Even if the authorities could afford to pay them, the professionals (excepting Lauder) did not want to go into the belly of the front lines. This problem would be solved from the wealth of talent within the rank and file of the Canadian soldiers.

And talent there was. Most regiments in the Canadian Corps had already been entertaining themselves. Singing had a privileged position in war culture and was a way in which men might form friendships with other soldiers.[19] By singing the same song, the soldier felt like he belonged. Certainly, a tangible and thriving musical culture had blossomed in Canada before the war. Subsequently, Canadian soldiers were arriving in France instilled with a deep appreciation for music. Many families were now able to afford a piano and the instrument was a central feature in the community.[20] And as discussed earlier, sheet music sales began to soar while associated industries of recorded music and gramophone equipment also prospered. As historian Tim Cook confirmed: "Canadians sang regularly, from Toronto middle-class houses to Quebec lumber towns, from maritime folk songs to the latest Vaudeville tune hummed through downtown Winnipeg, and also in church, school, and social gatherings."[21] It is little surprise, then, that the average foot soldier of the Canadian Corps sang heartily.

Often with the help of the YMCA, Canadian soldiers were able to hold impromptu singalongs in barns and abandoned farmhouses along the front line. As one talented soldier reminisced: "It was here that the one big family spirit prevailed. The audience and actors became one and thus banished all their worries for at least a little while, or as long as the *vin blanc* lasted. In these barns and at such functions there were men who sat and cheered on the singer of a sentimental ballad by shouting: 'Put a quiver in it, Jim'—men who died the following dawn with the song still on their lips."[22]

Soldiers genuinely looked forward to these "Y" singalongs, or "smokers," as they were affectionately called. Signaller John McArthur, by example, wrote home to say that "the batt'n are putting on a farewell concert for the next draft on Monday evening. I suppose it will be pretty good as they have some excellent talent in this bunch. There is to be a smoker afterwards so I guess we will have a good celebration … we have lots of singing here and there are lots of concerts in the Y."[23]

Smokers predated the more official concert parties of the Canadian Corps and would, in essence, harvest the crop of talent that officials drew from in order to fill the available concert-party positions.

Concert parties had been prevalent in the British Army as early as December 1914.[24] The Brits had authorized an order to "to extract a number of talented entertainers and directors from among their troops for the sole purpose of amusement and entertainment."[25] "The Follies" from the British 4th Division,

Figure 7 Originally with the 56th (London) Division's Bow Bells concert party, Jock Holland, seen here in 1920, became a Dumbell at the end of the war. (Courtesy John McLaren)

"The Fancies" from the 6th Division, "The Bow Bells" from the 56th Division (London), and, later, "The Gaieties" of the 5th Army were successful examples of permanent British concert parties whose members had been excused from active duty.

Divisional parties were becoming a common sight at the Front, as one machine gunner, serving in Arras in 1917 recalled: "Within five minutes walk of our Camp no less than four large concert halls had now been erected, and every night concert Parties [*sic*], belonging to the various divisions stationed on the Arras front gave first-rate concerts, to which all troops were admitted to the sum of half a franc. These concerts were greatly appreciated by our soldiers, especially after a long dreary spell of duty in the 'trenches.'"[26]

With their growing popularity, the British Army put forth a considerable effort into the logistical support of these concerts, and "repair parties" were engaged to ready the various makeshift venues for the performances.[27]

Initially, the difference between British and Canadian concert parties was negligible. Leslie Henson's description of his concert party, "The Gaieties" from the British 5th Army, was consistent, and nearly interchangeable, with Jack McLaren's description of the PPCLI CC as it is with Plunkett's recollection of the Dumbells. British and Canadian concert parties shared the same type of casts: singers, actors, comedians, and female impersonators, and the available equipment and technology were the same. As Henson remembered, the BEF provided the Gaieties with "a lorry on which to carry our lighting set, and at shortest notice [we] gave shows in barns, in schools, and in tents. The Tank corps built us a theatre in twenty-four hours with Chinese labour. It had comfortable stall seats of wood and canvas. Our life was a series of one night jumps, and we played to almost every branch of the forces."[28]

The majority of the permanent parties travelled by truck, performed in makeshift venues, made and collected their own props from discarded materials, and were always on the move, putting on a show almost every night.

There was usually a small fee charged for those performances put on in a theatre, whereas the open-air shows were generally free to the soldiers. The admission fee for a concert-party theatre performance put on by either the British or Canadian Army was approximately one franc, a modest fee, but tickets were often provided to the soldiers out of battalion funds. All concert parties were reasonably priced as to compete with the estaminet and other trappings that might have appealed to the soldier. For their part, the Dumbells performed free for soldiers throughout the war.[29]

If tangible differences between British and Canadian concert parties existed, they weren't perceptible in the appearance of the performers, admission fees, nor in the kind of venue where the performances took place. Next to the actual performance material, perhaps the only difference between the British and Canadian concert parties was that for the latter, the raising of permanent concert parties was more widespread. Given the comparative size of the two armies (the British Forces being far larger), it might be argued that the Canadian Corps was more comprehensively dedicated to manufacturing concert parties, especially later on in the war through the efforts of the YMCA.[30] Following a British mandate, the CEF would—over the course of the war—release 15 or so lucky and talented men from each division, so that they might provide entertainment and amusement for the fighting forces of the Canadian Army.[31] Remarkably, by war's end, over 30 concert parties were performing within the Canadian Corps.

Jack McLaren and His Haversack

John Wilson McLaren, or "Jack" as he was known, was one of the talented and lucky ones. McLaren immigrated to Canada from Scotland in 1902 at the age of seven, but returned there as a teenager to study architecture and later fine arts at Edinburgh College.[32] While there, McLaren joined the 5th Royal Scots before once again setting sail for Canada. This balancing act between military service and the arts would come to define most of McLaren's life.

Most Canadian soldiers can recall their whereabouts when war was declared at the beginning of August 1914. This was rendered easier for some, because the Great War broke out over a long weekend. Jack McLaren was no different. For him, it was Jackson's Point, just north of Sutton on Lake Simcoe in Ontario. And, like many others, McLaren was worried that the war would not last long enough for him to enjoy the adventure.[33] From Jackson's Point, McLaren rushed to make a train bound for Toronto where, upon arrival, he marched directly to the Armouries on University Avenue.

Not long afterward, McLaren, as well as a multitude of other early enlist-ees, found themselves in Valcartier, Quebec. The Valcartier training camp was rife with confusion, sickness, and generally unfavourable conditions. After one month of training, McLaren also fell ill with jaundice and was sent to the camp's field hospital. Unsatisfied with the treatment he was receiving, McLaren simply left the camp. As he explained, "I quickly came to the conclusion that I must get the hell out of there if I was ever to get well again."[34] Such was the administrative nightmare at Valcartier, McLaren was never asked to explain his hiatus from the Forces when he re-enlisted with the 4th University Company in Toronto, some six months after his first experience.[35]

After the convalescence that followed his first term as a Canadian soldier, McLaren spent some time with his friends, the Brown family, at their home on Lake Rosseau in Ontario's Muskoka region in 1915. While there, McLaren was introduced to the Scottish-born Canadian economist Professor James Mavor. A great patron of the arts, Mavor had been a friend of Tolstoy and had helped Russian Doukhobors escape religious persecution and resettle in Canada.[36] The professor found merit in McLaren's paintings as well as the theatrical sketches that Jack had written and performed about local summer cottagers.[37] Though Mavor bought some of McLaren's works, no one could have anticipated the bearing Mavor would have on McLaren's military career, and indeed the future of Canada's concert parties. Having re-enlisted in the 4th University Company in Montreal, McLaren would be one of the reinforcements sent to boost the depleted forces of the PPCLI.

The PPCLI had been the brainchild of Lieutenant Colonel Alexander Hamilton Gault. A Montreal businessman, Gault represented one of the

Figure 8   Jack McLaren during the war's early days, c. 1915. (Courtesy John McLaren)

remaining vestiges of 19th-century chivalry when he became the last private citizen to raise and partially fund an army under the British Crown.[38] The regiment took its name from its patron Princess Patricia, daughter of the Duke of Connaught, Canada's tenth Governor General. The Princess embroidered a camp colour for the regiment that would, over time, take on an almost mystical significance, having been the only regimental colour carried into battle by a British or Canadian regiment.[39] The PPCLI first saw action at the Ypres Salient in April 1915, suffering 238 casualties in the span of three months, after which only 10 of 27 of the regiment's officers remained. This entry quickly earned the regiment respect from battle-weary British and French regiments who had been impressed by the PPCLI's innovative surprise trench raids. During the Battle of Frezenberg at Bellewaerde Ridge in April and May 1915, however, the regiment suffered enormous losses. The Ridge became known as the "Grave of the

Originals" to future Pats, as only four officers and 150 men managed to crawl back.[40] Indeed, of the 1,098 PPCLI enlistees (only ten percent of whom were Canadian born), only 39 "originals" would survive the war. Within four weeks of their formation, the University Companies were on their way to the Ypres Salient to help the badly beaten Pats. It was here that Jack McLaren would see war for the first time.

McLaren was no ordinary foot soldier and his haversack was surely one of the most unusual to be found in the Dominion Army. Along with his Ross Rifle, McLaren's haversack toted along a cigar box of various paints, watercolours, brushes, sketch boards, theatrical makeup, wigs, and sheet music.[41] Remarkably, these items would serve the imaginative Scottish-Canadian far better than his Ross Rifle ever did. The coming of this peculiar artist to the Pats had been flagged for Captain Agar Adamson by his friend Professor Mavor. The latter had written Adamson to inform him that McLaren presented a certain skill set that should be properly exploited for the benefit of the regiment.[42]

Initially, Adamson had pegged McLaren out for mapping duties. And so McLaren joined the sniper unit to sketch reconnaissance maps of the Ypres Salient. As a sniper-mapper, McLaren recalled the brutal ingenuity of platoon commander Sergeant Christie. According to McLaren, Christie was a small, tough man, and he had the unit drive four-inch pieces of wood into the ground in no man's land in front of the barbed wire by the German trenches. One side of the wood, which faced the Canadian trench, was painted with phosphorescent paint. The Canadian sniping unit sat still, and with faces painted black, awaited their prey. As McLaren explained, "we trained our guns on the glowing stakes ... at night when the Germans moved about in front of the luminous sticks the light effect was blacked out, and we pulled the triggers of our rifles."[43] Similarly, the unit used a dummy head attached to a stick and held just above the parapet to draw German fire, thus allowing the unit to get a better sense of German sniping range.[44] But McLaren would not remain a sniper for long. However useful McLaren's shooting acumen or reconnaissance work was, his most important wartime calling was ahead of him. Soon, Adamson had McLaren organizing little impromptu concerts for the soldiers in the reserve area.[45] Within a year of arriving at Europe's theatre of war, McLaren and his singing soldier friends were poised to redefine the role of Canadian concert parties on the Western Front.

There were several divisional concert parties, soldier shows, and individual Canadian soldier-entertainers performing for troops long before either the PPCLI CC or the Dumbells began. Sergeant Gitz Rice of the 5th Battery in the 1st Divisional Artillery, for instance, had led minstrel shows with 20 singers and comedians drawn from various units by the end of 1915. Cyril "Biddy" Biddulph had also made a name for himself among Canadian troops with his "worried" soldier routine.[46] There was also the very first concert party in the Canadian Corps, which was formed within the 1st Canadian Field Ambulance. And though little is known about this non-permanent party, the group managed at least one grand-scale minstrel show with a huge cast.[47]

Still, the idea of a permanent or semi-permanent Canadian concert party germinated within the PPCLI. Princess Pats' historian Lieutenant Ralph Hodder-Williams recalled: "The officer commanding the Patricias was perhaps the first, among the Canadian battalions at least, to recognize officially these organized regimental entertainments after the hard day's work of training in rest camp. In quiet sectors the members of the Comedy Company were relieved of many trench duties, and generally had a new 'show' ready when the Regiment came back to rest."[48]

Lieutenant Colonel Gault himself was directly involved with the design of the Pats' Comedy Company.[49] And in May 1916, at the request of Captain Agar Adamson, the "PPCLI Comedy Company," with Jack McLaren as its chief comedy sketch artist, became the first semi-permanent company of soldiers to be relieved of their duty in order to entertain the Canadian troops along the Western Front.

The PPCLI CC performed on makeshift stages in abandoned farm houses, old barns and open fields underneath tents, sometimes perilously close to the actual fighting. This closeness to the battle would have a profound effect on how Canadian soldier-entertainers kept in touch with the war and the common soldier. Later, the PPCLI CC would serve as a mould for several other front-line concert parties.

The Pats' Comedy Company was considered by many, including members of the Dumbells, to be the best. Dumbell Alan Murray recalled watching a PPCLI CC performance, "they were superb, no one ever came near them with their satire, they would tear anything and everything to pieces in the most joyful manner."[50] Canadian theatre historian Patrick O'Neill agreed, "the greatest of these companies in terms of material and originality was the PPCLI Comedy Company."[51] Certainly, the PPCLI CC was more topical than the other parties and had developed a formula that future concert parties of the Canadian Corps tried to emulate.

Crucial to their success was Jack McLaren. As fellow Comedy Company member Conrad Stephens confirmed, "[McLaren] did practically everything; he could be straight, or he could be comedic, he was really versatile [and] wrote a lot of the stuff for the show."[52] Given his talent as a sketch writer, his relationship with influential agents like Mavor and Adamson, and the esteem in which he was held by his colleagues, Jack McLaren was—perhaps after only the Y's Captain Merton Plunkett himself—the most important soldier-entertainer in Canada's wartime concert parties. And through his craft, McLaren directly influenced the trajectory of the concert parties of the Canadian Corps.

The PPCLI CC was organized by the regimental paymaster Captain H.E. Pembroke, with the first official performance scheduled for Steenvoorde, France, in early June 1916. With very little time to prepare, Captain Pembroke, along with privates Lilly, Cunningham, Ham, Morrison, Fenwick (the female impersonator), Young (the pianist), Norman "Nobby" Clarke, and McLaren began rehearsing. Initially the keyboard player for the troupe, Nobby Clarke was soon be "demoted" to property manager—a job that he would relish—in favour of the more flamboyant piano-playing skills of Leonard Young.[53] Young had amazed his future comedic comrades in an impromptu performance at the Steenvoorde hall. Hearing Young's piano brilliance from their billet, the Comedy Company members fought their way through the mob at the entrance and up the stairs to find their future pianist. At the piano, Young was found with a mess tin hanging from his belt hook, and wearing a balaclava. The Comedy Company had found their hoped-for, as McLaren exclaimed, "musical saviour Rachmaninoff playing like a master of the keyboard."[54]

While Young was winning accolades for his piano chops, Nobby Clarke took his new position quite seriously. Within three months of the first Steenvoorde show, Clarke had swelled the Comedy Company's wardrobe and properties from two rations bags and a hat box to two truckloads of "property man's delights."[55] Old cart wheels, barrels, beds, and numerous other odd and ends were added to the growing collection and helped to inform future PPCLI CC skits.

In preparation for Steenvoorde, the Comedy Company set up shop in the corner of a field behind the transport lines. This proved a little too close to the actual fighting. As McLaren remembered, the Germans, flying in their observation planes watched "every movement of the first girls' beauty chorus that any concert party staged in France. Our anti-aircraft guns would open up on the German airmen. The falling pieces of shrapnel were often a provoking and very disturbing feature of nightmare effect, a deterrent to good rehearsing."[56]

The Comedy Company soon retreated to a new location in a nearby wooded area to finish their prep. Yet, only five days into rehearsal, the group received word that the Germans had broken through the Ypres Salient and that the Pats were badly cut up. The PPCLI had once again suffered heavy losses while helping the Allies hold the Germans from breaking through to the channel ports at Sanctuary Wood.[57] On 2 June 1916, the Comedy Company gave up showbiz for a time and once again donned their rifles and equipment and went back to the Front. Fortunately for them, when they reached the Salient, the entertainers were turned back around as a suitable number of reinforcements had already arrived. They were off the hook. In short order, the Comedy Company were returned to Steenvoorde with the express directive of putting on a show as soon as possible.[58]

Given the heavy losses that the PPCLI suffered while holding the Salient, there was some speculation among Comedy Company performers as to how the soldier audience would respond to their first performance. There was also another dreadful consideration. Having endured the hellish German push to the channel and having just received 20 crisp new francs, the surviving Pats were no doubt tempted by the appeal of the estaminet and *vin blanc*. Yet the troops were instructed to spend a beautiful sunny day in early June 1916 inside the Steenvoorde hall as a test audience for the PPCLI CC. The audience then, comprised mostly soldiers from the new University Companies were *forced* to watch the show.

The Comedy Company set up in the poorly ventilated upstairs of the local hall, which housed a small stage and a piano. They decorated the stage with colourful bunting, which was illuminated with acetylene lights.[59] And then they waited for their captive audience to arrive. McLaren expressed the entertainers' great reservations:

> We could hear the "enemy's" approach up the wooden stairway and I often sympathized a great deal with the German boys in later days when I heard that the Canadians had raided their trenches or taken a plot of ground from them. To be on the Canadian side when a raid is on is one thing, but to be the opposition and hear these same lads shoving and mauling each other to avenge themselves on the adversary and you are the adversary—well![60]

The first act, a burlesque on Uncle Tom's Cabin presented in army vernacular, did little to ease the tension between a crowd that did not want to be there and the lamentable performing soldiers. Following a solo song performed by Captain Pembroke came a duet, replete with a line of comedy chorus girls that seemed to soften the sanguinary mob. From this midway point onward, the PPCLI CC had turned the tide and their "enemy" crowd had been defeated. Surviving the initial hostilities, McLaren and his six colleagues had managed to turn the show around, winning the audience over with their various songs and routines, getting a company of men, who had just been through the belly of hell, to laugh, whistle, cheer, and—for a moment—forget.

This was real, if unexpected success. PPCLI Lieutenant Ralph Hodder-Williams wrote gleefully that "at one bound the Comedy Company became a regimental institution."[61] Indeed, this one show gave CEF authorities a bona fide reason to consider organizing other official concert parties and to extend the group's targeted audience. As such, the Canadian Corps decided that the PPCLI CC's show would be presented to the whole of the 7th Brigade.[62] And with word-of-mouth, compulsory parades to furnish an audience were no longer necessary, as McLaren explained: "By the time of the following evening's performance, which the second half of the Princess Pat's battalion was to witness, the fame of the little troop had spread so far and wide, a strong picket had to be placed in front of the hall to keep off the great crowd that tried to gain admittance."[63]

And following this first stint, the Comedy Company entertainers were presented with a miraculous opportunity amidst a dreadful war: a chance to get out of danger's way.

Colonel R.T. Pelly, as well as many other officers who had seen the early run of Comedy Company performances, believed that the lads would be performing a greater service to their country if they decided to stay out of the line as permanent entertainers. Ergo, if the merrymakers wished, they could stay out of the trenches and become permanent performers.[64] Still, the Colonel felt that the soldiers who had earnestly volunteered to fight in France and Belgium should be given a choice of whether they wanted to remain soldiers or to become musical jesters behind the lines. The company was given 24 hours by the Colonel to decide whether they wanted to remain fighting men or become full-time actors. As McLaren recalled, "the PPCLI Comedy Company went into conference, and, after a remarkably short convention the vote was unanimous, with both hands and feet, to carry-on as 'soldiers of song.'"[65] But the Pats experienced a constant flux of senior officers throughout the first two years of war. Lieutenant Colonel Farquhar and Colonel Buller had been killed. Gault had lost his leg and Agar Adamson too was wounded. Directives were therefore being updated continuously and the PPCLI CC's career trajectory was several times interrupted by a return to the Front.[66] Following these trips, however, the group was returned to the stage and the show, necessarily, went on.[67] In so doing, these morale-boosting "soldiers of song" became the first of their kind: a semi-permanent Canadian soldier show.

Singing at the "Y"

If the PPCLI CC provided a mould for future Canadian concert parties, the YMCA provided the infrastructure and necessary assistance to help the parties achieve their aim of raising the morale of Canadian soldiers. Each division in the Canadian Corps was allotted six YMCA officers to run the various functions of the organization. While some Canadian soldiers found the YMCA to be too preachy for their tastes, many others were, understandably, grateful for the organization's front-line presence.[68] Right in the eye of the maelstrom as they were, "Y" huts and canteens had become recognizable havens for Canadian soldiers looking for food, rest, and some diversion from the war.

At its zenith, the YMCA had within its ranks 140 officers and 745 other ranks. Their work was acknowledged in an official Report of the Ministry, which directly praised the YMCA's positive effect on morale: "The Army authorities, indeed, were quick to realize the effect of the 'Y' service on the morale of the soldiers and provided facilities with a gratifying willingness, while in nearly every case Commanding Officers, more closely in touch with the needs of the men, lent their influence and support."[69]

Raising and maintaining the spirit of the soldier was the mission statement of the Canadian YMCA, which provided a complete program of entertainment to Canadian soldiers, including cinemas, reading and writing material, and, of course, concert-party nights.[70] Later in the war, a 500-seat theatre was erected at the Beaver Hut, the Canadian YMCA centre in London. The Beaver Hut was famed for the hospitality it offered the Canadian soldier who "dines there, sleeps there, plays billiards there, buys his Canadian 'tit-bits' there, purchases his theatre tickets there at about half the regular price, reads English or Canadian papers and magazines, listens to an orchestra or to unscheduled music of which there is plenty at any hour."[71]

Figure 9 Captain Merton Plunkett's trademark smile. (Courtesy Stephen Plunkett)

Inaugurated by the PPCLI CC in 1918, the Beaver Hut staged many concert-party performances.

Long before the halcyon days of 500-seat venues, however, one officer was roughing it in the small "Y" huts just behind the lines. Orillia's Merton Plunkett was used to extra responsibility. At 13, Plunkett had become the family's bread-winner. As his daughter Annie O'Brien explained, there was no choice: "My father *had* to leave school because his father was ill."[72] The same set of uncles who would later invest in the initial Canadian run of the Dumbells tried to assist by setting Merton up in a grocery store in 1909. Music, however, was the real fire in Plunkett's belly. Mert sang in a choir in Orillia and later moved to Toronto to study music in 1913. While in Toronto, Plunkett lived at the "Y" and to help pay his way, took a job there as a social director. As Plunkett recalled, "It got so interesting I finally gave up the music lessons to work full time at Y social and musical activities."[73] His time there was so special that when war broke out, Plunkett felt compelled to do his bit in the First World War in the name of the YMCA. And so, the grocer from Orillia became an honorary captain in the YMCA and headed overseas with the 35th Battalion, attached to the Canadian 3rd Division.[74]

When serving with the "Y" in France, Plunkett began to make a name for himself by performing in concerts in various "Y" canteens. By the fall of 1916, Plunkett, as master of ceremonies, comedian, and singer, had become a celebrity among the many troops that saw him perform night after night at the "Y" can-teen in the village of Albert. As his brother Al Plunkett described: "[W]ith their buddies they sipped hot drinks and received warmth under the spell of songs and music by Captain (Mert) Plunkett, who on these occasions observed the glow of happiness and gladness of the men which resulted from these impromptu sessions."[75]

Figure 10 The "Y" hut, August 1916. (Courtesy Stephen Plunkett)

And while his fame soared in the miserable middle of the war at these "Y" gatherings, Plunkett kept a keen eye out for talented soldiers who might later fit into one of the many official concert parties he organized. Soldiers would arrive early at the hut for various "Y"-sponsored events, including the London Lady Parties, where a female group, usually consisting of a violinist, a cellist, and a soprano, would entertain the troops. To pass the time before the show began, Captain Plunkett would lead a singalong, where several soldiers with musical ability, or disability as the case may be, were able to sing, tell a joke, or play piano.[76]

One such soldier was Plunkett's own brother Al, who served with the 58th Battalion before being wounded by shrapnel at Sanctuary Wood. To help him recover, he was sent to help out at the "Y." Al recalled one of the first smokers he attended when he, as the baritone; alongside Silas Pickle, bass; Leslie Hughes, first tenor; and brother Mert on lead, harmonized the "old songs" for the audience, including "In the Evening, by the Moonlight" and "Sweet Adeline." Their renditions, according to Al, "had the boys yelling with such glee that it suppressed the constant rumble of the guns."[77] Canadian Headquarters recognized the glee that Mert Plunkett was capable of producing. Having demonstrated his ability as a morale booster, Plunkett soon became the pre-eminent officer of the YMCA.[78] With great determination and his trademark congeniality, Plunkett would refine and define the Canadian concert party.

The Chase to Vimy

War was all around the performers; a fact that dictated how shows were staged. All concert parties had to perform on makeshift stages that had been erected in the rest areas, which were dangerously close to the real action. As Dumbell Bill Redpath explained, "We were very often subject to bombing raids at night, because we were *just* behind the lines."[79] The PPCLI CC had to stop one show for a gas alert.[80] The soldier-entertainers chose to perform in the early evening, when it was dark enough for the artificial light to have its effect—often candles placed in biscuit tins—but light enough so that they could finish the show without drawing German shells their way.

The performers became expert in improvisation; a valued quality that they were fond of retelling in the interviews. Performing under tents and tarps, the concert parties made use of every available tool and prop. Plunkett recalled: "The first concert parties in the war zone used to borrow burlap hangings to use as backdrops. Ross Hamilton's first wig was made of rope and female impersonators used to be gowned in tenting or Y.M.C.A. window curtains."[81]

Hats for the Dumbells' drum corps were shaped from the Maconachie tins, which had previously contained the troops' vegetable stew ration.[82] Similarly, the sandbags full of props belonging to the PPCLI CC contained everything from horsehair to umbrellas, and the company's flatbed truck was converted into a stage for show time.[83] Predictably, not every show went according to plan. The set for the Comedy Company's *Dugout Scene*, for instance, comprised straw-filled sandbags that had been hung on a wooden frame in order that the entire scenery might be moved on and off the stage easily by one man. During one performance, a quartet was proceeding with the musical sketch when one of them suddenly belted out a sour note. Embarrassed, the singer hastily left the stage, shouting, "You can finish the Goddamn number yourselves." Unfortunately, the singer took with him the scenery for the sketch, leaving the others to exit the stage as best they could.[84]

The PPCLI CC possessed some resourceful scroungers who found useful objects in the most unusual places and from some of the unlikeliest sources. In Ypres, for instance, the troupe found the skin of a cat hung up in a farmer's barn and quickly cut it up to use for moustaches. At a field dressing station, the entertainers were able to convince one of the medics to part with some gauze that would later fashion skirts for the beauty chorus. The YMCA provided the Comedy Company with empty cartons from which hats were made.[85] Nothing was wasted, everything used and, if possible, made portable; ready to be carted to the next stop along the Front.

In September 1916, the Canadian Corps were ready to engage in the battles of Thiepval, Courcelette, and Ancre Heights. Correspondingly, the PPCLI CC followed the Corps' own marching orders. On 7 September, the performers left Ypres for Albert, taking with them all the properties they could manage.[86] At Warloy, Captain Fred Hancock of the YMCA, along with the assistance of a pioneer battalion, built a makeshift stage for the PPCLI CC. By placing a marquee against the side of an old house, Hancock and his assistants arranged seats for the spectators at the lip of the "stage."[87] It was at Warloy, just 10 kilometres west of Albert, that the PPCLI CC produced some of their best and most important work.[88] The audience, as McLaren described, were men "who just two hours before had been in battle … some with heads bandaged, or an arm in a sling, or a touch of shell shock."[89] Just as the war's fighter pilots improved with every flight they survived, the Comedy Company too, were flying high and got better with every subsequent show. PPCLI CC could now offer a quality show that was witnessed by soldier audiences who would soon be training for a date with destiny on the Ridge.

Wherever the Canadian Corps were sent, it seemed, the Comedy Company followed. In the late autumn of 1916, the troupe followed the Corps, heading northeast from Albert toward the Vimy sector. By now, the Pats' CC was immensely popular with the soldiers of the Canadian Corps. Yet, as popular as the company had been with the Canadian troops, their repertoire also become known *to*, and applauded *by* the Pats' top brass. To ring in 1917, PPCLI sergeants planned a dinner concert for the regiment's senior officers. Following the Hogmanay meal, all, officers and regular soldiers alike, converged on the "Y" hut for a special performance by the Comedy Company. As Hodder-Williams reported, the group repeated "some of its old favourites by special request, [and had] put on an entirely new 'show' written for the occasion."[90] Private Charles Douglas Richardson was also in attendance and expressed his admiration for his own PPCLI brethren-entertainers. Richardson, who had been serving with the Pats from the spring of 1916, had been severely wounded in the Ypres sector in June of the same year. The private, however, returned to his unit that December just in time to see the show: "There is a concert given by the P.P.C.L.I. concert party tonight at 10 o'clock and I think I shall take it in. The intention is to have it run into the New Year. We have a very fine concert party and the band of the R.C.R's which accompanies it, is one of the best."[91]

Four short months later, Richardson would perish at Vimy Ridge.

To keep things fresh for soldiers like Richardson in the season leading up to the Vimy charge, the Comedy Company changed the show every month. During this period, the company played to a vast number of Canadian soldiers at Barlin, Bruay-La-Buissière, Écoivres, and Mount Saint Éloi. The shows lasted through the winter of 1916–17.[92] From cook to colonel, the PPCLI CC left an impression on all who saw them. The Steenvoorde Nine, so called by Jack McLaren, would *not*, however, remain intact for the war's duration and some of the performers were sent back down the line, never to return to the soldiers' wartime stage. Many of the Pats' entertainers re-entered the fight, taking part in Canada's most famous battle. Indeed, the planning and execution of Vimy Ridge would come and go—with some Comedy Company members fully in its midst—months before Canada's more famous concert party performed its first show.

Plunkett's Trial Balloon

In 1917, Captain Plunkett, aware of the success of the Pats' CC, approached Major General Louis J. Lipsett, to see whether or not the organization of other, more permanent concert parties was permissible, as it had been in the BEF since 1916. Lipsett agreed, and gave his blessing to the formation of permanent Canadian concert parties.[93] Plunkett then busied himself with the formation of a test concert party, using the PPCLI CC as a mould.[94]

If not for the assistance and insistence of Lipsett, Adamson, and other key officers who knew the merit of the soldier-entertainers, many concert parties would not have survived their first show.[95] Plunkett was well aware of this reality. The Dumbells, for example, officially fell under the command of the

Divisional Officer, Lieutenant Colonel Gault, who, as previously discussed, was also in charge of the Pats' Comedy Company. But because the YMCA paid for the Dumbells' expenses, Captain Plunkett retained control of that particular concert party. Still, Gault was pivotal in securing the permanency of the Dumbells, and gave the concert party its name, which was taken from the insignia prominently featured on all of the 3rd Division's gear: a red dumbbell on a French-grey divisional patch, signifying "silence and strength."[96]

Through their influence, Gault and Lipsett were able to free several soldiers who, as far as their individual commanding officers were concerned, were on loan to the Dumbells for only one show. The two senior officers did not put their requests in the form of an order, but instead indicated in writing that they "would be pleased if [the various COs] could leave these men attached indefinitely."[97] The potency behind General Lipsett and Lieutenant Colonel Gault's "requests" ensured that those soldiers in question would be forever emancipated from trench slavery.[98]

Figure 11 Originally with the Y-Emmas concert party, female impersonator Charlie McLean became a feature of postwar Dumbells shows. (Courtesy John McLaren)

Still, time has slightly obscured the facts regarding the formation of various Canada's concert parties and, despite popular belief, Mert Plunkett's premiere attempt at a concert party was *not* the Dumbells. The trial balloon for Plunkett and the YMCA was a concert party appropriately dubbed "The Y-Emmas," which began performing in early 1917. Unlike the PPCLI CC, the Y-Emmas were a full-time unit and performed for not only for one specific regiment or division, but also all Canadian troops. The group, featuring Red Newman and Charlie McLean, successfully toured the front line under the supervision of Sergeant Carey, playing hundreds of shows for the soldiers. The success of the Y-Emmas afforded Plunkett the opportunity to build other concert parties.[99]

And there were many others. One ordinary foot soldier from Prince Edward Island spoke to the vast number of Canadian concert parties in the final year of the war: "… saw a number of concert parties when we were out. As you know much of our best talent is in khaki and each division and some brigades have a concert party which does nothing else. During the three weeks we were out I saw three variety concerts, free or for half a franc (ten cents), for which one would willingly pay from five to ten shillings for a ticket in London."[100]

So important were the concert parties for morale that a theatre school, specifically designed for the manufacture of Canadian concert parties, was begun in Mons in the summer of 1917. This too was officially sanctioned, as General Currie himself asked Plunkett to begin a theatre school to train performers. Plunkett, along with the assistance of singer Lieutenant Norman Jolliffe, was able to produce approximately 28 battalion parties, including a permanent party for the Canadian Corps Training School under the command of Lieutenant R.W. Day. In the winter of 1918–19 alone, the concert-party factory produced 19 parties.[101] Captain Plunkett remembered that "Once we had as many as seven parties training with us at the same time." [102] There was no space for live performances at the concert-party factory, only a stage for rehearsals and a place for costume and prop storage. The school adhered to the exclusive mandate of training concert parties for the Canadian Corps, turning 500 soldiers into morale-boosting entertainers.

Plunkett had convinced officials of the merit of the using several concurrent groups as concert parties. All of these successes came well before the Dumbells sang their first chorus. The 4th Division Maple Leafs, for instance, were very popular with the soldiers. Morley and Albert Plunkett, Captain Mert's brothers, were feature members of the Maple Leafs' roster. Blessed with matinee-idol looks, Al was a natural crooner and a fan favourite, especially with Canadian women on the Dumbells' several cross-country tours. The Maple Leaf concert party enjoyed an exceptional run with its version of *Alladin*, which was performed over 60 times at the Front and may have been, next to the PPCLI CC and the Dumbells, the most popular concert party of the war.[103]

Figure 12 Stretcher-bearer-cum-soldier-entertainer Alan Murray, c. 1920. (Courtesy John McLaren)

The Maple Leafs began the tradition of stealing performers from other parties to bolster their own. Legendary female impersonators Ross Hamilton and Alan Murray, along with pianist Leonard Young from the 9th Field Ambulance (and PPCLI CC) were headhunted by the Maple Leafs. This trio had been performing together in amateur theatre in Montreal prior to the war and were scoring successes long before anyone saw them with either the Maple Leafs or the Dumbells. The 9th Canadian Field Ambulance's official war diary testified to the quality of the troupe following their New Year's Eve performance of 1916:

> According to opinions offered on all sides the show was a great success. There were capacity houses on December 23rd, and 25th, and on Thursday, December 28th, 600 were admitted to the Hut and 500 turned away. From the laughter and applause, one clearly saw that the efforts of the actors were both appreciated and enjoyed. On Friday, December 29th,

a performance was given at C.C.S., #42 for the Officers, nurses, staff and patients of the Hospital and the show met with the same success. The success of the performance was aided largely by the efforts of the RCR band who played in their usual excellent style. Both the actors and band expect to give the show on several occasions in the month of January 1917.[104]

The 9th was closely linked with the Princess Pats and operated from a musical comedy approach. This was in contrast to the talented 10th Field Ambulance, which presented more of a revue-style show. The 10th included Toronto pianist Ivor "Jack" Ayre, Winnpeg comedian Ted Charter, the Scottish-born tenor Bill Tennent, and Edmonton's Jerry Brayford. Presciently, Plunkett later headhunted all of these gifted entertainers for the supergroup, the Dumbells.[105]

There was also the 1st Division concert party, The Volatiles. Over 50,000 Canadian soldiers; General Currie; the Duke of Connaught; Prime Minister Borden; and General John J. Pershing, the American commander-in-chief, converged at Tincques on Dominion Day 1918 for the Canadian Corps' sports day. It was in front of this esteemed audience that the Volatiles performed.[106] Given the size of the audience and the various VIPs in attendance, Canadian military officials would have wanted a top-notch act that befitted such an occasion, and the Volatiles were entrusted with this task.

If the Maple Leafs began the tradition of thievery, the Dumbells perfected it. The original eight Dumbells were initially attached to Ben Allen's 16th Battalion for a special performance to honour the new commander of the Canadian Corps, General Arthur Currie in June 1917. Most of these original Dumbells had previously performed with other concert parties. The 16th Battalion concert party had already absorbed the best members of the "Y-Emmas" (including Red Newman and Charlie MacLean) and much of the Dumbells' early performance material had been created in the 16th Battalion by Ben Allen himself.[107]

The Dumbells likely played their first official performance in early June 1917 at Major Beecher Gale's Theatre at Gouy-Servins, France. For almost every researcher who has studied the Dumbells the exact date for the troupe's first show has been difficult to determine. In some of the performers' accounts, the first official Dumbell show was given as sometime in August 1917. The majority of the cast involved, however, believe early June 1917 to be correct.[108] This latter date seems the more plausible, especially when taken with other independent sources.[109] Original Dumbell Jerry Brayford, for example, recalled how his first show was in front of his old regiment the 49th Battalion. Brayford's battalion were stationed at Villers-au-Bois, less than five kilometres from the Major's theatre in Gouy-Servins.[110]

The concert party may have begun performing as early as the end of May 1917. William John McLellan was an ordinary foot soldier who enlisted in the

Figure 13 A rare shot of the Dumbells in uniform during the war. (Courtesy Stephen Plunkett)

CEF in February 1916. McLellan was a repeat patron at Dumbell shows and gave his first glowing review of the 3rd Division's troupe in a letter home to his parents dated 26 May 1917: "We've been having a treat this week—given by the Divisional Concert Party. It's considered the best concert party in France and I can't see how it can be beaten very well. You'll never see better scenery at the Pan and the different scits [*sic*] are hard to beat. They get all the latest songs and can sure sing them too."[111]

Following their first official stint, the Dumbells were permanently billeted at a farm home in Ferfay, France, at the Canadian 3rd Divisional School.

While we cannot date their first performance, we do know that it took just over a year before the Dumbells' name had become famous among Canadian soldiers. In his personal war memoir, soldier Kenneth Walter Foster recalled when he got his first chance to see the famous comedy troupe's sports day show on Dominion Day 1918 in Tincques. For a spell, Foster was transported out of the fight: "… we attended the Corps sports … where a good time was enjoyed by all those able to attend … as a special added attraction, the famous 'Dumbells' put on a show. It was the first time I had seen them in action on the stage. So, for that day only, all thoughts of the War were cast aside."[112]

In the summer that followed this memorable show, the now-famous Dumbells were once again poised to morph into a bigger and better concert party.

By fusing members of the Bow Bells as well as the London Scottish Divisional Party and its 59th Scottish Divisional Band into their own camp, by the latter stages of the war the Dumbells had become an all-star concert party. Now the party was truly the best of the best in the Canadian Corps, borrowing heavily on the talents and the performance material of other Canadian concert parties that had gone before them. As the headline of the *Canadian Daily Record*, a military magazine issued by the Canadian War Records Office to the overseas forces trumpeted, "SCORED BIG HIT: Third Division Concert Party Play to Packed Houses."[113] Victoria-born Archie Wills, a newspaper reporter entrenched with the Canadian Corps during the "Last 100 Days," declared, they were "great relief, they were good too, they were tops of anything I've ever seen."[114] With a stellar lineup, tried-and-true material (albeit tested by other parties) and a growing reputation, the Dumbells soon became the pre-eminent entertainment group in the Canadian Corps.

History has been unkind to those others, unable to compete with the stacked Dumbell lineup. The stories, songs and skits of the Maple Leafs, the Red Patches, the Whizz Bangs, the C2s, the Woodpeckers, The Volatiles, and so many other parties, have been either forgotten, or retold as Dumbell tales. This was partly because the Dumbells absorbed so many members of different concert parties; however, it was also a product of the various Canadian tours and the success on Broadway that the Dumbells enjoyed following the war.

Improvising in No Man's Land

Concert-party performers and their crews were extremely pliable, adapting and improvising every step of the way. For music, the concert parties also had to make do with what was available to them. Some nights the parties had one of the various regimental bands accompanying them; as Alan Murray confirmed, "Every band in the division backed [the Dumbells] up at various times, some more frequently than others ... what a lift they gave."[115] At other times, however, the parties had to do without the lift of the regimental bands; in the chaos of trench warfare, they counted themselves lucky to find a lonely piano. This kind of improvisation was central to the survival of concert parties engaged in the hectic art of entertaining troops in the trenches.

Improvisation was key to survival itself, as confirmed by Dumbell pianist Jack Ayre, whose "C" company of the 116th suffered great casualties after he had joined the concert party: "there was only about forty-three came out, [of] about two-hundred and ten, [or] fifteen ... Killed and wounded you know, and I would've had to have been very lucky to have been one of the survivors. So I figure that being able to play the piano and do the job I was doing—it really saved my life."[116]

Other concert-party performers who had to return to active duty were not so lucky. Most of the members of the Steenvoorde incarnation of the PPCLI CC had been returned to active service. Bill Cunningham and Nobby Clarke were sent back down the line and Leonard Young also left the PPCLI CC in the fall of 1916. He returned to active duty with his original unit, the 9th Field Ambulance, and later lost his leg at Vimy Ridge.[117] The Pats' Stanley Morrison also lost his leg at Passchendaele on 30 October 1917, a wound that would later claim his life when he returned to Montreal following the war.[118] Others, like Percy Ham, also returned to active service and later won the Croix de Guerre.[119] The Dumbells' Al Plunkett was wounded at Sanctuary Wood, and second-generation PPCLI CC member Cyril Biddulph, the "worried" soldier, was killed in action at Monchy on 26 August 1918.[120]

Figure 14 Like so many other Canadian soldier-entertainers, Bill Cunningham, having performed for a spell with the PPCLI Comedy Company, returned to active service during the war. (Courtesy John McLaren)

Those performers who remained with their concert parties were hyper-aware of how lucky they were at having been chosen to sing and perform instead of fight. If Merton Plunkett smiled his famous smile upon you, you could genuinely consider yourself saved. Bill Redpath, by example, was delighted to receive Plunkett's telegram offering him a position with the Dumbells. For Redpath, this meant real meals and clean clothes courtesy of the YMCA.[121] But there was more at stake, a fact not lost on many of the troupe members. The PPCLI CC's William Filson, for example, fell through the soft boardwalk at Passchendaele, where his hand rested on the face of a dead soldier. Two men had to pull the hysterical Filson out of the mud.[122] Dumbell Jerry Brayford recalled how he too, nearly succumbed to the infamous Passchendaele mud while serving with the 49th Battalion:

> I'd been buried with a shell and thanks to the clay and loose mud … the shells went too deep, but it threw up manifolds of mud and there was another fellow named, Charlie Claridge and myself, were both buried by separate manifolds of this earth. And I had my shoulder and head sticking out and couldn't move because it had plastered us right in there and we were stuck. Two other fellows came to our assistance and they scratched the mud away until they get to our belts. And they took their belts off and hooked it onto ours, and put their elbows in that and they yanked me out that way and they did the same thing with Charlie Claridge. And my back … from the nape of my neck right down to my buttocks was all black and blue.[123]

As one of the walking wounded, Brayford was instructed to go to a Thanksgiving dinner shortly after his time in the mud. It was here that he met Plunkett. Unapologetically, Brayford confessed that after Passchendaele, he was now in the hunt for a soft job and acting and singing, when compared to getting buried in mud, was a lot softer.[124]

Still, the entertainers could experience a mixture of guilt and thankfulness for what providence had chosen for them. As Dumbell Al Plunkett confessed, "Heartbreak often marred gladness when we realized that some of our boys would never again return to our shows."[125] Dumbell Ross Hamilton said it was hard "to watch the boys laughing and enjoying themselves, knowing that they would have to head up the line."[126] Jack Ayre echoed this sentiment: "I get a lump in my throat when I think that some of the brave lads we entertained at 5 o'clock were dead at 7:30 in No Man's Land."[127] Lieutenant Ivan Clark Maharg of the 1st Canadian Mounted Rifles Battalion was one such chap. On one sunny day in July 1918, Maharg "had some tea at Mess & down to Billett. [sic] Dressed & went down to see the 'Dumbells' at Hamilton Gault's theatre. Fine show." Maharg was killed in action less than two weeks before the armistice came into effect.[128]

For those performers who didn't have to return to active duty immediately, there was always the looming threat of returning to the trenches. As such, the great majority of Canadian concert-party performers harboured no illusions about "stardom" when they saw the faces of the young men like Maharg, and when German shells acted as a constant reminder of how truly fortunate they were to be, if only slightly, removed from the actual fighting.

The soldier-entertainers did sometimes enjoy special treatment. Indeed, Canadian concert-party performers' celebrity grew with each performance and with this came certain small luxuries that were not available to the members of their fighting audience; most glaringly, the luxury of being excused from actual combat. It would, however, be wrong to overstate the smaller luxuries that these performers were afforded. When the bigger picture necessitated that

Figure 15 Al Plunkett and Ross Hamilton, c. 1918. (Courtesy Stephen Plunkett)

the Pats once again relocate—as it had in October 1916—the performers of the Comedy Company were understandably the least of the regiment's concerns. It was at this time that the Canadian troops, having participated at various battles along the Somme, were ordered up to Vimy Ridge. No specific orders, however, were given to the Comedy Company during the mad scramble, leaving the performers, who were now effectively free agents and relieved of front-line duty, stranded in Albert and left to fend for themselves. The free agents had to make their own way up to Vimy and remained very much an afterthought in the official CEF operations, especially in terms of receiving supplies and rations. McLaren, for one, was "very glad to eat some crusts of stale bread in a rat infested dugout near the Albert Brick Fields.[129] The PPCLI CC, who had been lionized in Steenvoorde, Warloy, and Albert, were now being refused clothes and rations at all quartermaster stores.[130] Less dramatically, but equally frustratingly, the Dumbells were also several times left to their own devices, cut off from their mail and occasionally their rations as well.[131] Like the soldiers they entertained, the comfort and morale of the soldier-entertainers were similarly vulnerable to the ravages of war.

So, under the constant threat of returning to duty and living with the uncertainty that came with their position as entertainers, these soldiers of song were never completely free of the real war.[132] Nor were the performers ever far from danger, as most of the shows occurred at rest spots hazardously close to the front line, where German shells and poison gas were a constant threat. The theatres that defined these early concert-party shows, were generally wooden huts that boasted a stage of about 30 feet across by 9 feet high, by 9 feet deep.[133] More rarely, one could see a show at a large open-air gala located safely behind the lines, where various parties would perform for several thousand soldiers at a time. But these shows were uncommon, as officials wanted no more than a couple of hundred men congregated at the same place for any extended duration.[134] Major Beecher Gale's Theatre at Gouy-Servins, which housed the first Dumbells' show in June 1917, was a step up from the typical outside concert-party venue; the theatre's spotlights had been fashioned out of machine-gun parts by Paul Harmon, a member of Gale's staff.[135] The more proper theatres, which would house concert-party performances near the end of the war, ranged in capacity from approximately 400 to 800 seats. On 17 October 1917, the Dumbells inaugurated the Pavilion, a newly made theatre at the Canadian Corps Training School that measured 30 by 90 feet, with a stage 30 by 15 feet.[136] While the Corps School also had a smaller but more elaborate "entertainment centre," which staged events for officers and important guests, the Pavilion was more representative of the type of theatre that the Dumbells would eventually be performing at.[137]

Even when the venues improved, the concert-party soldiers would be invariably called upon to perform several different military tasks. Most commonly, it was to cheer up the wounded at field hospitals, but in some circumstances, the soldier-entertainers were more directly involved. For example, at Boulogne, the Dumbells were entrained to double as stretcher-bearers.[138] And while the entertainers may have been spared a return to active duty, they became exhausted with putting on shows day and night in a continual cycle, as Murray explained, "A Battalion arrived, was given a meal, a show, and marched off."[139] Perhaps these experiences provide the most compelling contrast between those professional entertainers who were either hired or donated their time and the soldier-entertainers, for whom the war was not some distant, diabolical dream, only to be imagined. Instead, their war was a moment-to-moment experience, breathing all around them. This closeness to the war would sharpen the performers' material and earn the respect of their soldier audiences, whose spirits were lifted at watching their own comrades, rather than paid professionals, ham it up on stage.

The Rites of Spring

The German Spring Offensive in 1918 hit the Canadians hard. The PPCLI CC was performing at Neuville-Saint-Vaast in early 1918 when the Ludendorff Drive began along the Western front. The British 5th Army had been overrun by the German attacks and the looming threat of returning to active duty was felt among the soldier-entertainers. Members of both the Dumbells and the Pats' CC thought for sure that they would be returned to their units. To their surprise, Major General Lipsett requested the exact opposite, "Now as never before the troops need entertainment."[140] McLaren had left instructions to the others to move and safely store the troupe's scenery and props before even meeting with Colonel Stewart. As McLaren recalled: "I arrived at the Colonel's dugout at midnight, clicked my heels and saluted. On volunteering the information to my Colonel that the Comedy Company was all ready to dodge shells once more, he replied—'yes, but they'll be egg shells, at the Royal Command Performance in the Apollo Theatre, London, you lucky bastard.'"[141] Given the dire state of affairs facing the Allies along the Western Front, McLaren and his group took a bit of convincing that this was not a practical joke being played on them by the colonel. When the special tailor came along to take their measurements for the performance, the group began to believe their happy circumstances.[142]

After hundreds of trench-side performances, the PPCLI were on their way to the music-hall stages of West London. And in the spring of 1918, the PPCLI CC performed for King George V at the Apollo Theatre.[143] In an interview in 1967, Jack McLaren related the humorous ending to the PPCLI CC's Royal Performance:

When the curtain line came at the end of the show the curtain did not budge. There stood the company motionless and rigid in the final tableau. Nothing happened. Out of the side of his mouth "Kaiser Bill" ventriloquised the message to the wings to drop the curtain. No response. Again through clenched teeth he entreated "Please give us the curtain." Again: no action. Stepping off his throne and in character the Kaiser goose-stepped his way to the wings and in a clarion voice that echoed through the Apollo Theatre he shouted: "Come on Doc. Drop the bloody curtain." ... Our instructions were to get dressed in our uniforms as quickly as possible so that, should Royalty wish to see us, we would be ready ... George V, in parting, said to his Mary: "Come on Doc, let's drop the bloody curtain and go."

Figure 16 Jack McLaren (as the General), T.J. Lilly (as the Kaiser), and the rest of the PPCLI Comedy Company performed for King George V at London's Apollo Theatre, spring 1918. (Courtesy John McLaren)

It had been a long journey from the trenches to a Command Performance in front of royalty. The troupe were hobnobbing with some of the most popular celebrities of the day including Madame Edvina of La Scala, British comedian Billy Merson, and American vaudeville great Ethel Levy.[144] Only one year prior, as McLaren reminisced, the Pats' Comedy Company "were a deserted lot and alone on the battlefields of the Somme, thankful for a black crust of rat-nibbled bread—and now here we were being feted in Royal circles. Ah, it's a queer world, but *c'est la guerre!*"[145]

The Dumbells also made it to London, a little later in August 1918. The troupe played one week at the Victoria Palace and two more at the city's most popular vaudeville theatre, the Coliseum. The Dumbells' success at the Victoria Palace was indeed striking. Every night was sold out and every night many hundreds were turned away at the gate.[146] The following stint at the Coliseum produced much the same result. Captain Plunkett had to refuse various offers

Figure 17 The PPCLI Comedy Company's pianist N. Nicholson and Bill Filson at London's Apollo Theatre in 1918. (Courtesy John McLaren)

from theatres in Scotland and England for the troupe, knowing that the group were needed back in France for the final push. Before they returned, however, the company concluded their London tour with a free show for soldiers at the Palace Theatre on 15 September 1918.[147] By the time they returned home to Canada, however, the Dumbells had made the rounds of London's West End, performing at the Palace Theatre, as well as the Aldwych and the Little Theatre.[148]

It was at the Coliseum show, though, where the Dumbells upstaged the Diaghilev Russian Ballet that—for reasons unknown—was on the same bill. The ballet tour manager was so distressed with the popularity of the concert party that he requested that the ballet be moved to the slot *before* the Dumbells and not the other way around. As Dumbell Jerry Brayford remembered: "The house was pretty well filled, and as soon as the Dumbell half of the programme was finished everybody went out and the Russian ballet had no one to bow to, but they took them just the same ... bowing, three of four curtain calls, and nobody demanding it."[149]

The cheeky Brayford confessed, however, that he loved watching the ballet from the wings and in particular, Madame Lydia Lopakova, one of the famed leads in Diaghilev's Ballets Russes and who was also married to the famous British economist John Maynard Keynes. Despite the seemingly strained professional

Figure 18 Soldiers await a Dumbells performance at London's Little Theatre in 1918. (Courtesy Stephen Plunkett)

relationship between the two acts, members of the Dumbells became quite friendly with Lopakova and Léonide Massine, the male lead in the ballet.[150]

Later still, the Dumbells were asked to perform a command performance at Windsor Castle, but it was poor timing, as Canadian troops were facing heavy action at the Hindenburg Line and were once again in need of a morale boost.[151] The Dumbells were summoned back to France, where they played some 70 concerts for the soldiers during the months of August and September 1918.

The Meeting at Mons

Of the 30 or more Canadian concert parties—including the PPCLI CC, who performed countless shows in France, Belgium, and London, and was considered the *most original* party—why then were the Dumbells the *best remembered*?[152] As discussed, the Dumbells were the most explosively entertaining party; a fact that might be attributed to the shrewd decisions Captain Plunkett made in choosing the group's cast. The sheer quality of the party had, by war's end, dwarfed the others. Absorbing the best players of the other groups made the Dumbells an untouchable supergroup. And by war's end, they were about to morph again. Perhaps more importantly, though, was the fact that the Dumbells were in the right place at the right time. The group was at Villers-aux-Bois at the beginning of the famous German Spring Offensive in 1918, where they performed day and night for battalion after battalion of Canadian soldiers.[153] Here, the Dumbells were seen by more soldiers than any of the other Canadian concert parties and were thus able to forge a place in the memory of more troops. Besides the Villers-aux-Bois performances, the Dumbells were with Canadian soldiers for the "Last 100 Days" and performed in Mons for nearly a month beginning on 12 November 1918, the day after Armistice.[154] These two critical moments in Canadian military history solidified the importance of the Dumbells in the eyes of those soldiers who saw them perform. In the end, the Dumbells performed over 500 times for Canada's fighting men during the war.[155]

As early as the summer of 1918, many of the other battalion concert parties were already being disbanded.[156] McLaren, who was safe in his role with the Comedy Company, reflected the general feeling of the Canadian Corps during those last 100 days of the war: "We could hardly realize the news—nothing went wrong, the wildest hopes were realized, the cavalry went through, the trenches were left forever behind—while the toll of prisoners, the capture of guns and supplies, and the number of relieved villages were all prodigious. The Canadian Corps was on the move."[157]

So were the members of the Comedy Company who, in early November 1918, were sent to the village of Frévent, about 100 miles west of Mons. One day later, the Dumbells also arrived. Both troupes were inactive and awaiting instruction. By 9 November, the rumours of an Armistice were circulating throughout the Canadian Corps. It was during this time that the performers and their immediate supervisors began to contemplate an amalgamation.

Scarcely a year after they had put on their first show, Canadians and the rest of the world rightfully anticipated the coming of the end of the war. Because the fight was not entirely finished, Canadian soldiers, thousands of miles away from home, still had to wrestle with the prospect of a war that might drag on. Nevertheless, most recognized that the war was winding down and Captain Plunkett sought to combine the best talents of the Canadian Corps' concert parties to produce something special for the last few days of the war. Plunkett's goal was to stage a large-scale production of Gilbert and Sullivan's *H.M.S. Pinafore*.[158]

A great convergence of Canadian soldier-entertainers, many from the famous PPCLI CC and others from various concert parties who had been hand-picked by Captain Plunkett, assembled at Mons for the play. From the PPCLI CC, the Dumbells secured even more new blood in Charles Hillman, Jack McLaren, T.J. Lilly, and Fred Fenwick. Agar Adamson himself had asked Plunkett to absorb

Figure 19 Leonard Young, Al Plunkett, Bill Tennent, and Jerry Brayford in 1921. (Courtesy John McLaren)

some of the Comedy Company's performers into the Dumbells.[159] Some members of the PPCLI CC, however, were not enthusiastic about merging with the Dumbells at the Armistice. The PPCLI CC had previously resisted the opportunity of becoming a divisional show and wanted to remain loyal to Galt and the Pats regiment. The Comedy Company took pride in the fact that it had sent back various members of the group to active service, some of whom were seriously wounded, and that it had been around for about 15 months before the Dumbells performed their first show. The Comedy Company had also been performing in the tradition of the "real soldier" show; that is, where improvisation was the order of the day and props were made from scratch. According to McLaren, this was in stark contrast to the "professionalism" that was emblematic of the Dumbells.[160] There was also the consideration that while the Dumbells were reputedly strong in female impersonators with Hamilton and Murray, they couldn't compete with McLaren's topical comedic sketches. As Murray himself confessed, "The Pats had all the sensational skits that were ever heard of in the Dumbells in Canada, they were all Pats' skits."[161]

Ultimately, the group did not want to come under the sponsorship of the YMCA. It is little surprise then, that when the amalgamation of the PPCLI CC with the Dumbells took place near war's end, resistance was palpable. For these reasons (and perhaps others) Conrad Stephens chose not to join the Dumbells when the two companies amalgamated. According to McLaren, due to his pride of the PPCLI CC, Stephens likely resented those other parties who had been fully relieved of active duty from the beginning.[162]

Stephens could not have anticipated the future successes that lay in store for the Dumbells. And to be fair to him, his response was not altogether unreasonable. Ordinary soldiers too had taken pride in the concert party that represented their respective division or battalion. Clarence Reginald Gass of the 85th Canadian Infantry Battalion, for instance, was not very charitable in his review of another concert party when compared to his own division's: "This afternoon our divisional concert party put on a show for us. They are good actors and gave us a fine entertainment. I saw one by another party a few evenings ago but it wasn't as good."[163]

Even officers, often the butt of concert-party skits, took pride in their own concert parties and were quick to defend them, just as Hodder-Williams did: "Later in the war much of the talent in this Comedy Company [PPCLI Comedy Company] was merged in the more pretentious concert party of the 3rd Division, which has since become widely known in England, Canada and the United States as 'the Dumbells.'"[164]

Despite Stephens and Hodder-Williams's disapproval, however, the PPCLI CC was done, its remnants now Dumbells. And so, the *new* Dumbells, including over 30 new soldier-entertainers, loaded their scenery, themselves and the orchestra onto trucks and, on 9 November, travelled to Valenciennes, 26 miles west of Mons.

Peace

Although everyone knew it was coming, the singing soldiers were still stunned when the Armistice finally arrived. McLaren recalled: "There was no celebration or jubilation, but rather an incomprehensible numbness enveloped those of us who had spent two or three years in the midst of battle. This was the end of it and we just sat down quietly and looked at each other in disbelief."[165]

The supergroup that entered Mons upon Armistice found the jubilation and celebration that had been missing in their own group. The mood was encapsulated in a bulletin that had been posted everywhere:

> After 51 months of suffering caused by the iniquitous, pitiless, insolent, occupation of the German Army, the town of Mons is at last delivered by the heroism of the British and Canadian Armies, who at the time of the armistice ended the series of their victories in the very place where in August 23, 1914 they first encountered the enemy. The 3rd Canadian Division at the price of heavy sacrifices entered the town at 3:00 in the morning, avenging thus by a glorious success the retreat of 1914. Honour and glory to them.[166]

It now fell to the merrymakers of said division to give the people of Mons a fitting celebratory performance.

Serving with the 8th Canadian Field Ambulance, Bert Lovell described the general euphoric feeling surrounding those last couple of days of the war:

> Finally November the 10th we are near Mons and on the 11th we enter the city, the "War is over" and we are still alive ... The Carillon bells in a nearby tower played "The Maple Leaf Forever," while the dignitaries in their long frock coats and funny top hats cried "Hip, Hip, Hurrah"...We are able to share some of our rations with our friends, who made us comfortable in their homes. We attended the "Dumbell Concert Party" in the Big Theatre and witnessed many a happy reunion, as civilians were able to rejoin their loved ones who thought them dead.[167]

The new Dumbells' interpretation of *H.M.S. Pinafore* that Lovell would have seen debuted at the Grand Theatre in Mons one day late on 12 November.[168] The show played to capacity audiences for three weeks and was incredibly well received.[169]

Following the Mons engagement, the Dumbells took a short respite in Brussels in December 1918. Even here, however, mobbed by well-wishers and

Figure 20   The Dumbells in *H.M.S. Pinafore* in 1920. (Courtesy Stephen Plunkett)

townspeople who continued the postwar party, the supergroup were required to put on some impromptu performances at the Grand Place.[170] A few weeks later, the troupe would return to Brussels for a Command Performance for King Albert and his queen. It was here that the Belgian King awarded Captain Plunkett a medal for the troupe's service in maintaining the morale of the troops.[171] The success of *Pinafore* was reported back in Canada:

> The 3rd Canadian Division concert party "The Dumbells" that, like the 2nd Division party, "The Sea Toos," scored such a hit in London; went to Brussels, the capital of Belgium, a few months ago and gave [illegible] performance in the leading theatre there before the King and Queen of the Belgians, and full audience. The parties were given in aid of Belgian charities. The reception was quite the most enthusiastic they have ever had.[172]

Following their royal performance, the Dumbells played several town halls in Flanders. Even after the Armistice, the Dumbells were not given much of a reprieve. Indeed, if ever there had been a real threat of mutiny, it was the period directly following the signing of the Armistice, which saw a desperate idleness descend on Canadian soldiers, as Plunkett explained: "'We've won the blooming war; now let's get out of here and home,' was the attitude of the troops. The months of waiting menaced the rank and file's morale. Sir Arthur Currie sent for me. 'Full steam ahead,' he ordered. 'Take anyone you want and put on all the entertainment possible.'"[173]

And they did, performing at corps and divisional schools, hospitals and camps from Brussels all the way to London, and also on their passage home to Canada. Each concert-party performance was calibrated to each chapter of the Canadian war experience. When the going was tough, the number of shows were increased. It might even be argued that performances had become part of the official planning of the CEF, linked as they were to almost every Canadian advance.[174] There was one piece of the puzzle that the CEF did not anticipate. During the Dumbells' tour on the way back to England, some German POWs escaped from Hesdin under the cover of noise that the show created.[175] In the end though, the troupe reached Le Havre where they packed up for England and then, mercifully, it was home to Canada, where the second half of their history awaited them.[176]

Figure 21 Bertram Langley in the Dumbells' *H.M.S. Pinafore* in 1920. (Courtesy John McLaren)

Still, the other concert parties were not entirely forgotten, at least in the hearts of the soldiers that had seen them perform. Many of these other parties had been well received and were fondly remembered in soldiers' letters home. Andrew Wilson, by example, had seen the 4th Division's concert (likely the Maple Leafs) and thought it "very good."[177] Military Medal recipient Leslie Scherer took in a show by Montreal's Black Watch concert party, and confessed to his friend Catherine Crawford that "the Redheckles ... certainly are good."[178] The C2s were, according to Robert Shortreed of the 12th Canadian Siege Battery, very good soldier actors, "two of whom took ladies parts very well."[179] So, when the Dumbells toured Canada after the war, as O'Neill has suggested, "Veterans in the audience were not seeing the Dumbells on stage, but their own concert party in memory."[180] Dumbell members, especially those who had been with other parties before being attached to the Dumbells, did their part in keeping the memory of these other parties alive in various radio and television interviews. Still, given the experience of the cast, the Dumbells were able to improve on the quality of the Canadian concert party and, unlike the other parties, were afforded an opportunity to engrave a place for themselves in Canadian history following the war. For civilians who had never seen a front-line performance, it was the Dumbells who had become synonymous with the First World War concert party, and years of touring across Canada only strengthened this notion.

IV Only a Soldier Knows

The War and Humour

The humour that evolved during the Great War had, as discussed earlier, built on previous forms of comedy. Almost all of these forms had been launched in the music hall and had landed squarely on the makeshift stages of the Western Front. A certain strain of soldier humour, however, had existed in the British and Dominion Armies long before the outbreak of the First World War. McLaren warned, "If you think that soldier shows are unique and a product of the little argument of 1914–1918, you are labouring under a serious delusion ... they are not unique."[1] Many songs, slang terms, and comedic skits that were sung and performed by soldiers of the Great War had been inherited from previous conflicts.[2] Furthermore, the military was often closely associated with the general evolution of comedy and humour in both Britain and its colonies. This was especially true in 19th-century Canada where military theatre had the dual purpose of entertaining and enlightening its audience on the virtues of British high culture. It was only after the enveloping hopelessness and sanguinary nature of the First World War had set in that formerly sacrosanct themes like heroism, patriotism, the military system, superior officers, and, in some rarer cases, the war itself, were fair game for mockery. Concert-party performers would soon offer a more appropriate rendering of the music-hall musical menu, one more suited to its weary, jaded, and often emotionally exhausted audience engaged in a conflict where tragedy was continually draped in the ludicrous.

Shakespearian tragedies, popular English farces and comedies, melodramas, and, on rare occasion, musicals, were among the garrison productions put on in 19th-century Ontario. The importance of these military theatricals in regard to the development of Canadian theatre can hardly be overstated. Entertainers in the British garrisons in Ontario between 1812 and 1871 for example, were not only the "trained defenders of the empire," as historian Leslie O'Dell observed, but also the defenders of "the sophistication of upper-class British society."[3] The phases of development in 19th-century Ontario theatre were also closely linked to the military. From erecting the community's first performance spaces, and providing it with its only theatrical entertainment, to the promotion of civilian amateur groups, later culminating in the emergence of indigenous professional theatre companies, the British garrison laid the foundation for theatre to prosper in Ontario.[4]

Enlisted men *were* involved in the early garrison exhibitions, though their inclusion was usually confined to the periphery and all activities relating to public performances would have to be approved by the commanding officer and the officers of the regiment.[5] Military theatre productions of this age were generally funded and orchestrated by British officers who sought to impart upper-class precepts to the lower orders. Regular soldiers would have had little or no say in the choice of material for these productions.

Despite its significance as the cornerstone of theatre in Canada, 19th-century military theatre did not resemble the Canadian concert parties of the First World War. Although the concert parties of the Great War were usually organized by officers, they were unlike their military predecessor in that regular soldiers chose the songs, sketches, and parodies to satisfy the tastes of their regular-soldier audiences: parodies that concert parties directed at the very officers who had initiated their genesis. These tastes were in rather stark contrast to the prescribed, refined diet of upper-class entertainment. As Canadian author Ralf Sheldon-Williams asserted: "What man ... wasted one night of his precious ten or fourteen on the Opera or the 'legitimate'? The Palladium, the Alhambra and their kind knew us well, for our souls demanded 'bubble and squeak' after the strong meat which was our daily pabulum on the other side."[6]

Even the Dumbells' treatment of Gilbert and Sullivan's *H.M.S. Pinafore* was dressed down considerably, as to incorporate a few more "accessible" numbers.[7] Canadian soldiers wanted a certain style of entertainment and the concert parties of the Canadian Corps gave it to them, sometimes in the face of disapproval.

The emerging soldier humour of the First World War grew with the inhumane nature of the war experience. The style was not straight vaudeville, which had become dated during the early months of the war; but rather, vaudeville with an attitude. Certainly some songs and sketches of the music hall were already "self mocking and humorously defeatist."[8] Still, concert-party performers exaggerated these characteristics of the music hall to reflect the humour of the trenches.

The First World War was full of unprecedented circumstances; the totality of fighting, the rate of death (60,000 Allied casualties on the first day of the Battle of the Somme alone), the variety of new and terrifying wounds, and the number of countries engaged in the conflict, all of which spoke to the apocalyptic environment that made obsolete the more innocent strains of music-hall material. That is not to say that the structure and form of music-hall entertainment was not visible in the material written, adapted, and performed by the concert-party entertainers, only that the authors of the new material were mindful to accommodate the soldier's new sensibilities that had been a by-product of the fighting. Modris Eksteins' description of the surreal environment of the war in *The Rites of Spring* goes some way in setting the backdrop to the evolution of black humour: "In a war in which men buried themselves so as to live, in which soldiers went fishing with bombs, in which Senegalese troops at first ate the grease sent to lubricate trucks, in which a dead carrier pigeon was decorated with the Légion d'honneur.... Humour became bitter and black, and Monty Python would never have lived in the last quarter of this century had his forebears not gone through that 'great war.'"[9]

The collective human consciousness had crossed a threshold in the carnage of that Great war, necessitating that art, music, dance, and theatre evolve correspondingly.

What made the Canadian soldier laugh during the First World War? A key trait in the humour found at the Front was the deeply personal and exclusive quality encoded within the soldier comedy. This private element, as far as the soldier was concerned, was essential to the *funniness* of the material. Recently, comedy historian Andrew Clark illustrated how important shared knowledge between the performer and the audience was to humour, in his work *Stand and Deliver*: "Comedians can make countless Superman jokes because they know that every man, woman, and child in North America knows who Superman is. This familiarity is the cornerstone of any joke. Without it, a laugh is impossible."[10] Every soldier sitting in front of a concert party on the Western Front would have shared similar experiences, challenges and humiliations, comforts and triumphs, which together culminated in a timeless and unbreakable bond. Where the discourse of the British music hall was attuned to what it was to be cunning and what it took to survive inner-city life in London, the discourse of the soldier-entertainer and his audience was attuned to what it was to be cunning and what it took to survive the First World War.

Concert-party performers had purchased membership to that exclusive order because they were themselves soldiers and constantly in and around the war. As pianist Ayre recollected, one night during a performance, a German shell "sailed across" the stage on which the Dumbells were performing: "We cut our performance a bit short that evening ... after that close shave, I slept under my piano each night, right beside the pedals, to avoid shrapnel."[11] While Ayre's account may be a product of romance lusting after fact, he was, nevertheless, no stranger to the face of battle and had been in "C" Company when that outfit followed the Canadians' initial Vimy charge in 1917.[12]

Through their hands-on experiences, the concert-party performers had earned admission into the heart of the common Canadian soldier. The concert party thus became a circular celebration; the soldier in the audience seeing himself on stage, and the soldier on stage seeing himself in the audience. A prime minister, general, or civilian might *laugh*, but they could not honestly *know*.

Some of the best examples of the exclusive humour shared by soldiers could be found in the soldier newspapers or troop journals. The best known of these newspapers was the BEF's *The Wipers Times*.[13] Printed at the Front, troop journals were full of examples that highlighted the emerging irony that soldiers, and soldiers alone, came to recognize as the real war experience. It was in the pages of these troop journals that seeds of black humour were sown:

> Are you a victim to Optimism? You don't know?
> Then ask yourself the following questions.
> Do you suffer from cheerfulness?
> Do you wake up in the morning feeling that all is going well for the allies?
> Do you sometimes think that the war will end within the next week?
> Do you believe good news in preference to bad?
> Do you consider our leaders are competent to conduct the war to a successful issue?

> If your answer is "Yes" to any of these questions then you are in the clutches of that dread disease. We can cure you. Two days spent at our establishment will effectually eradicate all traces of it from your system. Do not hesitate—apply for terms at once to:

> Mssrs. Walthorpe, Foxley, Nelmes and Co.
> Telephone 72: "Grumblestones"
> Telegrams: "Grouse"[14]

British troop journals were only marginally different from those found in the Canadian Corps and what was funny to the British soldier was almost assuredly funny to the Canadian soldier. This is a fact that is made less remarkable when one considers that approximately 42 percent of soldiers enlisted in the CEF were British born.[15] Popular Canadian troop journals included *The Brazier*, *The Dead Horse Corner Gazette*, *The Forty-Niner*, *The Trench Echo*, and perhaps best known, *The Listening Post* of the 7th Canadians, which had a peak circulation of 20,000 on the Western Front.[16]

Trench newspapers further sharpened the Canadian soldiers' sense of coded humour. Published by soldier-editors for their soldier comrades, these papers were, in effect, the concert party in the written form. Dealing with a variety of topics that usually revolved around day-to-day survival in the trenches, trench newspapers contained soldiers' jokes, articles, and poetry (though usually *not* of the Owen/Sassoon ilk), as well as songs and cartoons. And like its concert-party counterpart, trench newspaper humour sometimes drifted near that even darker brand of comedy that was in its embryonic stage in the trenches. In one *Listening Post* cartoon entitled 'Don't Pull the Little Glass Ball," a simple-minded soldier pulls a grenade, mistaking it for an alcoholic beverage. With the soldier blown off his feet after the grenade explodes, the caption observed that the drink had "some kick to it."[17] In another *Listening Post* cartoon, a new, green recruit is being teased by two veteran soldiers. One of the veterans asks the recruit if he could borrow some money before the new soldier heads off for the trenches. The insinuation was that the rookie soldier wouldn't require money where he was headed and, more sardonically, that he wasn't likely coming back.[18] Just as it was for the Dumbells and the PPCLI CC, death was fair game in the Canadian trench newspapers.

Trench newspapers were not the exclusive preserve of the British Army or the Canadian Corps, nor were they, for that matter, exclusive to English-speaking soldiers. French historian Stéphane Audoin-Rouzeau, for example, reviewed the day-to-day lives of the *poilu* during the war as evidenced in the French soldiers' trench newspapers in his *Men at War 1914–1918: National Sentiment and Trench Journalism in France.*[19] Sharing the same conditions as their Canadian counterparts, French soldiers too expressed their contempt for the conditions on the Western Front and the disconnect they felt with civilians who knew nothing of *la guerre réelle.* French trench newspapers reveal—in much the same manner as Canadian ones did—the *mentalités* of *poilu* on the front line. Perhaps more than the Canadian soldier though, the French soldier, as Audoin-Rouzeau explained, was buoyed by a certain *sentiment national,* or patriotism that was, according to the author, "an indestructible barrier against the discouragement aroused by the trials of endless war."[20] While this sort of sentiment might not have been wholly anathematic to the Canadian soldier, overt patriotism was usually soft-pedalled while self-referential humour was always played up.

The most celebrated soldier-cartoonist was Bruce Bairnsfather who served with the Royal Warwickshire Regiment during the war. Bairnsfather's work was often featured in the British magazine *The Bystander.* Among his most famous pieces was "Where Did That One Go To?," which featured terrified soldiers hiding in a dugout wondering where the loud shrieking shell had fallen. A song by the same name, originally sung by Miss Lee White in the music-hall revue *Cheep,* was incorporated into the Dumbell repertoire:

Where did that one go to 'Erbert?
Where did that one go?
Oh, oh, oh, oh, oh.
Say ole chummy, that was rummy.
'Er-bert, 'Er-bert, tell me if you know.
Where the, what the, how the, why the,
where did that one go?[21]

The most famous of Bairnsfather's work was "Well, If You Knows of a Better 'Ole, Go to It." The cartoon featured "Bert," stuck in a shell hole with Bairnsfather's well-known anti-hero, the walrus moustached "Old Bill." The caption was internalized by Brits and Canadians and is still used today, meaning "if you have a better idea, then let's hear it." Bairnsfather had earned a strong soldier readership in no small way through his service with the Royal Warwickshire Regiment. It was likely the very fact that he had served at the Front that allowed Bairnsfather to draw a more real depiction of the war; a talent that eluded other illustrators who had not actually been there. [22]

Although Bairnsfather's work was more accessible to civilian audiences than a majority of pieces featured in other soldier papers, some civilians felt that his characters were a vulgar caricature of the nation's heroes. An interesting dichotomy emerged, and because Bairnsfather's work was offensive to the civilian, it became even more irresistible to those regular soldiers who saw in it the exclusive humour that only a serviceman could convey. As a *bona fide* "Tommy" himself, Bairnsfather greatly appealed to the regular soldier in France and Belgium: he, like the concert-party performers up and down the front lines, belonged.

The in-joke could also be found in the songs and sketches of the First World War. Invariably, concert parties had within their ranks, as Brophy and Partridge explained, men with a gift "for personal abuse, who would produce, for the battalion or battery concert-party, jests and ditties about topics of the moment or outstanding personalities of the unit."[23] This joke strengthened the bond among soldiers, often at the expense of isolating them from the rest of civilization. As one Canadian officer confessed: "I hated the contrast between the soft lights and comfort at the tea room and the trenches. I grew especially angry with the women—some very pretty ones too—who seemed so pleased and placid with themselves while I knew of the carnage at that moment going on."[24]

Mere contact from home could often be awkward, even irritating, as Eksteins argued: "Letters from home were often painful because of their naïveté. The ironies jumped out at the soldier: 'Try not to get wounded!' or 'We are having a hard time, too!' ... The soldier's sensation, on reading such comments from home, was often one of complete isolation. The troops might as well have been on the moon. They lived and fought in a place beyond understanding, beyond imagination, even beyond feeling."[25]

A conflict thus took shape within the soldier's mind between being less able to associate with civilization while still longing for the memory of what it once was. The soldier might really have believed the words when he first sang "It's a long, long way to Tipperary, but my heart's right there," yet for many, "Tipperary" remained remote even after they had returned home.

Those who remained at home could not readily relate to the humour that began to flourish among soldiers in their darkest hours. Similarly, they would not be able to relate to the everyday incidents common in the trenches. For example, when British soldiers, for a laugh, shook a severed hand that had accidentally been packed into a sandbag or, when a soldier got a chuckle out of his comrades by placing a lit cigarette between the lips of a dead soldier's mouth. Both the dead soldier and the sandbag could not be safely moved or disposed of, leaving the living soldiers to deal with the macabre circumstance the best they could. It was in these absurd and desperate situations that a new and darker humour began to germinate.

Certainly, soldiers of previous wars had found themselves in desperate circumstances. There are some examples of soldier songs from the Boer War that allude to the desperation and resulting humour of that conflict:

> Hiding in the ammunition van,
> Listening to the din and strife,
> When the fight was o'er out once more,
> And that's how I saved my life.[26]

Yet, given the Great War's exaggerated gruesomeness, and its unprecedented quality of hopelessness, the hardships soldiers faced seemed more profound and enduring. Soldiers of the First World War would see sights that no soldier before them had seen, and be exposed to surreal situations for longer stretches of time. It is not surprising then, that dark, anti-heroic soldier songs were greater in number during the First World War than they had been in any previous conflict in history and further away from the popular civilian perception of the war. Now more than ever, humour would serve as a soldier's safety valve, a tool to survive the war.

Most of the concert-party performers had experienced for themselves one bizarre situation after another. Ross Hamilton and Alan Murray had received only one lecture in Montreal after they enlisted in the 9th Field Ambulance as stretcher-bearers. During the lecture, the recruits were instructed on how to take poultices from boiling water. Three months later, they were on the front lines. Here, you had to be a truck horse, able to carry men of all weights, sometimes as far as two miles back to the medic station, over all sorts of territory, to where they could be attended to, or at least to where they could get help. Needless to say, this lone bit of medical wisdom was hardly enough to prepare a would-be stretcher-bearer for the Western Front. Many months later, resting on a stretcher floating on the mud near Vimy, Murray was overwhelmed with the senselessness of the war. Despair had set in. Yet the misery was broken when Hamilton drew Murray's attention to the hilarious juxtaposition between what they had learned and what little practical application it had. With a deadpan delivery, Hamilton began to recount the only instruction given the fledgling stretcher-bearers of Montreal's 9th Field Ambulance: "to remove the poultice from the boiling water." In recounting the ludicrousness of their education, Hamilton was able to cheer up the worried Murray, giving him the inspiration to finish the vital task at hand.[27] This was typical of the private sarcasm that soldiers enjoyed. Beyond a lifting of the spirits, this brand of humour enabled them to survive the absurd.

As the war dragged on, trench humour became more coded and further isolated from non-soldiers' understanding of it. Doubtless, civilians could recognize elements of funny within the humour at the Front, but to truly know it, without having experienced the fighting, was impossible. Soldiers often chose not to share their stories with their children, wives, parents, and siblings back home. When it came time to talk, it was usually with their grandchildren years later or, for some, not at all. But soldiers could always talk and laugh with their comrades at various reunions and memorial celebrations. These brothers in arms knew.

Simply put, songs and parodies authored by Canadian soldiers were not meant for civilian consumption. This made them even more appealing to the soldier-participants: audience and performer alike.[28] That they resonated with civilian audiences—particularly after the war—was, for the soldier toiling in the trenches, irrelevant.

Still, many soldiers did try to share their war laughs with their family, especially when the Dumbells toured North America following the war. The postwar success of the Dumbells had been secured in the hearts of the soldiers who saw them perform in the trenches. Murray spoke for most of the Dumbells, when he said that members of the comedy troupe were unaware of how meaningful the impression they had left on their soldier audience was, until they were reunited with their ardent fans after the war: "We were 'their' party and they showed us off. Sure we had a good show, better than expected, but certainly it was the loyalty of the lads from overseas that advertised and supported us ... An unexpected and very moving angle turned up when parents of boys who did not return but who had written of the Dumbells came to see the show their loved ones had enjoyed."[29]

Albert O'Connor was one such soldier who had seen the Dumbells at the "foot of Vimy Ridge in an old wooden shed." When the troupe started touring

Canada, O'Connor took his wife to see them perform in Toronto.[30] Soldiers like O'Connor had forged a loyal and durable partnership with the Dumbells in the belly of the trenches. The concert party represented a moment in time, not only for the soldiers, but also later, for those civilians who were willing to take the time to interpret the private humour of the soldier-entertainers.

Satire on War and Its Heroes

It did not take long for soldiers to relinquish any romantic misapprehensions of war that they may have been labouring under. Perhaps the most important group of songs for Canadian soldiers were those that satirized the war itself, military life, and a patriotism whose veneer wore thin upon arrival at the Front.[31] More than simply investing in good morale, singers of irreverent song and mockers of military procedure armed ordinary soldiers with the tools to survive their term in war. While the songs and sketches of the concert parties may have ridiculed heroes and satirized the lamentable day-to-day existence of trench life, they also invited the individual soldier to laugh at his own lot. The subversive material of the concert party acted as a veritable safety valve, preventing the war from obtaining a psychological stranglehold on the soldiers.

In most cases prior to 1914, *war*—as portrayed in paintings, literature and song—was a corrupt, exaggerated, and inaccurate representation of the truth. Brophy and Partridge argued that there must have existed a precedent or, at the very least, an understanding shared by ancient warriors that the reality of war was not as it seemed in its popular and enduring romantic image: "If British soldiers [in the First World War] were jesting about the death which slew their comrades and seemed their own certain fate, if they cheated hysteria with songs making a joke of mud and lice and fear and weariness, it must have been because their forefathers had evolved the same ironic method of outwitting misfortune."[32]

One might argue that the degree of derision and resignation to the reality of combat—as a reaction to the "great lie" peddled by flag-waving warmongers—reached a zenith during the First World War. The soldier's response to the reality of the First World War has survived in the large body of concert-party comedic material and soldier newspapers that is unprecedented in range, eloquence, and frequency. Comedy could be found everywhere in the war. Cecil Lewis, who saw the Western Front from above, said: "The trench system had all the elements of grotesque comedy—a prodigious and complex effort, cunningly contrived, and carried out with deadly seriousness, in order to achieve just nothing at all."[33]

The songwriters and sketch authors of the concert parties lived in this grotesque theatre of war, and it was here that they penned their incisive reactions to the war myth.

Adaptation was a formula commonly used by Canadian concert-party writers. By adapting popular songs, usually, but not strictly of British origin, the concert-party performers could humorously describe the war experience. Witness Steve Graham's ode to Ireland:

> *Sure, a little bit o' Heaven fell from out of the sky one day,*
> *and nestled on the ocean in a spot so far away;*
> *And the angels found it, sure it looked so sweet and fair.*
> *They said suppose we leave it, for it looks so peaceful there!*
> *So they sprinkled it with star dust just to make the shamrocks grow;*
> *'tis the only place you'll find them, no matter where you go;*
> *Then they dotted it with silver to make its lakes so grand,*
> *and when they had it finished, sure they called it Ireland.*[34]

As transformed for the Dumbells:

> *Sure a little bit of shrapnel fell from out the skies one day,*
> *and it nestled in my shoulder, in a most peculiar way.*
> *And when the MO saw it, sure it looked so sweet and fair.*
> *He said, "you're off to Blighty" they will fix you up back there.*
> *Then he sprinkled it with iodine to keep the bugs away,*
> *it's the only way to treat them, no matter what they say.*
> *But when I left the CCS, he changed his fickle mind,*
> *and he marked me down for duty and he sent me up the line.*[35]

Allowing the new comic lyrics to piggyback on a popular melody was one clever and effective way of capturing the attention of soldier audiences. Most would at once recognize the familiar refrain and empathize with the lyrically altered parody.

Yet some songs of the British music hall needed no concert-party treatment at all, and were suitably sarcastic and able to stand on their own in the soldiers' production. This was the case with Long, Scott, and Felman's "Oh, It's a Lovely War," which was perhaps the single most memorable satirical war song from the First World War:

> *Oh, oh, oh it's a lovely war.*
> *Who wouldn't be a soldier, eh?*
> *Oh it's a shame to take the pay.*
> *As soon as reveille has gone we feel just as heavy as lead,*
> *but we never get up till the sergeant brings our breakfast up to bed.*
> *Oh, oh, oh, it's a lovely war.*
> *What do we want with eggs and ham when we've got plum and apple jam?*

Form fours. Right turn. How shall we spend the money we earn?
Oh, oh, oh it's a lovely war.

When does a soldier grumble? When does he make a fuss?
No one is more contented in all the world than us.
Oh it's a cushy life, boys, really we love it so:
Once a fellow was sent on leave and simply refused to go. (chorus)
Come to the cookhouse door, boys, sniff the lovely stew.
Who is it says the colonel gets better grub than you?
Any complaints this morning? Do we complain? Not we.
What's the matter with lumps of onion floating around the tea? (chorus)[36]

As playful as the British original was, Red Newman and the Dumbells managed to attach an even greater weight to the song's irreverent dimension. Where the song was sung to a march tempo in the British revues, Newman, as Clark explained, "slowed it down and sang it like a torch song, giving it, according to (Jack) Ayre, 'a very sarcastic edge.'"[37]

The hero very often fell victim to the concert-party tunesmiths. Many soldiers preferred the non-heroic characters to the adventure seekers, as Officer Wyndham Lewis explained: "A V.C. [Victoria Cross Recipient] is after all a fellow who does something heroic; almost *un*English. It is taking things a bit too seriously to get the V.C. The really popular fellow is the humorous 'Old Bill' à la Bairnsfather. And it was really 'Old Bill' who won the war—with all that that expression 'won the war' implied."[38]

Waite's "Medals on My Chest" was a popular number that Dumbell Newman recorded for HMV. The song illustrates how some soldiers might have been underwhelmed by an unapologetic braggart, who had been awarded so many medals that the army had run out of letters:

First I went and won the DCM, Then I went and won the DSO,
and then I went and won the ABC, the EFG, the HIJKLMNOP,
and then I went and won the RST my word how I fought and bled.
Every word I say is true, I won the UVW,
and now I've been and won the XYZ.[39]

The strongest message poking its head out from behind the laughter in these sorts of songs was that the soldier could be unimpressed not only by the romantic allegory surrounding war, but also by its sanctioned awards. Glory and heroism were accepted ideals continually celebrated in every facet of both British and Canadian society so mocking these ideals afforded the average soldier a reprieve; by singing along to the likes of "I Don't Want to Be a Soldier," the soldier took part in a confessional, allowing him to say "war is not glorious" and "I am not always brave." It also gave the regular private an opportunity to take a concealed potshot at those, both military officials and civilians, who greatly invested in this idealism.

Satire on the Military System

Soldiers were often forced to adhere to ridiculous and archaic military customs. "British Regular army discipline," as Fuller surmised, "was more uniquely characterized by its constant emphasis upon spit and polish, "bull," and the rigid separation of the ranks."[40] Satirical songs were one way the soldier might safely voice his disapproval, and many official army procedures were vulnerable to satirical commentary good reason. The singing of such subversive songs was one way that the power relationship between the ordinary foot soldier and the higher ranks was negotiated. If soldiers had expressed such sentiments outside of the context of a parody or a comic sketch, they might have found themselves in hot water. MacDonald claimed that for those who sung irreverent and daring soldiers' songs: "There was a tacit understanding that they [the regular soldier] had a 'fool's licence,' and it must have relieved the rebellious spirit chafing at the bit of army discipline to express in anti-authoritarian song the scurrilous insubordinate sentiments that would have sent a soldier smartly to clink if he had expressed them directly in the hearing of an officer."[41]

The party performers afforded a chance to exercise this "fool's licence" publicly, which may have been for the soldier-audiences the most cherished of the concert party's many functions.

The troops, as Jack McLaren noted, "were always quick to adapt any song, that might apply to any of their own situations or activities."[42] One particularly insipid military activity—the kit inspection, was feared by soldiers, as attested in the popular soldier song of the same name:

> You all know that terrible feeling
> When your socks are out of repair,
> And you ain't got no laces of blacking,
> Nor a hairbrush for doing your hair.
>
> When your boots want re-soling and heeling,
> And your shirts are wanting a mend;
> Your toothbrush is black and mouldy
> Since you used it to spread Soldier's Friend.
>
> 'Tis then that the words "Kit inspection"
> Bring fear to the hearts of the brave,
> And you start to tremble with wind up
> Till you can't hold a razor to shave.[43]

Figure 22 Ted Charter delivers his "Kit Inspection" from the pulpit. (Courtesy Stephen Plunkett)

Dumbell Ted Charter was a Winnipeg real estate man. As such, Charter was a wonderful talker and a good impromptu writer who wrote for special occasions. Jack Ayre remembered that Charter would write and smoke until daylight.[44] A vaudeville actor, the former Dumbell stayed in London after the war. He wrote many skits for the concert party, but was best remembered for a monologue that he performed in the character of a minister conducting a mock sermon on the same subject:

> I desire to read to you, from the book of Numbers (*picks up a telephone book*), in chapter six, verse seventeen—At all times, by be prepared, for no man knoweth when Kit Inspection cometh ... Behold, there came towards them, one adorned with three golden stars, who swaggerth much before men. And he of the three stars spoke unto one known as R. S. M. (*Regimental Sergeant Major*), saying unto him, "bring before me at the ninth hour, one hundred and fifty men, bearing upon themselves their burdens and all of their possessions, and have them spread them before me, so that I may see which one among them falleth short—of that which he should have ..."[45]

Over fifty years later, Monty Python would frame a similar sketch on grenades in *Monty Python and the Holy Grail* (1975):

King Arthur
How does it ... um ... how does it work?

Sir Lancelot
I know not, my liege.

King Arthur
Consult the Book of Armaments.

Brother Maynard
Armaments, chapter two, verses nine through twenty-one.

Cleric
[reading] *And Saint Attila raised the hand grenade up on high, saying, "O Lord, bless this thy hand grenade, that with it thou mayst blow thine enemies to tiny bits, in thy mercy." And the Lord did grin. And the people did feast upon the lambs and sloths, and carp and anchovies, and orangutans and breakfast cereals, and fruit-bats and large chu …*

Brother Maynard
Skip a bit, Brother …

Cleric
And the Lord spake, saying, "First shalt thou take out the Holy Pin. Then shalt thou count to three, no more, no less. Three shall be the number thou shalt count, and the number of the counting shall be three. Four shalt thou not count, neither count thou two, excepting that thou then proceed to three. Five is right out. Once the number three, being the third number, be reached, then lobbest thou thy Holy Hand Grenade of Antioch towards thy foe, who, being naughty in my sight, shall snuff it."

Brother Maynard
Amen.

All
Amen.[46]

While Python and like comedy troupes were able to tap into the Great War soldier's daily grind for comedic effect, the soldier-entertainers of a half-century previous served up something more than mere comedy for the actual fighting men. The concert party, in effect, could act as the soldier's town hall meeting: a safe, public assembly, where the collective beefs of the community could be raised without fear of censure or condemnation. And while some of the songs revealed a form of resistance, the prevailing mood was, as Cook rightly observed, more "an airing of grievances than a precursor of revolution."[47]

Various shortcomings in the army's organizational system could be bemoaned in song as well. Andre Charlot's music-hall revue of 1916, *See-Saw*, parodied a particular military inefficiency that had caught the attention of the Canadian concert parties. The song entitled "Shirts" lamented a particular fault found in the BEF's system of soldier provisions. Easily morphed into a Canadian context, the song was also sung by the Dumbells at the Front. As McLaren revealed at a reunion for the Dumbells held in 1975, the CEF could be equally as inefficient as the BEF:

They used to take us behind the line for baths—"so called." The bath parade consisted of a very small trickle of water; someone shouted water on and water off in one short staccato sentence, and we were issued with what was called deloused shirts. (*painfully long pause*) God! When I think of some of these shirts that used to get up all by themselves …

Then McLaren sang:

They give you a trickle of water,
with which you must wash off the dirt.
You dry yourself on a towel,
then they hand you a sterilised shirt.
There are shirts, shirts, all kinds of shirts,
shirts that are little and tall,
shirts of all patterns, both "thinuns" and "fatuns,"
and shirts that are not shirts at all.
Shirts made from blouses and seats of old trousers,
shirts that were old women's skirts,
sacks that had ruffed it since Wellington snuffed it,
are issued to soldiers as shirts.[48]

Soldiers, required to keep their kit in top form, were at the same time issued clothing, food, shelter, and equipment that was less than adequate. For McLaren, Charter, Young, and the other sketch writers of Canada's concert parties, the irony of these *real* military procedures was apparent, and as such, needed little comic improvement to be turned into a sketch: they were already naturally vaudevillian.

Satire on Superior Officers

If the subjects of war and the military system were vulnerable to soldiers' mockery, it follows that those in superior rank over the private soldier were both obvious and irresistible targets. This could mean the very top echelons of the military down to the sergeant major and everyone in between. CEF officials had sought the essential element of positive morale in their soldiers to further military ambitions, and the concert parties delivered it to them. Yet, this was often purchased by way of provocative satire on the military authorities themselves.

Irreverent songs that could never be mistaken for patriotic anthems may have been tolerated by the officers because they rejuvenated the soldiers who loved every sarcastic refrain. There were, of course, some limits. Concert-party performers tempered parodies of their immediate superiors, and relaxed comedic boundaries if the soldiers were comfortable with their commanding officer. Few would have taken their superiors to task and individual soldiers did not need to be reminded of their own vulnerability.[49] Certainly, men could come to love their commanding officer but they could also privately resent him and fear that he was entirely unqualified for the position. Ergo, the concert parties' digs at their superiors was a feature that appealed to the average soldier, penetrating his consciousness and arming him for the task of surviving the ill equipped.

Following the Ludendorff Offensive in 1918, the British military brass undertook a spring cleanout of Canadian officers above the rank of lieutenant.[50] Canadian soldiers were now more and more, coming under the thumb of new officers who had little experience in the front lines. Charles Henry Savage of the 5th Canadian Mounted Rifles was able to draw on Dumbell irony to survive the ignorance of one particularly green officer. When Savage entered the dugout of his new commander, the latter pulled out a trench map and started listing off ridiculous objectives for his newly acquired unit:

> "I feel sure that there's a machine gun in this building," indicating a spot on the map almost in the German line. "The first thing for you to do is to go over and capture that gun. Then you had better go through the three huts just to the right of the machine gun and make sure that there are no German posts established in them."
>
> "And what shall I do after that?" I inquired innocently.
>
> "Well, you might go up and down the line a few times on the chance of capturing a German patrol or two, and after that just use your own judgment as to what you do for the rest of the night."
>
> It reminded me of a song The Dumbells—the Third Division's concert party—used to sing, in which after enumerating a long list of daily tasks each verse finished with, "And the rest of the day's your own to do with as you please."[51]

Green officers like Savage's arrived in an environment where meritocracy had at times been replaced by favour; leaving veteran soldiers to bit their tongues or quietly hum a scathing little ditty from their favourite concert party.

Various Canadian soldier-entertainers incorporated Ivor Novello and Clifford Grey's "On the Staff" into their show. The song illustrated how some soldiers engaged in brutal fighting might grow to begrudge the officer ranks, specifically those in the employ of a cushy job, well behind the vanguard of war:

> *If a blunder I should make, or some silly arsed mistake,*
> *I'll blame the office boy and have 'im shot!*
> *I'm on the staff (I'm on the staff),*
> *It's the job that's made for me, it's easy as can be,*
> *I'm on the staff (I'm on the staff),*

and 'pon my soul I really have to laugh.
I'll perhaps look in the office, say, from half past two to three,
there'll be four and twenty lady clerks who'll all attend to me,
and the nicest of the lot will put the sugar in my tea.
I'm on the staff, I'm on the staff.[52]

Another example of this playful resentment of officers can be found in the PPCLI CC's sketch *Old Nick*, where the spectrum of superior ranks was sentenced to hell. In it, the Devil awaits his latest damned arrivals, who slide down a chute and land in the middle of stage to be greeted by their new host. One by one they arrive; the sanitary sergeant, the sergeant major, the paymaster, the general, and so forth, until finally, Kaiser Wilheim arrives. The Devil, after this last meeting, quickly abdicates; handing his crown over to the Kaiser whom he confessed made him feel like an amateur.[53] In the judgment of some of the concert-party sketch writers, the Kaiser was still the enemy, and, at least marginally, more sinister than their own superior officers.

Officials were aware of the good the concert parties were doing and turned a blind eye to such irreverence in order to achieve the favourable result of having a high-spirited fighting force. The commanding officer of one particular dressing station confessed to Jack McLaren that his concert party was doing more for the boys than he could and the O.C. implored McLaren to "keep it up."[54] Likewise, Colonel Nicholson attested that the Dumbells were "contributing tremendously to the morale of the troops."[55] At the same time, some officers recognized that elements of the concert-party material teetered on the edge of acceptability. As Lieutenant Hodder-Williams confessed, "Skits, choruses, plays—many of them daringly personal—were hugely appreciated."[56] While these "daringly personal" sketches caricatured high-ranking officers (some of whom would have been in attendance), not to mention the war itself, there is no evidence to suggest concert parties were ever censored or admonished by CEF officials. Rather, the entertainers seem to have remained autonomous and received only one direct mandate from their superiors: "Be ready to put on a show any place, any time."[57]

Furthermore, officers wilfully engaged in organizing concert-party tickets for their troops from the battalion's funds and sometimes took part in show themselves; appearing in the very send-ups directed at them. The officers did not stand on their dignity and by virtue of their participation, gave implicit sanction to the show's content.[58] For some officers, it was a fair trade-off, to keep their men battle-ready.

Despite the irreverent sketch material that directly made fun of the officer ranks, the one-on-one relationships that many of the performers shared with the officers directly linked to the concert parties were generally respectful and at times warm and friendly. On one hand, McLaren may have written the skit *Old Nick* which likened British and Dominion Generals and high-ranking officers to Kaiser Wilhelm and Satan. On the other hand, he possessed a great reverence for at least one officer, Lieutenant Colonel Agar Adamson, whom McLaren considered, "a Patron Saint of the Arts."[59] This reverence came as a surprise even to the officers themselves. In a letter to his wife Mabel, Adamson explained how he was at a loss when the regimental pipe major at a concert put on by the PPCLI CC had "in very broad Scotch … asked to be allowed to play on the pipes a tune he had been composing since June hoping for the occasion to play it to me as CO. I had no idea that the great majority of men gave a damn who commanded them."[60]

Adamson was not the only officer so revered by the soldiers in his charge. Major General Lipsett also found a special place in the hearts of the concert-party performers. Lipsett helped to perfect the night "trench raid" that had impressed the likes of Winston Churchill. According to Churchill, "Lipsett made a realistic attack with his bombs. The splinters flew all over the place. The Canadians grinned from ear-to-ear. Wonderful fellows like leopards."[61] Lipsett was, as discussed earlier, the one who armed Captain Plunkett and his leap of leopards with the official backing necessary to raise a series of concert parties. While inspecting his new division in the very last month of fighting in the war, Lipsett was killed in action on 14 October 1918. On hearing of Lipsett's death, Alan Murray recalled: "In all the turmoil of turning over a division he had taken time to leave us a note expressing thanks and appreciation. To the phrase, 'an officer and a gentleman,' we felt privileged to add, 'and friend.'"[62] Murray—and the rest of the soldier-entertainers for that matter—walked a tightrope, constantly reconciling their relationships with their officer friends, who were vital to both the very existence of concert parties in the first place and to the material performed therein.

As they had reviewed the question of superior rank in their performances, so too did concert parties examine the question of 'superior class.' The values of the middle class dominated not only the way in which individual soldiers behaved, but also the overall organization of the war and the classification of its combatants.[63] Soldier-entertainers of the Canadian Corps parodied the privileged classes. A perfect example of the concert parties' reaction to the prevailing class system during the war can be found in Dumbell Stan Bennett's version of "Archibald." Musically speaking, "Archibald" leaves a little to be desired but the exaggerated arrogance of its main character is, nonetheless, effective comedy:

> *When first I heard what Germans called their beastly "Hymn of Hate"*
> *my blood began to sizzle, I was in an awful state.*
> *I said, "I'll join the army, then we'll win the blooming war,"*
> *What a laugh I am, I didn't think of it before.*

I called upon the general, and said, "I'd like to get in this game."
He said, "Old boy, I know your face, but I just can't think of your name."
I said, "I'm Archibald, Archibald, Archibald Vere de Vere,
no doubt you'll think it is queer, that I should bother you here,
but I'm Archibald, Archibald, the son of a noble peer."
He said, "Can you fight?" "You're jolly well right," I said, "I'm a Vere de
Vere."[64]

This was hardly an anthem for class warfare, but it is indicative of a growing awareness that soldiers were not in the most capable hands.

Such caricaturing of generals, officers, and the privileged classes remained, for the most part, good-natured.[65] A more deep-rooted derision for the upper ranks and authors of military strategy took time to develop, and would not really flower until the war could be viewed in hindsight. In the years following the war, many veterans and some historians regarded the military's brass hats with suspicion and scorn. Some saw them solely as "butchers and bunglers."[66] The famous officer-author T.E. Lawrence said of those directing the war, "The men were often gallant fighters, but their generals as often gave away in stupidity what they had gained in ignorance."[67] While Sam Hughes, the Canadian Minister of Militia and Defence, was widely praised for many of his initiatives (including the organization of Valcartier), Jack McLaren's opinion of the man stood in stark contrast. McLaren said of Hughes that he "was the author of enormous planned confusion."[68] And while it is unlikely that outright condemnation of the war would have been tolerated in the performances of the Canadian concert parties, one can still hear within their parodies at least the whisperings of contempt. This quiet contempt was something rather different from any sort of cheerleading the concert parties may have initially been recruited for. Yet, this was an absurd war and sharing contempt for it raised the troops' morale and allowed them to get on with the business of warring.

V The Canadian Concert-Party Experience

To the person with an active imagination, war is truly hell.
—Jack McLaren

Many issues that Canadian concert parties chose to explore on stage were ones that were relevant and applicable to most soldiers' everyday experience during the First World War. Surviving the rats, lice, snow, rain, and mud, not to mention bullets, shellfire, and gas, were aspects of trench warfare that transcended no man's land, and were common burdens for soldiers on all sides.[1] Together, these features of the war manufactured a climate that could be understood only through experience. Yet each army's experience was somewhat different from one another and the Canadian soldier had his own unique Great War to survive; a fact not lost on the entertainers of the Canadian Corps.

Individual themes specific to the Canadian experience included equipment malfunctions that were exclusive to Canadian troops, the horrors of the poison gas attack at the Second Battle of Ypres, leave and sick leave in London and, by extension, Canadians as viewed by others, and, finally, how Canadian men at the Front dealt with the absence of women.

The Ross Rifle

An Australian soldier watching the PPCLI Comedy Company might have laughed heartily and appreciated many of the shared trials of trench warfare with his Canadian brethren but would have known little or nothing at all of the inefficiencies of the Canadian Ross Rifle. In the end, only a Canadian soldier would have fully understood the trepidation associated with carrying the faulty weapon. This exclusivity of the Canadian-specific brand of soldier humour acted both as an agent in the concert-parties' success, and, as we will later see, in its failure too.

The Ross Rifle was the Canadian soldiers' official rifle when the First World War began. Problems relating to the rifle had been revealed as early as 1902 when the weapon was first tested. These problems were ignored until the weapon proved to be inefficient in the trenches. Enter Sam Hughes, the Minister of Militia, who championed the Ross and defended it against those forces that sought its replacement. Considered by many to be headstrong, arrogant, and slightly mad, Hughes fits the archetypal "donkey" classification—that rare breed of general who, ignorant of modern warfare, was, through a defiant and inflexible ego, able to till the graves of many young men in the First World War.[2] As a celebrated marksman of the Boer War, Hughes was among those who lobbied for the adoption of the Ross for Canadian soldiers.[3]

Various forces conspired to make the Ross the official rifle of the Canadian Corps. The British military had an interest in keeping the various armies within the empire outfitted with common weapons and equipment following the difficulties surrounding the South African conflict. Yet, when the Small Arms Company, makers of the British Lee-Enfield Rifle, had no interest in opening a Canadian branch, the Ross Rifle became the default rifle of choice for Canada's Forces.[4] Furthermore, Hughes' campaign for the Ross was in part aided by the economic and military nationalism that had captured the country's imagination. In adopting a Canadian-made rifle, the government was in keeping with popular "buy Canadian" sentiment.

The Ross, however, would prove rather unpopular with Canadian soldiers in the face of battle. As a target rifle, the Ross was excellent, but it was one foot longer, one pound heavier, and one-third more costly than the Lee-Enfield.[5] These weaknesses would later come to haunt the Canadians during the Great War. There was also a laundry list of complaints. The most common complaint was the stiffness of the bolt mechanism after rapid fire. There was also the tendency of the rifle to jam from the mud of the trenches. The Ross's problematic bayonet often fell off. The sights on the rifle were also too complicated. Al Plunkett, Dumbell and soldier, complained that when slung over the soldier's shoulder, the Ross "either caught on the parapet of the trench or protruded slightly above, thereby drawing enemy fire."[6] The rifle simply did not meet the requirements of the Western Front.

For many Canadian soldiers, the British Lee-Enfield was the preferred rifle. During the war, Sir Edwin Alderson, a senior British officer in command of the first Canadian Contingent shortly after the war's outbreak, commissioned his own series of tests comparing the Ross to the Lee-Enfield and found that the latter managed 100 to 125 rounds of rapid fire before jamming, whereas the Ross could manage only 25 to 50 rounds before jamming.[7] Official tests aside, the soldiers made the most compelling argument against the Ross when, at the

Battle of Ypres, Canadians took Lee-Enfield rifles off dead British soldiers to replace their Ross rifles. Under mounting threat of punishment, the soldiers of the Canadian Corps continued to choose, and trade for, the Lee-Enfield.

Alderson's tests and their results had crossed a line with the Minister of Militia: as Desmond Morton illustrated, "loyalty to the Ross was the ultimate test of loyalty to Hughes."[8] For Hughes, the Ross was a matter of personal pride and he was already disappointed that Canadian-made equipment had been abandoned in England before Canada's 1st Division crossed the channel.[9] Political lines were thus drawn with Alderson, Major General M.S. Mercer, and Arthur Currie condemning the rifle on one side while Hughes; his son Garnet; and Richard Turner, a Quebec-Tory and Victoria Cross recipient in the South African War, vehemently supported it on the other. Indeed, Turner threatened punishment to those in his division found with a Lee-Enfield rifle, while Mercer had to explain why the PPCLI carried the Lee-Enfield instead of the Ross. Lieutenant Colonel Francis Farquhar, the first CO of the PPCLI, said this of the rifle: "The experience which we have had with the Ross can hardly fail to have shaken the confidence of the men in that rifle."[10] Another anonymous colonel declared, "It is nothing short of murder to send our men against the enemy with such a weapon."[11] The men knew this too well and support for the British rifle had permeated the entire Canadian Corps, a fact later celebrated in song by the PPCLI CC. In the summer of 1916 the Ross Rifle was discarded and all four Canadian divisions were equipped with the Lee-Enfield.[12]

Jack McLaren was one Canadian soldier who knew both the deficiencies of the Ross and the merits of the Lee-Enfield. The former sniper shared his opinion about the weapon following the war: "In 1914 when war came to Canada we were completely unprepared to meet the challenge ... a few Ross rifles which were not much good, in the hurly burly usage of wartime conditions when we came across an unused British Lee Enfield mark 3 rifle, we threw our Ross rifles away and grabbed the Lee Enfield."[13]

McLaren immortalized the Ross with his play on one of Sir Harry Lauder's most popular songs, "Roaming in the Gloaming."[14] McLaren used the familiar melody and rewrote the lyrics to tackle the issue of the Ross rifle. Lauder's original:

> Roamin' in the gloamin, on the bonnie banks of Clyde,
> Roamin' in the gloamin, wi ma lassie by my side,
> When the sun has gone to rest, that's the time that we love best,
> Oh it's lovely roaming in the gloaming.[15]

Was replaced with McLaren's words for the PPCLI CC sketch:

> *Roamin' in the gloamin, Ross Rifle by my side,*
> *Roamin' in the gloamin, could nae fire it if I tried,*
> *It's worst than a' the rest, the Lee-Enfield I like best,*
> *I sure must loose it roaming in the gloaming.*[16]

In rewording Lauder's wildly popular lyric, McLaren had put into song what was already a popular feeling among Canadian soldiers. Moreover, McLaren had given his audience something that they could never have received from music-hall stars such as Lauder, George Robey, or Harry Wheldon: he had held up a mirror and refracted a uniquely Canadian perspective of the war. Successful interpretations like McLaren's were informally adopted by other Canadian soldier-entertainers. The Canadian Westerners of the 49th Battalion, by example, tailored the parody to their own needs:

> *Roamin' through the tranchees, Ross Rifle by my side,*
> *Roamin' through the tranchees, couldn't fire it if I tried,*
> *Oh, I've put 'em to the test, the Lee-Enfield I like best,*
> *When I go a-roamin' through the tranchees.*[17]

These sorts of tailored parodies really hit home with the troops. As McLaren himself confirmed, "The lads out front fairly gobbled this part of the menu up and then cried for more."[18] For this reason, above all others did the soldiers of the Canadian Corps return time after time to see their own version of the war reinterpreted by the likes of the PPCLI CC.

While the music used in the Canadian concert parties generally comprised popular British songs, McLaren, and other Canadian entertainers of the First World War like him, were keenly aware of the need to include topical Canadian material like the Ross Rifle issue in their onstage show. This fusion of popular British music with relevant Canadian material had great currency with the Canadian soldiers and established the concert party as a recognized source of Canadian entertainment. Concert parties and individual soldiers claimed existing songs and parodied and reappropriated them for their own purposes. As Lieutenant J.S. Williams observed, "Parody [is] much circulated over here. It absolutely reflects the impression and feelings of the men, and officers as well, in my opinion."[19] With the inclusion of topics relating directly to the soldier, McLaren and the others had created an exclusive bond with their following. It was a relationship that—at least for the Dumbells—would survive the war.

The Philanthropists

Canadian soldiers experienced a sharp feeling of alienation from civilian life when they were on leave in Britain, and it was far more acute for those wounded Canadians who were convalescing at a British hospital. This was rendered even more bizarre when soldiers were introduced to philanthropic civilians who tried, no doubt earnestly, to lend a helping hand. It was difficult for some Canadian soldiers to reconcile the hell on earth that was the experience of the Front, with the innocence of many civilians who were often oblivious to what war was really like.

This should not, of course, diminish the tremendous positive change that some philanthropic women of means were able to affect during the war. Montreal-born Grace Julia Parker, later Lady Drummond, for example, assembled a staggering list of public achievements during the First World War. Drummond, who lost a son to the war, was able to establish a department of information for the wounded and missing through the raising of personal financial gifts. As Elizabeth Kirkland observed, at the core of Drummond's work was a sincere devotion to "help her fellow citizens and to enable them to help each other."[20] For her wartime efforts, Drummond received the Médaille de Reconnaissance, the British Red Cross medal, and the Serbian Red Cross Medal.[21] Yet, many civilians from Drummond's class were naïve to the simple wants of battle-weary soldiers.

The wounded Canadians recovering in a British hospital were often subject to the whims of well-meaning philanthropists. The archetypical philanthropist was a woman from London's high society, who sought to raise the morale of the wounded by providing high-culture entertainment. The philanthropists believed that such fare might not only amuse but also instruct those soldiers who were either wounded or on leave in Britain. Their efforts, however, did not always achieve the desired effect. The content of one such concert party put on for the troops was described in the British newspaper *The Bedfordshire Times & Independent*:

> By the kind thought and generosity of the members of the Wing Badminton Club, all the troops billeted in the village, were invited to a very substantial meat tea at the Hall on Boxing Day. After tea an entertainment was provided, tobacco and cigarettes were handed out to all the men in the Hall, and after the concert, coffee and cake and other eatables were provided. The Boys Scouts made themselves very useful as waiters. The entertainment included Morris dances by Miss H. Tatham's class and songs by Mrs. T. Gale who completely won the hearts of the soldiers with "Tipperary." Captain and Mrs. Daniels gave a club swinging exhibition and Miss Adams recited "Play the Game."[22]

Knowing what we know of "Tipperary," it was unlikely that the soldiers were as impressed with Kipling and the tunes as they were with the smokes and grub.[23]

Another example of well-meaning but unappreciated philanthropy can be witnessed in the case of the English actress Lena Ashwell. While working with the Ladies' Auxiliary Committee of the YMCA and the Actresses' Franchise League, Ashwell helped supply professional entertainers for the base camps in France, with the mandate of providing "the best in literature, art, music and drama."[24] While Ashwell was a fine performer and her heart was in the right place, the show was somewhat lost on veteran Canadian soldier, who sought a form of escapism, not high art.[25]

Certainly popular culture could and did inform high art in much the same complementary way "legitimate" theatre informed the music hall. In this respect, there was a circular relationship between "pop" and the "serious." Recall that Dumbell Jerry Brayford, while poking fun at the Diaghilev ballerinas for taking curtain calls to an empty house, still stuck around to watch them dance because he thought they were marvellous.[26] With this in mind, the Canadian concert parties became expert at fusing the high and low. While quality was never compromised, the entertainers understood that the majority of fighting men, officers, educated and otherwise, were not terribly fussed on instructional, highbrow art in their short respites from the fight.

The gap between the classes was, at least cosmetically, shrinking during the war and so too was the gap between highbrow and lowbrow entertainment, which was redefined during this period. Still, the entertainment provided by some well-meaning philanthropic agents, as Dumbell Al Plunkett observed, might have done more to disturb than delight the soldier.[27] Sheldon-Williams surmised in his contemporary account: "Chopin, Grieg, Mendelssohn? Where are your laurels when the fighting man finds solace in 'Keep the Home Fire Burning,' 'Pack All Your Troubles' and 'Roses Are Blooming in Picardy?' The writers of these hackneyed, stale effusions, anonymous so far as we were concerned, could move us and lift us more surely with their homely notes than all your classic masters."[28]

In actuality, private citizens who had organized special treats for the troops were usually too out of touch with soldiers' tastes for the amusements to do any amusing. Lauder was one civilian who was not so out of touch: "A man who has two days' leave in London does not want to see a serious play or a problem drama, as a rule. He wants something light, with lots of pretty girls and jolly tunes and people to make him laugh."[29]

And Lauder aimed to give them just that, night after night. In their own way, the educated McLaren and the savvy Plunkett also followed Lauder's wartime mantra.

The Canadian concert parties were naturally able to amuse. Perhaps the all-time most memorable Dumbells' sketch was written by McLaren and Leonard Young while they were performing in the PPCLI CC together.[30] The skit was entitled *The Duchess Entertains*, and was a parody of the philanthropists of London's high society. *The Duchess* was set in a British hospital where wounded soldiers, attired in their hospital "blues" with white lapels and red neckties (the latter of which was unpopular with many soldiers as they signified effeminacy), were subject to the awful entertainment provided by their host, the Duchess, originally played by Conrad Stephens and later by Leonard Young.[31] The Duchess introduced various guests to the wounded soldiers in an unsuccessful effort to cheer them up. In the Comedy Company version, the punchline came with the final introduction of an undertaker.[32] Soldier audiences found this innocuous use of death in the PPCLI CC sketch hilarious. Despite being surrounded by death, most soldiers were too preoccupied with the misfortune of living in war to be too concerned about dying in it.

Certainly the misfortune of living in war provided more compelling comedy. Regardless of how the soldier audiences really felt about death, the undertaker was left out when the Dumbells began using the *Duchess* sketch. Perhaps satirizing the entertainment provided by philanthropists was simply funnier than using the undertaker as the punchline. By the time the Dumbells began using *The Duchess Entertains*, the sketch had become clearly focused on the highbrow entertainment. The poor quality of entertainment was embodied in an atonal opera singer whose voice was akin to fingernails scratching a chalkboard. Alternatively, there was the French singer "Mademoiselle Julie Tres Moutard," who couldn't remember the words to the selections she chose. Three wounded soldiers painfully endured the recital, as well as the ludicrous queries of the Duchess.[33] Red Newman, playing a wounded Cockney soldier with a cast on his

Figure 23 The company's signature sketch, "The Duchess Entertains." (Courtesy John McLaren)

leg, was asked, "Where were you wounded?" to which he replied, "Where was I wounded? Well, if you want to know, Missus, I was hit on the head lady and the bandage slipped—I was hit right in the Dardanelles." The Duchess asked "Scotty," a wounded Scotsman who was a nod to Lauder's character and was played by Jack McLaren, what branch of the army he was in. Scotty replied, "Well I used to be a sanitary man, Missus." The Duchess was unsatisfied and pressed on, "Oh, and what were your duties?" To which McLaren shared a dumbfounded expression with the audience before replying, "You're asking for it, woman."[34]

One guest that the soldiers really did appreciate the Duchess presenting them to was Miss Genevieve Few-Close. A hopeless ballerina played by Alan Murray, Miss Few-Close excited the soldiers with her ridiculous dance routine, and indeed, her lack of clothing. In some ways, Murray's character reflected London's dark, hedonistic underbelly that had been swelling as the war dragged

Figure 24 Originally with the 9th Field Ambulance and later the PPCLI Comedy Company and the Dumbells, Leonard Young—the Duchess—lost his leg at Vimy Ridge. (Courtesy John McLaren)

on. As early as 1915, there were already 150 nightclubs in Soho alone, females were less and less chaperoned by elders, and alcohol was free flowing long after the legal closing hour had passed.[35]

Although not all Canadian soldiers who had spent time on leave in London would have encountered the seedier quarters of the City of Earthly Delights, almost every soldier wanted to see women—even if it was men who were dressed as women (the matronly Duchess notwithstanding). Miss Genevieve Few-Close eventually exhausted the Duchess's patience. The latter, following a strict high-moral code, pulled aside the frightfully underclad ballerina and prepared to introduce yet another astonishingly boring guest. But rather than endure any more treats from the Duchess, the soldiers frantically hobbled to the door, preferring a return to the Front over staying.

The sketch was an unqualified success. And not just with the soldiers; years after, box offices across Canada would receive phone calls from curious fans who wondered if the Dumbell review that was playing in their town that particular evening included the *Duchess* sketch.[36] Jerry Brayford remembered that various theatres were threatened by their patrons: "If you haven't got the Duchess Entertains on I'm not coming to see your show."[37] One reviewer who attended a performance in Vancouver said of the sketch, "it is only necessary to state that the theatre fairly shook with merriment."[38] During one performance in Toronto following the war, the Duchess of Atholl was in attendance. The Dumbells were uncertain how the Duchess would accept the sketch, but could not afford to pull the piece from the show. Following the performance, the cast was instructed to wait on stage to receive the Duchess. When she arrived, stage she swished over to Leonard Young who had played the Duchess that night and said, "My dear Duchess, you're a solace to another Duchess and if ever you want to write another sketch, come and see me, I can tell you funnier things than the ones you wrote."[39]

The *Duchess* continued to wield a wide range of influence, as other notable guests were equally amused with the sketch, including Hollywood impresario Irving Thalberg. Thalberg offered Jack McLaren a screen test for Metro-Goldwyn-Mayer after he saw the sketch performed at New York's Ambassador Theatre. McLaren passed on Thalberg's offer, but later in life admitted that it may have been his biggest mistake, "Norma Shearer was smarter than I. She married him. I never did go to Hollywood."[40] Hollywood's loss was no doubt Canada's gain.

"The Duchess Entertains" remained in the Dumbells' repertoire for a decade, reappeared at various Dumbell reunions, and was finally recreated in Alan Lund's play in honour of the famous concert party, the Legend of the Dumbells. Unlike many of the songs and sketches of the Canadian concert parties, which spoke primarily to the soldier, the Duchess possessed a pure humour that was accessible to virtually all who saw it performed.

Gas

If in some smothering dreams you too could pace
Behind the wagon that we flung him in,
And watch the white eyes writhing in his face,
His hanging face, like a devil's sick of sin;
If you could hear, at every jolt, the blood
Come gargling from the froth-corrupted lungs,
Obscene as cancer, bitter as the cud
Of vile, incurable sores on innocent tongues,
My friend, you would not tell with such high zest
To children ardent for some desperate glory,
The old Lie: *Dulce et decorum est*
Pro patria mori.[41]

—*Wilfred Owen*

Although front-line humour had evolved into a darker tone than that which was played out in the music hall during the war, there were still limits to what subjects were acceptable, and those that—like the execution of shell-shocked victims—were not. Canadian soldiers would, over the course of the war, become familiar with the devastating effects of poison gas. While serving at the Second Battle of Ypres in April 1915, Canadians were among the first to fall victim to the hideous weapon. The discharge of poisonous gas via shells and other projectiles had been forbidden in the Hague Declaration of 1899 and later at the Hague Convention of 1907.[42] Although it was condemned by both sides, both sides used it; the use of gas transformed over the course of the war from unthinkable to standard fare. British and French chemists had been developing various gasses for use as weapons, yet it was the German chemist Fritz Haber who provided the Germans with a chlorine gas to be methodically deployed during the Second Battle of Ypres.

German authorities believed that gas would be an effective way of preparing an advance. If the enemy was overwhelmed by gas, the Germans might simply walk over a demoralized army and take their objective.[43] Part of Germany's rationale was that killing by gas was more humane than killing by shelling. Various historians including Basil H. Liddell Hart and Peter Graf Kielmansegg have subsequently given credence to this claim, whereas Eksteins considers the argument hollow: "[gas] was not used instead of artillery; it was used in addition to artillery."[44] In support of Eksteins, British artilleryman, V.M. Fergusson wrote of his disdain for the German rationale:

These humanitarians claim that it is more merciful to asphyxiate a man than to blow him up with high explosive shell. That is their pleasant way of trying to appear before the world at large. In reality—having turned on the gas they bayonet everyone who has been too overcome by the fumes to move and then turn their high explosives onto the wretched crowd of people who remain struggling for breath. Words fail to describe one's feelings about the whole thing.[45]

Generally speaking, gas was considered by many to be out of step with an unwritten "soldier's code of war" and, with its horrifying effect of suffocating men to death, most participants viewed it as an "immoral weapon."[46] Simply put, the idea of poison gas terrified men.

Tactically speaking, poison gas was by no means the most efficient weapon in the First World War. Twelve times the amount of men killed as a result of poison gas were killed by shellfire alone.[47] Reassessments of its effectiveness have led some military historians to view the weapon as a failure.[48]

It was the nature of the wounds inflicted by the gas—first in the chlorine form, then the deadly phosgene form, and finally mustard gas—that produced the most non-lethal casualties and which haunted those soldiers who witnessed the attacks and survived.[49] Poison gas attacks testified to the totality of the war, as victims made exhaustive efforts to capture a single breath. With faces blue and contorted, they frothed yellow mucus from their mouths, indicating an impending, agonizing death. Fellow soldiers often had to witness gas victims choking to death and, in more extreme cases, watch as their comrades coughed up their lungs: literally. Perhaps no other horror of trench warfare could compete with the devastating psychological effect that poison gas had on the soldier.

Canadians led the way in coping with and surviving the Western Front's gas environment. With functional respirators and advanced anti-gas training from the Canadian Corps Gas Services, the Canadian soldier had a much better chance of surviving a gas attack than, for example, did his American counterpart.[50] But the cumbersome gas masks, replete with piglike snouts, gave the soldier, already fighting in a surreal landscape, an additional extraterrestrial appearance. These masks, combined with the fickle and unpredictable behaviour of the gas in poor wind and weather conditions, limited the success of poisonous gas as a weapon, though not before Canadian soldiers saw their share of casualties.

Canadians were the first intended targets of German chlorine gas. On 22 April 1915, Brigadier General Currie of the 2nd Brigade and Brigadier General Turner with the 3rd Brigade were positioned at Langemarck, near Ypres. The Germans had been waiting several days for the wind to blow in a southwest direction, in order for the gas to be carried over no man's land and into the Canadian trenches. When the Germans released the gas from the metal cylinders, the wind carried it instead to the Algerian trenches. Those French Colonials who could manage to flee did so. Some Canadians tried to fill the breach left by the Algerian troops, but overcoming the fumes proved impossible as Lance-Corporal J.D. Keddie of the 48th Highlanders recollected: "We noticed dense volumes of dense yellow smoke rising up and coming towards the British trenches. We did not get the full effect of it, but what we did was enough for me. It makes the eyes smart and run. I became violently sick, but this passed off fairly soon."[51]

In an effort to defeat the gas, the soldiers were issued cotton bandoliers within hours of the attack. Still, many Canadians lay choking, gasping, and ultimately surrendering to the greenish-yellow clouds of chlorine gas.[52] Poison gas played only a part of the slaughter during the Second Battle of Ypres, a battle that claimed 208 officers and 5,828 men of the Canadian Corps.[53]

The "death clouds" were always viewed with great trepidation. Those soldiers who had had experience with gas (which included some of the performers, such as Rice and Newman) were acutely aware of the psychological hold the weapon had on fighting men, especially those who had witnessed firsthand men suffocating to death. As historian Tim Cook observed, "Poison gas never lost its ability to inspire dread and apprehension in the soldiers who encountered it."[54]

Gitz Rice wrote patriotic songs during the war, both before and after he had become a victim of a gas attack at Vimy Ridge. The gunnery officer accompanied the PPCLI CC on piano in Albert during that party's string of shows on the Somme in the fall of 1916.[55] On several occasions, Rice also accompanied Captain Plunkett at the famous smokers at the "Y."[56] Rice also was a key contributor to the standard musical fare of the Canadian concert parties and the entertainers of the allied forces at large.

Rice was a character and gifted storyteller. Although there is insufficient evidence to confirm it, Rice may have written "Mademoiselle from Armentières," though the authorship of the song has been officially credited to Harry Carlton and Joe Tunbridge.[57] Another interesting, if questionable legend surrounding Rice puts him at the piano during the famous "Silent Night" singalong of Christmas 1914. It was here that German and allied soldiers enjoyed a self-declared truce, mingled with each other, played football, and swapped plum pudding for German sausages before returning to war.[58] Rice's most verifiable and popular hit, however, was "Dear Old Pal of Mine," a tune made popular by the famous tenor John McCormack and one that was written on a stolen piano on the Western Front.[59]

Due to his immense popularity, several of Rice's songs were adopted by the Dumbells. Specifically, the Dumbells performed Rice's "Keep Your Head Down Fritzie Boy" (also written on said piano), a song that humorously explored a Canadian sniper's observation of a German trench:

Keep your head down, Fritzie Boy
Keep your head down, Fritzie Boy
Last night in the pale moon-light,
I saw you, I saw you
You were fixing your barb'd wire,
when we open'd "rapid fire!"
If you want to see your "Vater in the Vaterland"
keep your head down, Fritzie boy.[60]

Crucially—at least as far as the concert parties were concerned—Rice's work was recognizable *to* and widely sung *by* Canadian soldiers.

Rum rations, homesick ballads, women, Canada, and so forth, were the standard subjects for this gas victim who preferred topical, if safe, themes for his wartime compositions. Yet, Gitz Rice, the most prolific Canadian songwriting soldier of the First World War, observed strict parameters within which to create his odes to war. Despite his own horrific experience, Rice never entertained the notion of exploiting the subject of poison gas in a song.

For other concert parties too, making light of the soldiers' day-to-day experiences was a successful method in terms of winning audience approval, but gas, even though it was topical and many concert-party performers had experienced it personally, was a topic that Canadian concert parties generally avoided. Like Rice, singer Red Newman, who began entertaining with the Y-Emmas concert party before joining the Dumbells, was a victim of a gas attack.[61] Several other concert-party performers, including Alan Murray, Ross Hamilton, Bill Tennent, and Leonard Young, had firsthand experiences with the gruesome results of poison gas while serving with various Field Ambulance units, but did consider using the subject of poison gas in a dramatic sketch. The trio, however, later reconsidered. Too real, too terrifying was the subject, as Murray explained:

We called [the sketch] *gas*. It was a gas attack in Ypres, one of the very last ones, and the gas was shot at the Canadians but the wind shifted and carried it to two Irish regiments—and they got all this gas. And we were lugged over from the Canadians to help take care of them, and this young Irish officer, he was nineteen—he was dying. One of our lads who was a minister went up and spoke to him—it was unbelievable, he was lying at the side of a ruined chapel in Ypres. The only way to help them breath, you see, because the chlorine used to choke them, was to turn them on one side, our Colonel used to give up one tube and let them get air. There were two men holding this officer and he threw them aside and stood over his own stretcher and recited eight lines from "The Ballad of Reading Gaol," the ones ending: "For he who lives more lives than one, more deaths than one must die"—and he dropped dead. Well we were going to use that as a sketch, it was unbelievably theatrical, and we told the story, just as I am telling it [now], and this fellow just leaned back and said, "and then what do you do with the audience?" Which was exactly right; you couldn't leave the audience on that note.[62]

There was nothing funny about gas.[63] Rarely—and only rarely—could it be treated in a "gallows humour" sort of way, as it was in "Bombed Last Night":

> *Gassed last night, and gassed the night before*
> *Going to get gassed tonight if we never get gassed anymore*
> *When we're gassed, we're sick as we can be*
> *For phosgene and mustard gas is much too much for me*
> *They're killing us, they're killing us*
> *One respirator for the four of us*
> *Thank your lucky stars that we can all run fast*
> *So one of us can take it all alone.*[64]

The subject also found tangential application in a Bruce Bairnsfather cartoon. In it, one soldier is thumbing through his chum's photographs and remarks: "Well, yer know, I like the photo of you in your gas mask best."[65] Still, while ordinary soldiers may have nervously made light of gas in a manner of surviving any given day, their entertaining comrades were unwilling to test the subject on stage.

The ineffectiveness of the Ross Rifle, making a mockery of philanthropists, the incompetence of the enemy and even one's own commanders: *this* was the stuff of good comedy. Even death could be used, carefully, as it had been in the original PPCLI CC sketch "The Duchess Entertains."[66] Comedian Cyril "Biddy" Biddulph also explored the delicate subject of death. Biddulph replaced Captain Pembroke when the latter left the PPCLI CC. Before joining McLaren and the lads, Biddulph had already experienced some success as a stand-alone actor and had travelled with Lillie Langtry back in Canada. While playing His Majesty's Theatre in Montreal, Biddulph chose to enlist with the 5th University Company.[67] By the time he had joined the PPCLI CC, Biddulph's "worried soldier" routine was already well liked by the Canadian soldiers. Loaded down with an impossible array of equipment, sandbags, barbed wire, A-frames, and a rifle, Biddy struggled about the stage before settling in to sing his slow, mournful dirge entitled "My Motta." The song was a good example of how soldier-entertainers were able to capture and package the senselessness of the war for their understanding comrades in the crowd:

> *The sun will shine although the sky's a grey one*
> *I've often said to myself, I've said*
> *Cheer up Biddy—you'll soon be dead*
> *A short life and a gay one*[68]

Prophetically, Cyril Biddulph perished at Monchy during the German retreat near war's end.[69]

While death may have been fair game, dying was another matter. Music-hall performances during the war rarely addressed actual killing or the dead as such topics hardly raised morale. And while the brand of entertainment on the front lines was rather more subversive than that which was performed on the home front, an unwritten code of what *was* and *was not* funny was strictly observed by the performers.

Time alone would bridge the gulf between respectable humour and that which was considered taboo. An irresistible, if impossible question to consider for those growing up in the last 30-odd years of the 20th century would be to ask whether or not the comedy-sketch writers of the various Canadian concert parties could have anticipated the future of black humour and its seemingly endless and flexible boundaries of decency where *their* war was concerned. Witness *Monty Python*:

> Fighting Each Other [Going over the top in Flanders]—
>
> Blackitt
> *Oh, if I … if we don't meet again … I just want to say it's been a privilege fighting alongside you sir …* [They are continually ducking as bullets fly past them and shells burst overhead]
>
> Trevor
> *Yes, well I think this is hardly the time or place for a goodbye speech …* [Trevor is clearly anxious to go]
>
> Blackitt
> *No, me and the lads realize that but … well … we may never meet again and so …*
>
> Trevor
> *Alright, Blackitt, thanks a lot.*
>
> Blackitt
> *Just a mo, sir! You see me and the lads had a little whip-round, and we bought you this, sir …* [He produces a handsome ormolu clock from his pack. Trevor is at a loss for words. He is continually ducking]
>
> Trevor
> *Well I don't know what to say … It's a lovely thought … thank you … thank you all … and now we'd better …* [He starts to go]
>
> Blackitt
> *Hang on a tick, sir, we got something else for you …* [Two of the others emerge from some bushes with a grandfather clock]

Blackitt
*Sorry it's another clock ... There was a bit of a mix-up ... Wellacott thought
he was buying the present, and Spadger and I had already got the other.*

Trevor
Well it's beautiful ... They're both beau ... [A bullet suddenly shatters the
face of the grandfather clock [and] kills one of the carriers] *but I think
perhaps we'd better get to cover now. I'll thank you properly later ...* [Trevor
starts to go again but Blackitt hasn't finished]

Blackitt
*And Sergeant Harper got this for you, sir. He didn't know about the rest of
us ...* [He hands over a wrist watch]

Trevor
Lovely. [A shell bursts right overhead. Trevor flings himself down into the
mud] *Christ! Right! Let's go!*

Blackitt
And there's a card from all of us ... [He produces a mud-splattered enve-
lope] *Sorry about that ...* [Trevor pockets it and tries to go on] *three cheers
for Captain Donovan. Hip Hip—Hooray! Hip Hip—Hoor ...* [An almighty
burst of machine-gun silences most of them. Blackitt is hit]

Trevor
Blackitt!

Blackitt
[hurt] *And one final thing, sir ... ah! Spadger, the cheque ...*[70]

Comedy troupes like Monty Python and Black Adder would have the First World
War to thank for the emergence of this brand of sketch comedy, and over time,
nearly everything about that war would become fair game.

Soldier Comforts

Keeping an army happy was essential to keeping an army fighting. Food, a good
place to rest one's head, proper clothing, letters from home, leave, recreation
and—for some—sex were among the fundamental comforts that helped men
survive the horrors of the war.[71] Most of these subjects were often featured in
the material found in the repertoire of the Canadian concert parties at one point
or another.

Alcohol, rum in particular, was coveted by soldiers and was central among
the available morale-building tools. Indeed, the war would have been a more
difficult sale for military authorities without the prize of rum and its mollifying
effect.[72] Whether it was facing machine gun fire, or battling the nuisances of lice,

rats, rain, snow, and sleep deprivation, or being forever under a looming threat of death, rum had many uses on the Western Front. It could muster courage, ease emotional trauma, nurse flu, sooth aches and pains, keep a soldier warm, and, perhaps most vitally, allow men to get some precious sleep.[73] For these reasons, and perhaps others too, soldiers had a special place in their hearts for "demon rum."

During the war, Gitz Rice and Henry Burr released two Canadian comedy series on 78s entitled "Fun in Flanders" and "Life in a Trench in Belgium." The series covered soldier comforts in comic songs and parody sketches. Most notable from the collection is the pre-eminence given to the rum ration, as immortalized in "Fun in Flanders—Part Two":

> When I first joined the army I thought that the life of a soldier was perfectly
>   grand,
> I pictured myself with a sword and gun keeping step to a military band.
> But after two years at the Front I confess, I'm sadder and wiser by now,
> for they feed me on biscuits that ought to be brick and tins of solidified cow.
> But there's one army custom I really think fine,
> you won't hear me grouch when I'm falling in line—
> For my rum, rum, my issue of rum, nobody's late for their issue of rum,
> You forget all your troubles, you go on the double for rum, your issue of rum.[74]

The importance of rum to the troops can hardly be overstated. SRD (Services Rum Diluted) or "Special Red Demerara," as it was officially called, was administered to the soldiers in measurements of a half gill (less than a half pint), three times a week.[75] Where beer, whisky, and wine might be found at the front lines only from time to time, soldiers could rely on and look forward to their rum ration.

When the rum ration was not delivered on time, soldiers could be surly and left to think up new meanings for the initials SRD: "Seldom Reaches Destination," "Sergeants Rarely Deliver," "Soldier's Real Delight," and "Soon Runs Dry." As Tim Cook noted in his article "Rum in the Trenches," "Rum was used as a combat motivator, a medicine, and as part of the reward system." M.A. Searle of the 18th Canadian Battalion at Passchendaele demonstrated how rum could save lives, "Most of us carried on ... because of not limitless but more than ordinary issues of rum."[76] As a multipurpose tool, rum could encourage, assuage, and remedy.

No rum? Someone was surely to blame. Of all ranks, the sergeant-major was most conspicuous in his role as the regimental goat, and the butt of many regimental jokes and songs. And so it was in the traditional marching song "The Old Barbed Wire" that the sergeant-major was to blame when the rum went AWOL:

If you want to find the Sergeant-Major,
I know where he is, I know where he is.
If you want to find the Sergeant-Major, I know where he is,
He's boozing up the privates' rum.
I've seen him, I've seen him,
Boozing up the privates' rum,
I've seen him, Boozing up the privates' rum.[77]

Yet, sergeant-majors were not the only ones guilty of hoarding the precious SRD. Privates could be tried and convicted in the soldier songs and cartoons of the war. With his celebrated wit and more than ordinary insight into the day-to-day life of a soldier, Bairnsfather produced an illustration that showed a regular soldier drinking the rum ration intended for the entire platoon, with the caption "The Spirit of our troops is excellent."[78]

While the Woman's Christian Temperance Union and the Young Men's Christian Association may have lobbied for the revocation of the rum ration for Canadian soldiers, the great majority of fighting men felt that they could not have fulfilled their duties without it.[79] Harold Simpson, for example, may have been censoring his own personal use of SRD from his mother while defending the idea of it at the Front:

> A few temperance fanatics have been condemning [rum] in some of the Canadian papers. Personally I have been fortunate enough to keep clear of places where I needed it or possibly I am in good enough shape not to need it. But I have sense enough to know that it is a necessity and that it has been the means of saving many a life. I would like to see some of those who condemn it so freely go over the top in the face of a modern barrage without a drop of any stimulus and I state they would change their minds.[80]

So cherished was rum that it could be used as an effective disciplinary tool: those exemplifying good behaviour got it; those out of order did not receive their ration. Jack Ayre said of his ration that it "was a life saver after standing all night in the trench, cold, damp, as soon as you drank the rum you got warm ... it was a life saver."[81] Rum was certainly far more coveted than most comforts, certainly more than, "bully beef" or "plum and apple jam," which might explain its salience in soldiers' song, skit, and cartoon. The Army-issued rum ration was a subject that every soldier of the Canadian Corps could relate to, and the mere allusion to it during a concert was sure to get a rise out of the soldiers.[82]

Pure Silliness

Not all of the Canadian concert-party material was topical or purposeful. Unadulterated silliness, too, had its place. Although the tone of the material had been dramatically altered by the Canadian solider-entertainers, the music-hall form and its nonsense remained. Behold, "Captain Thingamabob," once styled by Dumbell Newman:

> They used to call me "air-full" in the air brigade,
> in the air brigade, yes a gas bag I'm afraid.
> They used to call me "nervy" in the infantry,
> in the infantry, oh it was very sweet to me.
> They used to call me "skinny" in the skinnamarinks,
> in the skinnamarinks I got into arrears,
> but dear ole lore, I had to stop the war,
> when they called me "Mademoiselle from Armentières."[83]

The last line is of course referring to the war's most popular silly song, "Mademoiselle from Armentières," a song whose nonsensical lyrics were sung by millions:

> Mademoiselle from Armentières, parlez-vous?
> Mademoiselle from Armentières, parlez-vous?
> Mademoiselle from Armentières,
> she hasn't been kissed for forty years,
> Inky-Pinky, parlez-vous?

Armentières was a village on the Somme river that billeted allied soldiers and was notorious for its brothels, though most civilians would not have necessarily associated the playful lyrics with any lewd connotations. The best-known version of lyrics to "Mademoiselle from Armentières" are innocuous enough, and not entirely dissimilar to a nursery rhyme, as the remaining stanzas attest:

> Oh Mademoiselle from Armentières, parlez-vous,
> Mademoiselle from Armentieres, parlez-vous,
> She got the palm and the croix de guerre,
> For washin' soldiers underwear,
> Inky-Pinky parlez-vous.

> The Colonel got the Croix de Guerre,
> Parlez-vous, the Colonel got the Croix de Guerre,
> Parlez-vous, the Colonel got the Croix de Guerre,
> The son-of-gun was never there!
> Inky-Pinky parlez-vous.

Oh Mademoiselle from Armentieres, parlez-vous,
Mademoiselle from Armentieres, parlez-vous,
You didn't have to know her long,
To know the reason men go wrong!
Inky-Pinky parlez-vous.

At its most basic, the song was an easy-to-remember drinking song. There were, however, other versions that were unmistakably lewd.

Vaudevillian sketches of the pie-in-the-face variety were still very much part of the concert parties' act. These sorts of sketches were often informed by those props that the concert parties had available to them. McLaren explained that:

> one had to write around the props we had. This called for much more creative and ingenious writing. For instance, take the cart-wheel ... the playwright would sit down beside the beastly thing and try to think of something humorous for an act introducing the cart-wheel—while overhead was the whine of "Archies" for inspiration. But this method of approaching the playwriting question did a great thing—every subject that was dealt with, was a local one.[84]

Breathing theatrical life into an abandoned cart wheel beneath the whine of anti-aircraft fire rather summed up the peculiar writing conditions and habits of the uniformed comedy writer.

A similar sketch was the PPCLI CC's "Miss Skinny," which was later added to the Dumbells repertoire. Tom J. Lilly, the oldest performer of the PPCLI CC, was forever gathering odds and ends at the Front to be later used as props. He once carried a ladder discarded from a trained dog act, which he later incorporated into the *Ms. Skinny* sketch. Lilly, as Vera Skinny, the world's greatest stuntwoman, would climb the ladder and await instructions from the Master of Ceremonies, played by Jack McLaren. McLaren would announce that Ms. Skinny would jump from atop the ladder into a small wooden bucket. Before "she" jumped, Ms. Skinny complained that there wasn't enough water in the bucket, so McLaren added five drops of water from an eyedropper. Ms. Skinny would then prepare to dive into the bucket. The lights would dim, and a human-size doll, dressed as Ms. Skinny, was tossed from above into the bucket scattering, rice everywhere, much to the delight of the audience. McLaren confessed that one night Lilly had "over stimulated himself with army rum," and had refused to come down on cue. McLaren was left to ad lib until two other members of the company went aloft and brought Vera down into the bucket.[85] These sketches—whether aided and abetted by army rum rations or not—had no great underlying message or political aside, offering the audience just an escape in pure funny-bone hilarity.

Figure 25 The PPCLI Comedy Company's T.J. Lilly, who, like so many other strong concert-party performers, was absorbed by the Dumbells at war's end. (Courtesy John McLaren)

The Canadian concert parties also contributed to this category through music. Ayre wrote a wonderfully silly song for the Dumbells' act that became the party's famous introduction and closing theme "The Dumbell Rag":

> *Hi! Boys hear our latest rag, It's a sort of raggy drag,*
> *Just listen while we sing it once for you, we hope you'll sing it too.*
> *If anyone here has the "Blues," his "Blooming Blues" he will [lose].*
> *Oh, that Dumbell Rag, that "dummy" Dumbell Rag,*
> *sing it high or sing it low, just sing it together and let 'er go HI!*
> *Oh, that Dumbell Rag, don't let your voices lag.*
> *What do we care if it shine or rain?*
> *This makes you think you're home again.*
> *"D-U-M-B-E-L-L," that ever-loving Dumbell Rag.*[86]

Before Ayre's rag became the theme song for the Dumbells, Gitz Rice's "Take Me Back to the Land of Promise" had been the most recognizable piece of music associated with the concert parties of the Canadian Corps:

> *Oh take me back to the land of promise, back to the land of the ice and the*
> *snow,*
> *Where you and I, together we'll wander, down Albert lane where the maple*
> *trees grow*
> *Skating, baseball and canoeing, that's the place to do your billing or cooing,*
> *Oh take me back to the land of promise, back to my little grey home in the*
> *west.*[87]

Despite the early popularity of "Take Me Back," Rice's song could not compete with the jovial "Dumbell Rag," which was heard far more often given the number of shows the Dumbells performed along the front. As such, it was Ayre's refrain—not Rice's—that many Canadian soldiers whistled on the way back to the fighting for their next tour of duty, and for many it would be the last

Figure 26 Jack Ayre's famous "Dumbell Rag" c. 1920. (Courtesy Stephen Plunkett)

song they ever heard.[88] The success of "The Dumbell Rag" reached far beyond front-line tastes, and after the war Ayre sold over 10,000 sheet-music copies of the song.[89]

Alas, there is little room for critical analysis of these compositions, and although it might be argued that these songs were part of the larger safety valve that defined the concert parties of the First World War, they hold no hidden meaning, nor larger significance unto themselves, and are part of a tradition of variety theatre that is only funny—because it is. As Brophy and Partridge have concluded, "examine them and there is no content at all, but sing them in good company and they satisfy some deep, unsuspected thirst of the spirit. Such songs annihilate logic."[90]

The Ladies

There was, however, much hidden meaning and broader significance in the concert parties' use of female impersonators. In terms of success and celebrity, the Canadian Corps produced some exceptional female impersonators. The appeal of these "ladies" reached beyond the Canadian men and soldiers of other armies who, perhaps charmed by the likes of "Marjorie" and "Gladys," became fans of the Canadian "beauties." Remarkably, Canadian female impersonators found critical success on the stages of London's theatre district and even Broadway following the war. As a vital feature of the Canadian concert parties' front-line show, the female impersonator later became the cornerstone of the Dumbells' postwar revue.

Figure 27 "Marjorie" (Ross Hamilton) and "her" suitors, from left to right: Jerry Brayford, Jock McCormick, Elmer Belding, and Bill Redpath. (Courtesy Stephen Plunkett)

As titillating as the female impersonators were, they stopped well short of using overtly crude material. And while soldiers sang bawdy songs in the First World War, these were far fewer in number than one might expect. Most racy songs were parodies of existing soldier songs. The famous lyrics of "Tipperary," changed to, "That's the wrong way to tickle Mary, it's the wrong way you know."[91] Perhaps the most obscene of the trench songs was the revamping of the silly champion "Mademoiselle from Armentières" entitled "Three German Officers." The original marching song was reworked with crude lyrics that were widely known and sung among soldiers of the BEF.

> *Three German soldiers crossed the Rhine, parlez-vous?*
> *Three German soldiers crossed the Rhine, parlez-vous?*
> *Three German soldiers crossed the Rhine,*
> *to fuck the women and drink the wine,*
> *inky-pinky, parlez-vous?*[92]

The song continues, relating the eventual rape and impregnation of a landlord's daughter, who, nine months later, gives birth to a bastard "Hun."[93]

These sorts of songs were no more important to the soldier than the rest of the large repertoire of soldier songs were. Even within the rowdy, impromptu soldier singalongs, there was an unwritten code to be adhered to; if the moment called for quiet to accommodate the singing of a mournful ballad, most soldiers understood and respected the mood. This moment often came toward the end of the evening, when a calming, sentimental lilt was preferred over a raucous belter. New soldiers, unfamiliar with the protocol of the company smoker were gently introduced to the code by senior soldiers who subscribed to the principle: the right song for the right time.[94] And the time for songs with any farcical or sexual thematic content had, by nightfall, given way to matters of love, home, and those ones who had been left behind.[95]

Concert parties of the Canadian Corps did not perform songs of an overtly crude nature. Instead, the risqué quotient of the show was supplied by the party's female impersonator. When "Marjorie" sang "Hello My Dearie" to "her" loyal following, the mischievous, sexy portion of the performance had been adequately satisfied. Had the Dumbells been allowed to perform real bawdy numbers, which in all likelihood they would not have been, their appeal in Canada following the war would have been greatly reduced. Popular soldier humour was adventurous enough for most civilians and drag was risqué enough and widely appreciated by all audiences both during and following the war.

From early on, the rest of the troupe began to believe what critics back in Canada would later suggest in their reviews: Ross Hamilton and Alan Murray were the real features of the Dumbell show.[96] "The most beautiful woman is a man," read an advertisement for a 1919 Dumbells performance at the Old Russell Theatre in Ottawa.[97] Jack McLaren said that: "when Ross Hamilton of the Dumbells marched into a mess in costume, every officer would stand to attention until *he* was seated. Then, in a truck driver's voice, he'd call for a drink—and the illusion soon vanished."[98]

What Canadian men at the Front really wanted to see when they enjoyed a pause from the fighting were women. The need to include "girls" in the show appeared to be axiomatic for those organizing the concert parties; McLaren plainly stated, "We *had* to have 'ladies.'"[99] Hamilton's explanation was similar to McLaren's: "We knew we'd have to act as girls to attract the boys."[100] And like much of the material found in the programs of the Canadian concert parties, "drag" had been imported from the British music hall.

From the pre-Shakespearian stage to Oscar Wilde's West End London, theatre had longstanding links with homosexuality and the portrayal of homosexuality. By 1914, cross-dressing represented the most distinguishing feature of the concept of what it was to be homosexual.[101] Yet concert parties of the First World War and the British music hall in general embraced drag. This is especially interesting given that during this time, homosexuality was outlawed and male–male desires engendered great anxiety among the status quo; a fact that has been explored in several academic studies.[102] Still, by the turn of the 20th century, drag had become "a keystone of British theatrical tradition."[103]

Some historians argue that a crisis in masculinity engulfed Europe and North America in the latter part of the 19th century and in the years leading up to the First World War. The war itself, having placed an unprecedented number of men together in a male-only environment, rather fanned the flame of existing anxieties in an homophobic society. Remarkably, front-line theatre was in some ways able to repair, if only for the duration of the war, a ruptured homosocial continuum. In short, theatre allowed a safe environment where same-sex relations, via men in drag, could not only be embodied but also explored, therefore redressing current popular anxieties about homosexuality.[104] This safe environment did not exist offstage where cross-dressing, effeminate behaviour, or indeed actual male–male erotic desire as such was forbidden in the militarist and heterosexist culture of trench warfare.[105]

Drag was common. Every concert party had its requisite beauty and the unabashed carnival spirit within the soldier-drag performance was fully endorsed by military officials who believed, as historian Natalie Zemon Davis articulated, that transvestite rituals never seriously questioned the "basic order of society itself" and afforded soldiers a limited release.[106] Historian Alon Rachamimov concurred that soldiers in drag possessed both "disruptive" and "normalizing" potential.[107] In essence, drag at once relaxed pervasive homophobic predilections while confirming, often through over-the-top performances, the normative and acceptable behaviours within what gender historian Judith Butler described as a heterosexual matrix.[108]

As historian Laurence Senelick explained, cross-dressing operated within two distinct forms: mimicry and mimesis. Mimicry presented a de-eroticized, often oversized and unattractive version of a woman.[109] In mimicry, this "dame" originating from the pantomime tradition, caused no threat to gender identity.[110] In most cases, the drag portion of the concert parties was so exaggerated that there could be no confusion as to the real sex of the actor. Comedy critic Andrew Clark opined that drag represented a rejection of the traditional male gender role and, "As soldiers, the men represented the pinnacle of society's perception of manhood; a man in drag was the antithesis," and therefore funny.[111]

The specific purpose of mimesis, on the other hand, was to faithfully impersonate an "erotically alluring woman."[112] Obviously, this latter form was far more risqué but only slightly less common in concert-party productions than the former version. Fuller suggested that mimetic-styled drag performances presented a surrogate woman for soldier audiences who were perhaps pining for a sweetheart left behind.[113] Yet, whether or not soldiers were willing to suspend their disbelief to conjure up memories of the girl at home or privately (within a collective homosocial setting) engage in some form of homoeroticism can surely never be determined given the dearth of soldier diaries and memoirs that speak specifically to sexual desires, homosexual or otherwise.

What few historians have considered, however, is the possibility that some soldiers believed the mimetic-styled drag actor to be a woman. This notion may seem implausible, yet evidence suggests that actors like Ross Hamilton convinced some gullible soldiers with his portrayal of "Marjorie." While gender identities were certainly blurred for some during such performances, for a few, Marjorie was all female—really.

McLaren guaranteed that many soldiers really did think they were seeing the genuine thing: "These [impersonators] were 'girls' to the soldiers—they really believed it."[114] Hamilton, who often had to hide from his admirers noted, "I didn't dare leave the show without first changing back to men's clothes."[115] The queens of the concert parties most certainly titillated the sexually frustrated soldiers when they were not hyperexaggerated, nor predictably farcical, but instead charming, beautiful, and believable.

Soldiers and sex remain an onion of a subject for scholars. Historians such as Craig Gibson have helped add a new layer of understanding to that seemingly inaccessible subject. Through the excavation of soldier diaries and letters, as well as official medical documents aimed at ebbing the flow of sexually transmitted diseases, Gibson demonstrated that soldiers in the BEF and the Dominion

Armies had forged more sexual and romantic relationships than first presumed by historians.[116]

Certainly, there was sex at the front. Prostitution was rampant and organized brothels lined the front lines.[117] Ferguson has suggested that over one in four Canadian soldiers contracted syphilis in 1915 alone.[118] Still, not all Canadian soldiers spent their money on sex, as one soldier declared, "Others who went mainly to London and lived it up came back with lurid tales. I just listened. I was a virgin then, engaged to another one back home, and although I'd already had a couple of close calls I intended us to stay that way until we were married."[119]

Andrew Clark opined that because "there was plenty of sex to be had for a soldier with money to spend," the Dumbells' drag routines, "were irreverent send-ups, pure and simple."[120] It might be argued, however, that the drag routines of the Dumbells represented more than that to many Canadian soldiers. Perhaps the female impersonator was indeed a surrogate woman who represented the girl back home. Whatever this most involved and important piece of the concert party represented to the men at the Front, female impersonators were often able to sell the sorely missed idea of "woman" and many soldiers were willing to buy into what the likes of Hamilton and Murray were selling.

By having "girls" in the show, concert parties were able to preserve their longevity in the First World War. The PPCLI CC provided the Canadian soldiers with the luscious Fred Fenwick, and the Maple Leaf Concert Party of the Canadian 4th Division boasted "Gladys," played by Edmund Bullis, famous for his rendition of "Come and Cuddle Me."[121] Canadian soldiers would have seen various shows put on by not only Canadian, but also British, Australian, and American concert parties that sported female impersonators. James Lloyd Evans, for example, took in a performance by a Scottish concert party quite possibly the Bow Bells of the 56th Division in June 1918: "There is a Concert party belonging to one of the Scotch Divisions at this place, I went to see them the other night & they were simply immense, they put on a Musical Comedy, all the ladies' parts are taken by men & hang me it's hard to tell the difference if we didn't know, am sending you the Programme in a separate envelope, it certainly was some show."[122]

Performing for battle-weary soldiers could be a baptism by fire for various concert parties, especially earlier on. Yet, the presence of a "female" instantly improved the audience's temperament and a concert party's odds for success. McLaren likened the PPCLI CC's first show to a boxing match: "Round three introduced the 'Beauty Chorus' and the audience were putting up their hands in surrender—and using them to applaud."[123] Similarly, the outcome of the Dumbells' first performance at Major Beecher Gale's theatre at Gouy-Servins was undetermined until the critics were silenced by the "beauties" of the Canadian 3rd Division.

The concert parties of the Canadian Corps used creative means to dress their female impersonators. Before they were able to secure the services of a London dressmaker, members of the Dumbells sewed dresses from latrine canvasses. Some of the impersonators' hair was fashioned from rope, or in the case of the PPCLI CC, from the horsehair that had been stuffed into two chairs found in an abandoned French barn.[124] Princess Patricia herself donated costumes, grease paint, and civilian clothes to the concert party while Lieutenant Colonel Agar Adamson had enjoined his wife, Mabel, to send dresses and wigs scrounged from a theatrical costumier over to the PPCLI CC.[125] Nearing war's end, the pianist Leonard Young was able to secure the help of a court dressmaking establishment.[126] Later still, actresses from London's music halls, including Elsie Janis, answered letters from the Dumbells and donated their discarded costumes to the cause.

Creating the "ladies" was perhaps one of the entertainers' most difficult tasks. One audience member, Harold Simpson, spoke to some of the costume and character challenges that faced the Canadian concert parties in a letter home to his mother:

> Some of the more enterprising of the parties are now staging plays instead of variety shows and we saw three exceptionally good attempts while we were out. In staging a play they are up against difficulties which they don't meet in the variety concert for to be a success the costumes must be suited to the part and the actors must be able to adapt themselves easily to their respective roles and give a sense of reality to the play. It is in the latter that the greatest difficulty is encountered, for in the absence of actresses some of the more adaptable males have to take the female numbers under the camouflage of a skirt. And so perfect have been some impersonations that I have seen that if one did not know the difference one would not believe that those who took the female numbers so well were not really, truly actresses.[127]

When done properly, some soldiers—perhaps the greener or more wishful thinking among them—really did not know the difference.

Much thought was put into choosing the ladies. The concert parties employed various methods to determine which men would make good women. Alan Murray had great legs. An office manager for the Imperial Tobacco Company in Montreal before the war, Murray's unconventional acrobatic dance routines were at once humorous and superb. One London critic raved, that "'Marie' has a decidedly great gift for dancing, and 'she' and Tony [Al Plunkett] brought down the house with 'Take me back to Italy.'"[128] McLaren said of his colleague: "Alan Murray was also an outstandingly successful female impersonator and a man of boundless enthusiasm who danced with irrepressible verve. He invented and directed the ensemble and dance numbers and gave the show its spark."[129]

And "she" was pretty too, according to another witness of an early Dumbell show: "As 'Marie,' Alan Murray is a raving beauty, the custodian of many hearts."[130]

If Murray was the versatile and lovely legged one, Ross Hamilton was the statuesque, leading-lady type. Unlike Murray, who had a long face, Hamilton possessed a round face, and was able to carry the leading-lady role with sincerity and confidence. Murray remarked on Hamilton's transformation: "Ross was not a particularly good looking man off stage … but it was uncanny what a dose of make-up would do to him … he slapped [his make-up] on with a white-wash brush, but he was a raving beauty, there was no doubt about it."[131]

Figure 28 "Marie," a.k.a. Alan Murray, c. 1919. (Courtesy Stephen Plunkett)

Hamilton was born in Pugwash, Nova Scotia, and had acted in local YMCA theatricals there before moving on to the famous Trinity Theatre of Montreal where he met Murray and Young.[132] He harboured no desire to be a female impersonator before the war: "If anyone had told me at that time I'd come back to Canada as a woman I would have killed him."[133]

When the First World War broke out, Hamilton, Murray, and Young went straight out of amateur theatre and into the 9th Field Ambulance. At the front, Colonel Peters requested that the talented bunch from the 9th Field Ambulance put on a Christmas show to cheer up the wounded and others.[134] It was here that Hamilton began to develop his famous character "Marjorie," named after Hamilton's close friend Marjorie Weir. "Marjorie" would have to fend off and disappear from male well-wishers at every stage door.[135]

The musical number that became synonymous with "Marjorie" in the Dumbells' earliest performances was "Hello My Dearie," from the music-hall hit *Zig Zag*. When he sang it to a uniformed Bill Tennent, appearing as "Marjorie's" beau at the Front, Hamilton, according to writer Max Braithwaite, "represented every soldier's girlfriend back home."[136] Canadian soldiers came

Figure 29 "Marjorie," a.k.a. Ross Hamilton, c. 1919. (Courtesy Stephen Plunkett)

to associate various music-hall hits with Hamilton, including "I'm Looking for Somebody," "Give Me a Little Cosy Corner," "'Widows Are Wonderful," "If You Were the Only Girl in the World," and "You're the Boy!," yet Hamilton's persuasive interpretation of these songs often caused problems. After a solid performance of "Some Day I'll Make You Love Me," various Dumbell members had to gently break the heart of one officer who had shown up backstage with a bouquet of flowers, explaining to him that "Marjorie" just wasn't his type.[137] Admiration for "Marjorie" from the officer ranks occurred more than once, as journalist Herbert Whittaker recalled "a member of the top brass was among those sex-starved soldiers who tried to date 'her.'"[138] At one performance, a Scottish soldier fell suddenly and deeply for "Marjorie" who had to crawl out of a dressing room through a hole in the ground to avoid a kiss ... twice![139]

Most soldiers, though, knew the truth about the "lady" they were watching. Bill McLellan was one soldier who was not fooled by the Dumbell "beauties," despite being thoroughly entertained by them; as evidenced in his letter home:

> They are two "girls" in the party. One of the girls—a man named Hamilton—acts and looks just like Grett McKenzie—do you know her? The other one has a regular Melba voice and the looks to go with it. I saw it every chance I had. Believe me, if anyone saw it who didn't know anything about it before except that it was just a bunch o' fellows picked from the 3rd division—there would be a surprise in stock for him.[140]

When "Marjorie" toured Canada with the Dumbells, *most* people knew that the character was played by a man, though some were still unsure as this review from Fort William, Ontario, illustrated: "Marjorie's song 'Some Day I'll Make You Love Me' was a scream. It was sentimental from the word go and the last verse 'she' addressed to a man in the bald-headed row. He was covered in confusion until 'she' said in a harsh voice 'What's the matter? You're not bashful, are you?' which brought down the house."[141]

Still, Hamilton relied far less on these rare onstage confessionals and instances of breaking character for cheap laughs—he is instead best remembered for his portrayal of the authentic *songstress*—carrying the torch song, believably, to its conclusion.

That Hamilton was more than just a garden-variety female impersonator there can be no doubt, as McLaren attested: "As a female impersonator Ross Hamilton was an unforgettable consummate artist of incredible skill. He had a rich contralto voice almost operatic in stature and carried a great quality of conviction. He completely fooled the troops by the thousands."[142]

Some of the toughest theatre critics in New York agreed, and when in 1921 the Dumbells took their *Biff, Bing, Bang* review to Broadway's Ambassador

Theater, one journalist exalted, "Ross Hamilton is a female impersonator upon whom Julian Eltinge has nothing at all … Canada may well be proud of one pretty and talented 'girl'; Mr. Ross Hamilton."[143] That Broadway critics bandied about Hamilton's name with the period's best impersonators, including Julian Eltinge, the Creole Fashion Plate, and Bert Savoy, speaks to the high level and believability of the Canadian's act.[144]

The public demand for "Marjorie" in Canada lasted for several years after the war. In 1928, however, in an effort to save the touring company, Captain Plunkett chose for the first time to include real women in the revue. For some fans, and indeed performers, this was an unforgivable compromise. Conrad Stephens commented on women joining the Dumbells, "I was disgusted by that, it wasn't the Dumbells."[145] It might be argued that the inclusion of women contributed to the demise of the Dumbells, along with the economic realities of a waning vaudeville industry fighting the perpetually growing silver screen. When women were allowed into the show as participants, the Dumbells were no longer exclusively a soldier show. For many, the inclusion of women had compromised the integrity of the concert party and the Dumbells ceased to be unique.[146]

Captain Plunkett's front-line theatrical school in Mons, the concert-party factory, produced by war's end nearly 70 female impersonators, many of whom had no previous experience in drag.[147] Perhaps no other element of the concert party was as vital to soldier approval, soldier morale, and the survival of the concert party, than was the indispensable "beauty."[148]

The Dumbells afforded the soldiers of the Canadian Corps an escape, at least for a short while, from the nightmare of war. At the same time, they were able to facilitate the celebration of what the war had come to mean to each Canadian soldier. They were able to do this, often unwittingly, by holding up the "mirror of satire" to the soldiers, which reflected the unfortunate and hilarious reality of the soldier's day-to-day life.[149] McLaren confessed that he wrote not a single sketch for the PPCLI CC or the Dumbells—all his material had been collected from what he had overheard Canadian soldiers say.[150]

Members of the Canadian concert parties sang British music-hall hits in their performances, but Canadian themes were often addressed through adaptations of popular songs or in the performers' comedic skits. Whether it was the "Canadian in France," the "Canadian on leave," the "Ross Rifle," "Going back to Canada," or the Canadian "beauties," the concert parties of the Canadian Corps consistently incorporated Canadian subject matter into their performances.[151] Canadian soldiers would not share the same identification with Bob Hope, Marilyn Monroe, and Glen Miller in the Second World War as they had with the men of Canada's concert parties. These entertainers were warriors who had earned the approval of the regular soldiers of the Canadian Corps and, more importantly, admission into that extremely exclusive world.

The concert-parties' comedy was an effective marriage of vaudeville and realism that would not have been possible without the war experience. Each component of this new brand of comedy was equally important; "Miss Skinny" jumping into the wooden bucket was cherished by the soldiers every bit as much as the most acerbic lines of "Oh! It's a Lovely War" were. Thus, the Dumbells were able to touch on a broad range of feelings and emotions. In performance, the Dumbells combined desperation with bitterness, sadness with irony, loneliness with sex and, somehow, always managed to produce funny.

Officially and unofficially the concert parties satisfied two purposes. At once they were able to mollify military authorities by keeping the troops happy enough to continue the good fight while entertaining the troops at the expense of those same military authorities through a celebration of the futility and hopelessness of the fighting—a celebration that galvanized that *esprit de corps* shared only among regular soldiers of the Canadian Expeditionary Forces.

Beyond the front-line soldiers of the Canadian Expeditionary Forces, the Great War had profoundly affected the whole of Canada and its people. Considering its over 60,000 dead, Ottawa sought to further establish the Dominion's autonomy following the war; first, with the Balfour Declaration of 1926 and later with the 1931 Statute of Westminster, Canada had secured the power to decide when and with whom to war.

Having paid such a terrific price and bolstered by the legacy of nation-defining battles like Vimy Ridge, people from coast to coast began, perhaps for the first time, to entertain a sense of pan-Canadian nationalism. This mood found expression immediately following the war in Canada's cultural renaissance. After the Armistice, there ensued a boom in Canadian literature; with a marked rise in the output of Canadian authors in both official languages. Mazo de la Roche's *Jalna* (1927), Frederick Philip Grove's *Settlers of the Marsh* (1925), and Martha Ostenso's *Wild Geese* (1925) were among the more famous works produced in the decade that followed the war.[152] At the same time, modernist expression in poetry was being explored by Newfoundland's Ned Pratt; by the "Montreal Group" of Leo Kennedy, A.M. Klein, A.J.M. Smith, and F.R. Scott; and by Fernand Prefontaine, Léo-Paul Morin and Robert de Roquebrune of the francophone magazine *Le Nigog*.[153] With a mandate to research and preserve Canadian history, the Canadian Historical Association began operations in 1922, while the University of Toronto began publishing the *Canadian Historical Review* in 1920.[154]

The country's sporting traditions were also brought to the forefront. Hockey, in particular, continued to ascend and, with many of its players having served with the CEF during the war, the National Hockey League came into being in 1917 just prior to the war's end in 1917.[155] Canada also experienced an unprecedented number of initiatives in the fields of science and medicine. Sir Frederick Banting, who was awarded the Military Cross after being wounded at the Battle of Cambrai in 1918, co-discovered insulin alongside Scottish-born John Macleod. The two shared the Nobel Prize for Medicine in 1923.[156] And Canadian-produced arts, dominated by the matchless collective work of the Group of Seven, began to shape and capture the country's self-image.[157] In search of a Canadian aesthetic, the group had turned their back on European traditions, polarizing the Canadian art community and seeking to liberate Canadian art from the stale traditions of the Old World.[158] Indeed, much of the country was inching away from the old world.

The Dumbells were involved in these various currents in postwar Canadian culture. Jack McLaren managed to directly touch two of the more important ones. Following the war, McLaren returned to painting, moving in high circles of the Canadian art scene. As a member of the Arts and Letters Club in Toronto, McLaren became close friends with members of the Group of Seven who were also members of the club. Indeed, McLaren's own work echoed the work of his good friend Arthur Lismer, while his approach possessed a depth similar to the work of his fellow soldier Fred Varley. McLaren was also friends with Emily Carr, Carl Schaffer, Harold Town, and Sir Frederick Banting, all of whom were members of the Arts and Letters Club. Yet it was Banting to whom McLaren was closest.

Banting served with the 13th Field Ambulance during the war and had built a friendship with McLaren based upon their mutual love for the exciting new directions taking place in Canadian art. Banting accompanied joined Group of Seven luminary A.Y. Jackson on various trips across the country, including the far north, to capture the Canadian landscape before devoting his life to medicine and collaborating on the discovery of insulin.[159] Banting gave McLaren one of the sketches he painted while he was with A.Y. Jackson in St. Jean Port Joli, Quebec, and the painting hung on the wall of McLaren's recreation room for many years.[160] McLaren's own paintings were not without merit and some of his wartime sketches of Somme, Vimy, and Ypres were displayed for many years at the PPCLI Regimental Base in Edmonton.[161]

The Dumbells were also touched by new technology. The concert party was several times featured on radio during the embryonic stage of Canadian broadcasting. The Toronto Star's radio broadcasting—however sporadic it may have been in those early days—began to broadcast shows with Dumbell stars such as Al Plunkett, Ross Hamilton, Jack Ayre, and Red Newman as early as 1922.[162]

The Dumbells were beginning, as many Canadians at this time were, to understand who they *were* from who they *were not*. Canadians were deeply suspicious of all foreign markets (and most foreigners for that matter) and their effects on the Canadian economy and subsequently, the Canadian psyche. And now, more than ever, Canadians were fearful of Americanization. It was perhaps a legitimate fear. For every domestic magazine sold in Canada in 1925, for example, eight others from the United States were imported.[163] Similarly, Canadian radio did not have the financial wherewithal to compete with American radio. Consequently, early American radio shows were as, or even more popular than, indigenous Canadian programming.[164]

The Dumbells' Red Newman articulated the dread with which some Canadians viewed outside markets like Great Britain or the US in his 1926 HMV recording "Canada for Canadians":

> *Let's keep the money in the country,*
> *don't let our money go abroad*
> *If every true Canadian would get right up and say,*
> *"I'll buy goods made in Canada, not a country over the way"*
> *There would be no unemployment,*
> *no families on the street,*
> *no crippled soldier pleading for a dime ...*
> *Canada for Canadians*[165]

Ironically, Newman was the only Dumbell *not* born in Canada. Albert "Red" Newman, was born in Dover, England, and joined the Dumbells in July 1918 after his time with the Y-Emmas. In both parties, Newman was called upon to play the Cockney for any skit that required one. Newman's Cockney was so authentic that it caused him one particularly embarrassing encounter. While performing in New York, Lady Cavendish had asked members of the Dumbells to an after-show party. Red was enjoying the lavish affair and began to put on airs in an effort to delight the guests. Spouting an accent that had a touch of Oxbridge to it, Newman pretended to have been an alumnus of Cambridge University. Unfortunately for Red, Lord Burley, who won a gold medal for Britain in the 1928 Olympics for hurdling, was also in attendance. Burley said to Newman that he had been at Cambridge too, to which Red replied—perhaps too quickly, "Ya wuz, wuz ya?" In this belly of New York's high society, Red could not resist laying it on thick.[166] Newman left the Dumbells and joined the Originals in 1922, but he returned to perform with the Dumbells before they officially disbanded in 1932. Newman moved to Swift Current, Saskatchewan, before settling in Ontario. The singer bought and operated a hotel at Wasaga Beach, Ontario, where he died on 26 September 1952.[167]

VI   The Dumbells in Peace

In those European shows that followed the end of the war, the Dumbells used for a finale a sketch that saw the entertainers one by one leave the stage to board a railway carriage bound for Canada. The conductor, John McCormick asked each soldier-entertainer where his final destination was. One was headed for Toronto, Bill Tennent was for Winnipeg, the centre of the universe; Jerry Brayford was for Edmonton, God's country; and so forth. When they were boarded they sang:

> *Home again, I want to roam again, you see,*
> *O Canada first, take a tip from me:*
> *If you're wise and you can use your eyes,*
> *you'll see an Emerald Isle lying 'round every mile.*
> *We change your climate too and you can choose your view.*
> *We show you something whenever you roam.*
> *I think your London town has won renown,*
> *but I want to go home.*[1]

The sketch promised happiness back in Canada, but there were no guarantees for the continuance of the legendary wartime concert party. The question arose: Was there a future for the Dumbells in Canada? Many said no, maintaining that it was strictly a soldier's show. Others were not so sure, as one journalist from a New Brunswick newspaper forecasted prior to the concert party's North American success, "Had the Dumbells remained together they might have toured the empire and scored a continuous success."[2] Captain Plunkett had enough faith in the commercial potential of the Dumbells that he turned down postwar volunteer opportunities for the concert party with the Canadian Military and the Red Cross. The reason was simple enough: the Dumbells had done their duty and now the idea of a "continuous success" was in the cards.

Still, the Dumbells had hardly followed the usual path to fame in the entertainment world. As Al Plunkett confessed: "The cast of the Dumbells were not
the usual type of showmen that one would expect to find in show business.
They were not 'born in a trunk'... they were ordinary individuals having some
gift or talent which had been brought forward as a result of the entertainment
demands of wartime."[3]

Nevertheless, in selecting the best entertainers from the various Canadian
concert parties, and perfecting a show through literally hundreds of performances, the Dumbells had grown into more than just an amusement for the soldier; they had become *really* good. As one Broadway theatre critic aptly observed,
"whatever they may have been in the beginning, the performers have developed
into serviceable actors, with plenty of assurance and sometimes a bit to spare."[4]
Even New York's toughest theatre critic, Alan Dale, who was dubbed "Prince
Hard-to-Please" by other theatre critics, said of the concert party's *Biff, Bing,
Bang* revue that "the Dumbells hit the standard of real art."[5] In London, before
they returned to Canada, the Dumbells had won accolades in that city's most
prestigious theatres. An impressive tribute to the troupe's success can be found
in a newspaper clipping from Jack Ayre's scrapbook:

> Seldom if ever in the history of the Victoria Palace has such a scene of
> enthusiasm been witnessed as that which greeted The Dumbells upon
> the conclusion of their act on Monday. It was a reception, too, that was
> splendidly deserved. All the best features of modern entertainment are
> embodied in the turn, or rather series of turns, contributed by this clever
> amateur combination of trans-Atlantic visitors. Each and every number
> has been finely produced, and detail and finish would do credit to many
> West End revues. The settings are novel and artistic, and the dresses and
> lighting effects all that could be desired. Add to these desirable quali-
> ties brilliant singing, sparkling comic touches, and not a moment's wait
> during the whole of the time the curtain is up, and the pleasure of the
> audience is easily accounted for.[6]

With the help of veterans who brought their friends and families to see those
first North American shows, the originality and charm of the famous Canadian
concert party had transcended soldier audiences and became accessible to civilian ones. As such, the Dumbells were, as television host Frank Willis once stated,
"unique in the history of Canadian show business, unique perhaps in the whole
of the entertainment world," and much more than just a wartime amusement.[7]

Captain Plunkett's uncles, Albert and Sam Kerr of Orillia, invested between
$30,000 and $60,000 to get the concert party's first professional revue up and
running. The concert party was not idle for long: their last performance overseas, or rather, on the sea, had been in March 1919, and their first show in

Figure 30 The Dumbells on Broadway in 1921. (Courtesy Stephen Plunkett)

Canada was in September of the same year. After Plunkett had secured the funds, Ambrose Small, the biggest man in Canadian show business, was willing to give the Dumbells their first real showbiz break. Plunkett persuaded Small to give the Dumbells a trial run in London, Ontario's Grand Theatre on 1 October 1919.[8] There had been a one-night appearance in Owen Sound prior to the group's first engagement at Ambrose Small's Grand Theatre.[9] But it was really the London performance that made them. The show was such a success that before the end of the first act, Small had allegedly booked the concert party for a much longer run at Toronto's Grand Theatre. The Dumbells enjoyed a terrific 16 weeks at the Grand with their first professional revue, *Biff, Bing, Bang.*

Following their successes in Owen Sound, London, and Toronto, the Dumbells calendar for 1919 was soon completely booked. From 29 September to 29 December, the group played 34 towns and cities across Canada. From Vancouver to St. John's, crowds lined up to see the soldier show.[10] And almost

Figure 31   The Dumbells at Toronto's Grand Theatre in December 1919. (Courtesy John McLaren)

all of Canada was represented within the Dumbell cast: there were, among others, Edmonton's Jerry Brayford, Winnipeg's Bill Tennent, Montreal's Alan Murray, Toronto's Norm Nicholson, St. John, New Brunswick's Elmer Belding, and Saskatoon's Bill Filson. This was perhaps one more reason that the nation so readily adopted the group as *the* Canadian concert party of the Great War.

The difference between the Dumbells' overseas show and the Canadian show was negligible in terms of material, but drastic in terms of the venues and amenities. The troupe travelled across Canada by rail on a dedicated sleeping car that was housed at the local railway yard during their stay in a given town. And now the Dumbells were celebrities wherever they went. Other famous Canadians wished to entertain the troupe whenever they were in town. In Edmonton, for example, the Lougheeds had the group over for a golf-putting competition in the Lougheeds' large drawing room.[11] In Perth, Ontario, it was the Wampole family, famed for their pharmaceuticals and, more recently, natural health products, who offered the Dumbells' wives gifts of powder and beauty products.[12]

As with any group of touring entertainers, there was much merrymaking after the show, and sometimes too much. On one evening, in snowy Peterborough in December 1919, the group had a contest to see which member could jump deepest into a large snowbank. The rules were simple, contestants were allowed 12 strides from the middle of the road before launching themselves face first into the snow. The winner would be presented a laurel wreath. While Jerry Brayford seemed to be the winner, he had unfortunately, with his extra effort, found a buried fire hydrant that blackened his eyes and nose.[13]

In London, Ontario, there was the famous midnight "fox hunt" that the Dumbells participated in with wartime friends they had met from the Royal Canadian Regiment (RCR). Using a bottle of scotch to represent the fox's brush or tail, one person was chosen to be the fox while others would, shortly afterward, pursue their quarry. Many residents of North London were woken up to the sustained baying of Dumbell hounds.[14] There was also a late-night/early-morning round of golf in the Regina fog with several young ladies from a charm school.[15]

Wherever the Dumbells went, people wanted to share their hospitality. As Alan Murray confessed, "What a perfect alibi for a party we were."[16] In order that at least half of the cast would not suffer from a hangover, the troupe broke up into a couple of groups. Group A would party with the locals on night one, letting Group B rest up for the next night.[17] The appeal of drinking to excess, plagues many travelling entertainers and the Dumbells were not immune.

One cast member was particularly affected by the ongoing party; Al Plunkett struggled with alcoholism for much of the rest of his life. There was, understandably, some tension created in the family by Al's affliction. After the Dumbells disbanded, the good-looking Plunkett remained in showbiz, singing on radio and in nightclubs around North America.[18] Eventually, he realized that he needed to get out of the biz in order to put his life right. As he later confessed: "My drinking increased and I could no longer face the confusion, indifference and loneliness of my life. These feelings were now a hazard to me and brought about the one decision I was capable of making: to retire from show business, on which I secretly blamed much."[19]

Plunkett did, however return to showbiz and later joined the RCAF during the Second World War. Following that war, Plunkett became a road inspector for the Ontario Department of Highways and managed a nursing home with his wife, Marie. The crooner, who had won the hearts of so many Canadians, admitted that he was never completely free of his demons: "I cannot state that I will never drink again. Of that I am not at all sure—although I sincerely hope I will not. With each twenty-four hours I murmur a prayer to my Superior Power to protect, guide, and give me faith and courage to overcome my weakness, and to help me step by step along my way."[20]

Al died on 19 April 1957 at the age of 58.

The Dumbells played large centres across the country, and also managed to perform in some of Canada's smaller and more remote towns. For the smaller towns, the Dumbells show would be the highlight of the year.[21] Journalist Dennis Braithwaite offered: "For us kids who used to pay 50 cents for admission to 'the gods' of the Empire Theatre in Saskatoon and get there an hour and a half before curtain time to grab a front-row seat, The Dumbells were not only the greatest show but the greatest event on earth, circa 1925."[22]

In Pincher Creek, Alberta, the entertainers and their equipment had to be taken from the rail station to the venue by sleigh. McLaren spoke of the freezing conditions during the six relays that were necessary to bring the performers and their gear to the show: "The driver wrapped us up in buffalo robes—special large sleighs moved our scenery, costumes and lighting plant to the small town hall … The low temperatures also did nothing for our make-up grease paints which froze solidly on our faces and other parts of our anatomy."[23] The harsh Canadian winter and the impossibly busy touring schedule that the troupe had been assigned—including several one-nighters—took its toll on the Dumbells.

The troupe usually performed for a full week in the big centres, and in the bigger towns it was three-nighters. But the majority of the shows were one-night stands. Jack Ayre lamented that one "had to live in a suitcase for so long, and in those days you couldn't get your laundry done."[24] Likewise, McLaren confessed that he often had to go to the front desk in the hotel he was staying at to ask what the name of the town was.[25]

When playing in Hanover, Ontario, the troupe had to make do in a very small venue that also housed the local fire engine. The Dumbells took advantage of the truck-cum-dressing-room, laying out all of their costumes and makeup on the fire engine due to the lack of space at the venue. Predictably, in the middle of the show, the firefighters of Hanover were called into action, taking with them all of the Dumbells' essentials. But a small-town fire paled in comparison to shouting over German artillery, and so the show went on.[26]

The year 1920 proved even busier than the year before: the group worked their way west from Ontario to British Columbia and back, and then to the east coast on a route that finally brought them back to Ontario at the end of the year. In all, the Dumbells had played 98 different cities and towns in the calendar year. The following year started much the same, but when the Dumbells returned to Toronto from out west, they headed south of the border for the first time. In the Big Apple, the Dumbells became the first Canadian revue ever to have a hit on Broadway.

The concert party's New York stint was wildly successful. Impressing the critics, the Dumbells played to packed houses and were rubbing elbows with the likes of Lionel, John, and Ethel Barrymore; Mae Murray; Mary Pickford; and D.W. Griffith. Such high praise from a legion of New York critics was as incredible as it was unexpected for a Canadian production. Weed Dickinson of the New York Evening Telegraph wrote: "No American soldier show seen in New York has the Dumbells, 'Biff, Bing, Bang's' snap and vigour—nor its talent … if this be treason, make the most of it. There is not space enough to praise 'The Dumbells.'"[27]

American praise of the troupe was not limited to New York. Frederick Von Stade, Boston's drama critic, wrote of the Dumbells in 1921: "If you want to know how comedians should act to be funny, or hear how delectable ditties should be sung, or learn how chorus boys can be manly and still be excellent chorus boys, go to the Dumbells."[28]

Although these sorts of glowing reviews from south of the border caught the attention of Canadian journalists, as early as 1920 one Canadian journalist had labelled the Dumbells a Canadian institution:

> Canada has never had, if we comment correctly, any outstanding national characters in the theatrical profession until the "Dumbells" came along. Britain has its first comedians such as Robey and Lauder ... But Canada, hitherto, has not possessed this characteristic ... Canada has finally received to itself a group of players who have set a standard of their own, and should stay in that niche until memories of the Great War are faded into grey.[29]

Given their successes, the concert party had truly become a household name in Canada. Still, the soldier-entertainers privileged the praise they received from soldiers over the great press that followed the Dumbells' postwar touring career. Speaking to the approval they received from the solider-audiences, McLaren believed: "I don't think you can get any better honour, or citations, than [their] laughter and applause."[30] And they got it in bucketloads.

Individually, the soldier-entertainers were also flying high. Jack Ayre, who before the war had been playing accompanying piano for silent films in a small West End Toronto theatre, found himself leading an orchestra on Broadway and being congratulated by none other than the famous American bandleader Paul Whiteman. "Marjorie" was so popular in New York that "she" was asked to don a pair of boxing gloves and get in the ring with boxing legends George Carpentier and Jack Dempsey for a publicity stunt. Dumbells' related sheet-music sales skyrocketed, as one trade journal offered: "The majority of sheet music dealers throughout the country have the famous 'Dumbell' show to thank for popularizing a number of Feist songs that have kept the cash register humming during the last few years ... dealers in various parts of the country have reported a big demand for such numbers as 'Give Me a Cosy Corner,' 'On the Road to Anywhere,' 'Come Back Old Pal,' 'L'il Old Granny' and others."[31]

The perpetual success of sheet music and recording sales from various revues demonstrated how the Dumbells set the Canadian standard: "The Dumbells have established an enviable reputation during and since the war, and everyone knows that they would not use in their revue a number that was not a sure 'catch.'"[32]

Yet, the soldier-entertainers were not without their share of controversy. In Montreal, performing at the Princess Theatre, the Dumbells had used a joke about American General Douglas MacArthur's Rainbow Division, which had arrived in France only "after the storm was all over." The joke was hilarious for Canadian ex-servicemen in the audience who harboured a little contempt for the American military; however, it did not go over as well with a group of American women who happened to be in the audience that night. For his safety, Dumbell Ben Allen, who had told the joke, did not appear again for the rest of the show. News of the controversial joke travelled south ahead of the concert party's first American performance, as Braithwaite explained: "In New York on opening night when everybody was tiptoeing around with fingers crossed, two stern females with blood in their eye caught Plunkett and demanded if this was the Canadian show that went around insulting American fighting men. Plunkett assured them that the foul joke was in another Canadian soldiers' revue and managed to get rid of them."[33]

Had Plunkett not been as believable, the Dumbells' run at the Ambassador might have been much shorter.

The Dumbells enjoyed continued success throughout the 1920s. Many revues followed *Biff, Bing, Bang*, which had produced a hit with Ross Hamilton's rendition of "A Little Cozy Corner." Most of these subsequent revues, however, came after the concert party had been fractured in 1922, when the majority of the cast, unsatisfied with their pay, presented Plunkett with an ultimatum. Plunkett did not capitulate and, with only 10 days before their next production, all but Plunkett, his brother Al, and Ross Hamilton walked out on the Dumbells. To fill the vacancies, Captain Plunkett recruited other ex-servicemen including Pat Rafferty, originally of the Red Patches; Sammy Birch; Bert Wilkinson; Glen Allen; and another Plunkett brother, Morley, who had starred with the Maple Leafs concert party.[34] The revue opened on time in Hamilton, Ontario, and was extremely successful despite the loss of the better part of the cast. In that same year, Captain Plunkett's own composition "Come Back, Old Pal" began to gain momentum and, by 1924, had sheet music sales in the "five figures."[35] Plunkett had proven that *his* concert party could survive a seemingly irreparable breach.

Figure 32 Before his Dumbells days, Pat Rafferty performed with the Red Patches and Maple Leafs concert parties. (Courtesy John McLaren)

Meanwhile, those Dumbells who had left the Plunketts formed a splinter group, calling themselves the Originals. The Originals found some fortune with several of their own revues, which toured between 1923 and 1928.[36] In particular, the 1923 production, *Full O' Pep*, was extremely successful, and numerous songs from it were recorded and released on the HMV label.[37] Indeed, the Originals were far more representative of the Dumbells' front-line cast than were the Dumbells circa 1923. The strong Originals' cast boasted former Dumbell standouts Newman, Murray, and Charter, along with Bill Tennent, Bertram Langley, Jerry Brayford, pianist and musical director Ayre, Jock Holland (originally of the Bow Bells),

Figure 33 Morley Plunkett. (Courtesy Stephen Plunkett)

Fred Fenwick and Leonard Young (originally of the PPCLI Comedy Company), and Charlie McLean (originally of the Y-Emmas), among others. The Originals also experienced some critical success with their *Rapid Fire* revue. *The Edmonton Bulletin* said of the show: "Rapid Fire is a hum-dinger of a revue … a show decidedly above the average and can be enjoyed by all."[38] *The Peterborough Examiner* concurred: "'Rapid Fire' is a great show, the Originals bigger and better than ever, and should enjoy a record run throughout Canada."[39] Still, there was a great deal of weight attached to the name "Dumbells," and the Plunketts would outsell and eventually outlast the splinter group.

The 1922 split remained a point of contention for original Dumbell members. In a 1951 *Maclean's* article Plunkett had confessed that he had been greedy, a fact that Murray was only too eager to confirm in 1965.[40] Although Plunkett had been referring to all of his investments and not exclusively the Dumbells, the article was nonetheless inaccurate in parts and must, given the different claims by Murray and Brayford, be viewed with some suspicion.[41] Dumbell Jerry Brayford recalled in an interview in 1962 how Major White, then the editor of the *Halifax Herald*, broke a story on how the members of the Dumbells were being fleeced by Captain Plunkett in 1921–22. After Gladstone Chartered Accountants reviewed the books, it was discovered that there was a substantial

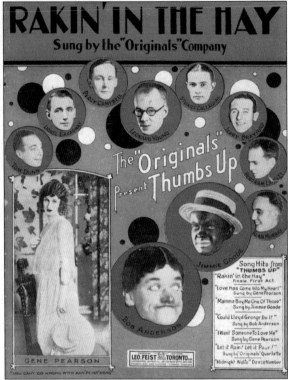

Figure 34   Leonard Young, Jerry Brayford, Bertram Langley, and Alan Murray formed the core of the splinter group called the Originals. (Courtesy Stephen Plunkett)

sum owed to the men, who had then been receiving a modest $100 a week.[42] Sadly, friendship and camaraderie, two hallmarks of Canada's fighting men during the First World War, had given way to suspicion and bitterness, and some soldiers who had fought, sung, and danced together were forever estranged.

On the wave of the Dumbells postwar fortune, Captain Plunkett attempted to increase his profits. With the aim of touring two concert parties around Canada simultaneously, Plunkett tried to revive the Maple Leafs, but the troupe proved unsuccessful. The short-lived revival had allegedly set Plunkett back $30,000. Another investment that went south for Plunkett was the Merrymakers open-air theatre that he built at Sunnyside in Toronto. For a time successful, the Merrymakers Theatre was soon sold to the Toronto Harbour Commission.[43] Eventually even the Dumbells became unprofitable. At this juncture, the Plunketts had to forego their own pay.[44]

Alas, the concert party could no longer count on filling theatres, and by the spring of 1930 many people's memory of the war was indeed fading to

Figure 35   Captain Plunkett outside Toronto's Royal Alex in 1926. (Courtesy Stephen Plunkett)

grey. Soldier humour, once vitally fresh, had become less relevant to Canadians whose memory of the war began to fade. Decoding the exclusiveness of soldier humour had been a pleasant pastime for civilian audiences eager to relive what their sons, husbands, or fathers had gone through in the war, but a decade had weakened that interest and, simply put, the Dumbells were neither able to adapt to public tastes nor compete with the various elements conspiring against the concert party. The advent of "talkies," which began to circulate in 1927, was one distraction that a vulnerable vaudeville theatre group did not need.

The old soldier show really began to wane when the Dumbells chose to include real women in their 1928 revue *Why Worry*. This move proved unpopular with the concert party's loyal audiences who felt women threatened the integrity of the concert party. As one journalist surmised in 1936:

> [The] Dumbells lost their hold on many of their vast audience. If I may judge by my own reaction, because they became more prosperous and their productions became more elaborate, they lost more and more of their originality and individuality. The first few Dumbells' shows were unique. Then they became more and more an imitation of the big American revues. I think if the Dumbells had remained strictly Canadian, they would have remained a national institution.[45]

Ross Hamilton had vowed never to play in a show with girls in it, and he never did, confessing that, "I knew I couldn't compete with a beautiful girl."[46] Ross,

Figure 36   The Dumbells' curtain call. (Courtesy Stephen Plunkett)

who was according to Jim Kennedy, who dined with Ross years after the latter's showbiz days, confirmed that he "was so incredibly well spoken, he was a perfect gentleman."[47] He lived alone in Pleasant Valley, Nova Scotia. He died at Camp Hill Veterans' Hospital on 29 September 1965.[48]

Before the concert party was finally abandoned in the early 1930s, they would tour the whole of Canada 12 times in 14 years, playing close to 1,000 shows with an estimated audience of over one million people.[49] There were over 56 weeks' worth of performances at Toronto's Grand Theatre alone and of course the historical 12-week run in New York at the Ambassador Theatre.[50]

Of all the reasons that accelerated the demise of the Dumbells, none could compare with the damage inflicted by the Great Depression, which severely restricted theatregoers' disposable income and had, by 1932, ultimately ruptured the concert party's financial viability.[51] But when the Second World War came around, several First World War concert-party performers had a mind to renew efforts in raising the morale of Canadian soldiers. Jack McLaren put together a group of performers, and wrote a revue to entertain the troops that was sponsored by Lever Brothers.[52] Jack Ayre, Pat Rafferty, and Jimmy Denson took part in the group. The Lifebuoy Follies, as they were called, toured Canada, Holland, Belgium, Scotland, and England for four and a half years. As a Dumbell, Ayre had stood at the Stock Exchange in Brussels just after the Armistice in 1918, and found himself there again at the end of the Second World War with the Lifebuoy Follies.[53]

Ayre remained a working musician for the rest of his life and filled his calendar with club dates, banquets, and shows at Loews Theatre and various hotels in the Toronto area. Ayre, who had started playing professionally when he was 15, was on his way to another gig when he died of heart failure on a Toronto streetcar at the age of 82 in 1977.[54] He was the last surviving Dumbell from the 1917 Gouy-Servins show.

For his part, Captain Plunkett took more official action at the beginning of World War II, when he once again headed the organization of Canadian concert parties for the troops. In 1939, Plunkett became the overseas entertainment supervisor for the Canadian Legion's Auxiliary Services. Plunkett lobbied for the re-establishment of concert parties in the Canadian Army and surmised, "It amounts to this, that among the men of Canada's new armies there is the raw material for all the concert parties the troops will need—concert parties that will certainly equal and perhaps surpass anything the old Dumbells were able to do."[55]

Plunkett's song "We're on Our Way" was sung by soldiers on their way to Europe during the Second World War. Plunkett retired to Collingwood, Ontario, with his wife, Lila Taylor. The congenial captain, who saw his Dumbells rise out of the trenches onto a Broadway stage, died on 20 December 1966. Despite Plunkett's good work in the latter conflict, the uniqueness and popularity of the First World War concert parties would not be reproduced in Canadian military entertainment during the Second World War as trench culture could not flourish in this different type of war.

As far as Canada's military authorities were concerned, the Dumbells had become a prototype for soldier entertainment in World War II.[56] As historian Laurel Halladay explained: "The beneficial impact of the Dumbells on the morale of Canadian troops was not forgotten … the connection between formally organized entertainment and morale had definitely been noticed by the Canadian military."[57]

More broadly, the surreal and black humour of the Great War's English-speaking concert parties provided the form for concert parties of the Second World War and subsequently inspired the brand of comedy that emerged from it. The more bizarre elements of First World War concert-party material, for example, were essential to later understandings of popular humour. As such, traces of the Great War can be found in the DNA of relatively recent examples of popular English-speaking comedy. Indeed, future British and North American comedy troupes were all touched, either directly or indirectly, by the First World War concert-party phenomenon.

Leslie Henson, for example, was a member of the Royal Flying Corps and led the British Fifth Army's popular concert party the Gaieties in 1918. Henson, alongside English actor and later film producer Basil Dean, founded the Entertainment National Service Association (ENSA). ENSA's raison d'être was to provide entertainment for British soldiers. ENSA's principles and form were organized around Henson's own First World War concert-party experience.[58]

The results of Henson's association with ENSA and later its immediate successor the Combine Services Entertainment (CSE) were profound. For instance, after suffering shell shock and a significant mortar wound to his leg in the Second World War, Spike Milligan cut his comedy teeth with the CSE.[59] Milligan would become one of the key architects of the legendary BBC radio program *The Goon Show*, in which he starred with fellow World War II veterans Harry Secombe and Peter Sellers.[60] Milligan was no stranger to the concert-party formula, as his father Captain Leo Milligan was known as the "soldier showman of India" during the First World War.[61] While serving in the Second World War, Gunner Milligan had himself organized entertainment shows for his own immediate comrades before joining the more official military entertainment providers, the CSE. Moreover, Milligan was intimate with what many Great War entertainers had already known about the importance of comedy in terms of surviving and even *winning* a war: "There were the deaths of some of my friends, and therefore, no matter how funny I tried to make this book, that will always be at the back of my mind: but, were they alive today, they would have been first to join in the laughter, and that laughter was, I'm sure, the key to victory."[62]

These sentiments dovetailed nicely with those of First World War concert-party veterans such as Henson who, apart from setting up the very organization that launched Milligan's career, also later worked with the Goons' Peter Sellers at London's Palladium in the twilight of the former's career in 1954.[63]

The Goons revolutionized comedy and took the surrealism of the concert party variety to a whole new level, influencing a generation of fledgling British comedians, most notably the cast of *Monty Python's Flying Circus*.[64] John Cleese, for instance, was "absolutely amazed by [*The Goon Show*'s] surreal humour." For Cleese, the Goons came at a key stage of his comedic development and he never missed a show.[65] When Milligan and the Goons were winding down in the 1960s, Cleese and company were on the ascendance and would soon wield an unmatched influence on the world of English-speaking comedy, including the Canadian variety.[66]

Meanwhile, Canada had its own share of famous entertainers who came out of the Second World War. Meet the Navy, the Bluebell Bullets, and the Johnny Canuck Review, among others, had all—like their Great War predecessors—sought to counter poor morale among the troops.[67] Certainly the most popular of the Second World War's Dumbell-esque troupes was the Canadian Army Show. The show, which toured Europe and was broadcast on CBC during the war, featured soon-to-be-famous soldier-entertainers Johnny Wayne and Frank Shuster.[68] Like the Dumbells and PPCLI CC before them, Wayne and Shuster raised morale by being vaguely disrespectful of military authority, a fact that greatly appealed to their soldier audiences.[69]

There could be no comparison though, between the memorable songs born of the First World War and those songs that were popular in World War II. With radio and greater access to the musical culture of the home front, soldiers of the Second World War were not as isolated from popular trends and thus were not able to develop the same unique musical subculture that soldiers of the First World War had.[70] Glen Miller's swinging melodic genius is undeniable, but the rustic and homely quality of a song manufactured or adapted in the muddy trenches of Flanders is missing from the popular, polished works of the Second World War. "Moonlight Serenade" might soothe and was certainly fondly remembered, but "Oh! It's a Lovely War" fully interpreted a particular experience of one historical moment.

The routes of Canada's postwar trends in comedy, however, can be traced back to the Wayne and Shuster variety of wartime entertainers.[71] And Wayne and Shuster can thank the Dumbells and other concert parties of the First World War who gave their particular brand of comedy its form. And the deep associations do not end here. Frank Shuster's daughter Rosalind married Lorne Michaels, the Canadian-born producer of *Saturday Night Live*. Rosalind wrote for *Saturday Night Live* before the couple split up, and Michaels credited his former father-in-law Frank Shuster as being a big influence on his professional development.[72] Michaels was also greatly inspired by the Monty Python team, to the extent that *Saturday Night Live* was referred to by its biographers as "*Monty Python* meets *60 Minutes*."[73] It would seem then, that the *Goon Show*, *Monty Python*, *Blackadder*, *Wayne and Shuster*, *SCTV*, *Saturday Night Live*, and later *Kids in the Hall* (also produced by Michaels) were all reading from the same irreverent hymn book that had been passed down by those who had sung from it in the mud of Flanders.[74]

There were numerous Dumbell reunions before and after the Second World War with varying degrees of success and each with its own significance. Perhaps the most important of these was the 1934 Canadian Corps Reunion in Toronto. This reunion was particularly significant to veterans at a time when they had begun to voice their displeasure about their postwar lot. The reunion also revealed how the war was beginning to be remembered by Canadians in general.[75] The Dumbells were central to this memory-making process.

Yet memory meant different things to different people. For organizers of the reunion, the event was intended to showcase and remind the nation of the stick-to-itiveness and resiliency of veterans. In essence, the reunion's planners wanted the event—and its heroes of yesteryear—to positively inspire the nation at what was an extremely difficult time for many Canadians who were trying to survive the effects of the Depression. For the Corps' rank and file, however, the reunion offered an escape and a chance to indulge in 72 hours of nostalgia.[76]

Indeed, it was unlikely that the Corps' old soldiers were motivated to attend the reunion to display—for public consumption, it was hoped by the organizers—the high ideals of patriotism, order, discipline and stoicism that the "brass hats" had banked on. A far more plausible motivation for attending was the pride that Canadian soldiers shared with their respective battalions and the opportunity to revisit the comradeship they had enjoyed with others who had been there and "knew." Even here, 20 years after the fact, the divergence between the mindset of officialdom and the soldiers' actual experience found expression.

The Canada that soldiers dared to imagine in the trenches had not materialized; a trip to the past appealed to many soldiers for whom peacetime was a failure. For many veterans, the interwar years in Canada were difficult; many felt that their service was not fully appreciated by their government or a significant part of the Canadian population who were caught up in materialistic pursuits. Veterans believed they had received a raw deal. Many ex-soldiers naturally believed that they were entitled to better treatment from the Canadian government and that they should have more access to social welfare. While the paradigm shift to social welfare was a relatively new concept for Canadians, one should be aware that the 1934 reunion predated the famous On-to-Ottawa Trek by only one year. Many veterans continued to struggle to reintegrate into society and faced the reality of abject poverty. Many others struggled just to live—some laboured with disabilities—and many tried to get by on scarce means. The reunion environment ripened an overwhelming desire for change; the veterans' role in that change was significant and was articulated through organizations like the Royal Canadian Legion.[77]

The Legion's "Report of the Ontario Provincial Command" in 1933 was particularly accusatory: "The Great War was fought for Freedom and Democracy, as against control and power by Might through Wealth and Rank ... we see little or no evidence of those principles for which we fought, our country being dominated and ruled by the power of wealth ... the interests of money are held in higher esteem than Health, Employment or material welfare and life itself."[78]

Similarly, in a sermon delivered to a quarter of a million people who attended the Sunday morning service at Riverdale Park during the reunion, Canon Scott articulated the disillusionment that many veterans were experiencing "a wild orgy of covetousness and opulence has been succeeded by unemployment, poverty and even starvation ... revelations of greed and dishonesty in high places, with the consequent oppression of the poor ... the very foundations of orderly government have been imperilled ... where is the world that we fought to establish?"[79]

Many attending veterans posed the same question. It is little wonder then, that this weekend pass to the good old days, back to when at least the dream of a better Canada was still alive in the soldiers' consciousness, was a welcome respite from the stasis of their collective reality.

The weekend festivities began on 4 August 1934, exactly 20 years after war had been declared. Well exceeding the organizers' modest expectations, some 90,000 veterans from across the country and elsewhere descended on Toronto. The number exceeded the entire field strength of the CEF on the Western Front at any one time.[80] Towns and municipalities, as well as church organizations and veteran associations, held fundraisers to send their veterans to Toronto for the weekend.[81] Over one fifth of the attendees, or approximately 20,000 veterans, jammed into the CNE's Coliseum to watch the Dumbells take the stage where Red Newman, Gitz Rice, and company led the captive crowd through old sketches, jokes and the group's most popular songs.[82] G.R. Stevens recalled a conversation that took place among soldiers at that reunion who were debating the origins of one of the Dumbells' pieces at the reunion:

> I said it was a pity that Jack McLaren had not done his classic turn "The Night the Old Cow Died." Akers said that it had not been McLaren's act, it had been Red Newman's. Dorman offered to bet that McLaren not only had played the sketch but had written it. He got his idea (said Dorman) from a painting of a stag, with gouts of blood the size of buckets welling from its nostrils, on the wall of a boozer at Camblain L'abbe. I said Dorman was wrong. I remembered the stag perfectly; it was on the wall of an *estaminet* at Voormezeele, together with a Frenchman dressed in plus fours for *la chasse*, his gun muzzle belching fire at the stricken animal from a distance of four paces. Akers said my ignorance was refreshing; it is Germans and not Frenchmen who shoot in plus fours.[83]

So familiar were some troops with Canadian concert-party material that it supplied them with good, and likely endless, debating material. The Corps reunion gave soldiers a chance to relive the good times they experienced in the trenches with a familiar soundtrack.

Reunions could be wild affairs, and the one in 1934 was no exception. Toronto was overrun with what was mostly good-natured, if over-the-top behaviour: there was the bonfire at the corner of King and Yonge, the craps game that veterans started up in the middle of an intersection and an incident that saw an ex-cavalryman unsuccessfully attempt to take a horse up onto the roof of the King Edward Hotel.[84] The Dumbells were not immune from the adverse aspects of such merriment. T.J. Lilly's wife wrote Jack McLaren's wife to inform her that:

> Evidently Tom had a very enjoyable time at the Toronto Reunion, for he came back on the early morning train and took a taxi from the Westmount Station. The taxi drew up at our front door and Tom came

out of it—wearing a small brown derby hat perched precariously on the top of his head, his trouser legs rolled up above his knees, a green cardboard moustache stuck on his nose, and he crawled out of the taxi on all four, barking like a dog.[85]

More official reunions came in 1936 and 1937, when a few of the Originals tried to revive the famous concert party under the auspices "Stars of the Dumbells." The cast included Red Newman, Jack Ayre, Ross Hamilton, Pat Rafferty, and others, but they enjoyed only limited success.[86] Larger, more memorable one-off Dumbell reunions came in 1939, at a Massey Hall performance in Toronto in 1955, and at a final reunion in 1975 at Toronto's Lambert Lodge. This last reunion was put together by the CBC's Bill McNeil and featured the four surviving members of the Dumbells; Jack McLaren, aged 79; Jack Ayre, aged 80; Bill Redpath, aged 84; and Jerry Brayford, aged 87. It was fitting that Bill Redpath, who had been with the Dumbells from December 1917 until the end of the war, was honoured. Redpath had remained in London for nine months after the war and therefore missed the touring years that might have been his had he returned with the comedy troupe to Canada.[87] Like McLaren, Redpath was born in Edinburgh and though he took a position as a banker following the war, he remained involved in the arts over the course of his life.[88]

For his part, Jack McLaren had said goodbye to the Dumbells back in 1922. McLaren had, even by then, already had enough. Opting to neither carry on with the Dumbells nor branch out with the Originals, McLaren returned to painting and, alongside his friend John McCall, opened the successful McLaren and McCall advertising company. In 1923, McLaren married his wife, Lillian Clarke McGregor. Jack Ayre, Nobby Clarke, Percy Ham, and Red Newman from the Dumbells were all at the wedding with their wives, a group that sharply demonstrated the schism that the Dumbells sustained given those names who were *not* in attendance.[89] McLaren wrote and performed several music-hall-styled reviews with Mavor Moore at the Arts and Letters Club from the mid-1920s until the outbreak of the Second World War. It was at the Arts and Letters Club shows that Toronto's extremely popular annual revue *Spring Thaw* was born.[90] Like many of his colleagues, McLaren

Figure 37 Jack McLaren's *Let's All Hate Toronto* (Kingswood House, 1956). (Courtesy John McLaren)

once again put his efforts toward raising the troops' morale during the Second World War and even wrote some of the official entertainers' sketches.[91]

McLaren returned to the stage for various Dumbell reunions and was perhaps the most vocal and accessible of the performers when newspapers, magazines, radio and television journalists wanted to do a piece on the famous troupe. McLaren, thankfully for historians, was always willing to oblige. No, he never went to Hollywood for an MGM screen test. Nor did he accept an invitation to join the Group of Seven.[92] And the legacy of his beloved PPCLI Comedy Company has been and likely will always be overshadowed by the more famous name of "Dumbells." But McLaren's wit is apparent throughout the body of work that has survived: both Dumbells and Pats' CC alike. This last surviving Dumbell and the single most important comedy sketch writer in the Canadian Corps died in 1988.

A tribute to the famous concert party premiered at the Charlottetown Festival in 1977. *The Legend of The Dumbells*, directed by Alan Lund and written by George Salverson, was a spirited, if somewhat historically flexible account, that raised the profile of the concert party and restored it to memory. Jane Champagne described the audience's reaction to opening night: "When the show reached its finale with The Dumbell Rag, the audience rose to its collective feet and stayed there; they'd just found out that Canadian musical theatre roots had been planted firmly by a troupe of Canadian soldiers of the line during the First World War—and were proud of it."[93]

Various productions of the play have been produced over the years, including the most recent rendition at the 2002 Charlottetown Festival.[94]

Nearly a century after their first show, the legacy of the Dumbells endures. The importance of the famous First World War concert party to Canada's heritage is deserving of more academic attention. Though the spirit of the Dumbells lives on the stages of Canadian theatre, historical accounts have hitherto lacked both the veracity and depth that such a subject warrants. The Dumbells' interpretation of the war during their touring years engraved an enduring image in the memories of many civilians who had never seen the front lines. As Frank Willis attested: "Perhaps when memory calls many of us back to the Great War, it's not to France and Flanders, to the mud and blood and horror of trenches we never saw, we remember rather the Dumbells, who brought back with them from overseas something of the unflagging spirit and unfailing good humour that was the genius of the Canadian Corps. They were soldiers too."[95]

Thirty-five years after their final tour, journalist Grace Lydiatt Shaw, who had travelled across North America in search of Canada's theatrical history,

Figure 38   The inimitable Jack McLaren, c. 1966. (Courtesy John McLaren)

explained: "So many places I would go, and I went all the way from Victoria to St. John's Newfoundland, and Hollywood to New York, and I would say to people, 'What would you remember that was a Canadian show?' And I think most of them said, 'Oh, the Dumbells,' they all remembered the Dumbells."[96]

Mert Plunkett's daughter Annie O'Brien (née Plunkett) was in the navy during the Second World War. Wherever Annie went, her surname was always a point of interest to people who would invariably inquire if she had ever heard of the Dumbells.[97]

The Dumbells also influenced future stars. A young musician growing up in Winnipeg, Laurie Thompson, had seen the various revues that the Dumbells brought to town. His musical aspiration "was to tour with the Dumbells, it was the 'top spot' in Canada you might say."[98] Thompson eventually fulfilled his dream when he became part of the 13th edition of the Dumbells in 1929.[99] Musician-actor Hugh Mill similarly remembered: "As I recall, it was the finest show that was ever seen, the first bang-up musical comedy and it did go with a bang and the lightning speed and smoothness. It was superbly produced—really magnificent."[100]

Canadian theatre itself was also positively affected by the Dumbells. The Orillia Opera House, for one, was buoyed by the success of the Dumbells.[101]

Contemporary Canadian storyteller Lorne Brown has retold the Dumbells' story across the country since the 1990s. His father Lew Brown was a member of the Queen's Field Ambulance during the war and was given the order to build a stage for the Dumbells' show.[102] It would seem that the party atmosphere so symbolic of the postwar touring Dumbells had already, by 1918, become a feature of the trench-side performing troupe. The Dumbells, as Lorne Brown related, "arrived in the backs of two lorries, and they were, in [Lew Brown's] words, 'drunker than lords' … they rolled and fell out of the lorries, and stood there gently swaying in the breeze."[103]

Lew Brown was then entrusted by his CO with the unenviable task of sobering up the entertainers. He did. And incredibly, more than 40 years later, Lorne Brown followed in his father Lew's footsteps when he served as a stage and lighting technician for a Dumbells' reunion performance in Toronto.[104]

Despite critical acclaim and an adoring following, it took 56 years for any level of Canadian government to officially recognize the importance of the Dumbells to the country's history, long after many of the original concert-party performers had died. This recognition came only after CBC journalist Bill McNeil had lobbied endlessly for official recognition on the Dumbells behalf. It was presented to the four surviving members during the 1975 reunion:

> On behalf of the people and the government of Ontario I extend sincere best wishes on the occasion of the reunion of "The Dumbells"—1916–1919. In the trenches and on the battlefields of World War I your gift of laughter enabled men to transcend the awful realities of war and it is in their memory, those who gave their lives and those who survived, that we say thank you. May your reunion, today, be filled with laughter and joy, blessed with the knowledge that you have used your talents to enrich the life of your fellow man.
>
> —*William B. Davis*
> *Premier of Ontario*[105]

The Dumbells meant so many different things to so many Canadians. As historian Edward Moogk confirmed, "They were not only entertainers—they were also sacrilegious, socially aware, sentimental, irreverent, and intensely

Canadian."[106] The significance of their phenomenal postwar success is dwarfed only by their impact on Canadian soldiers during the First World War. Perhaps Jack McLaren best summarized the concert-party's raison d'être: "Men who had been in the thick of the Somme battles just two hours before made up our audiences; some with bandaged heads or arms in a sling, or perhaps with just a touch of shell shock. How those lads enjoyed the show! Its popularity lay in the fact that we held the mirror up to the troops themselves and echoed their conversations in exaggerated ways that caricatured all the quirks and absurdities of the soldier's life."[107]

Whether by accident or design, Canadian concert parties satisfied a mandate of morale boosting as prescribed by Canadian military authorities engaged in the largest program of recreation on the Western Front. Of course, the most irresistible facet of this Canadian legacy is that the "morale boosting" was often executed with surreptitious cheek, concealed insolence, and a playful contempt for those who would send them "up the line." But the soldiers went, happily whistling the "Dumbell Rag" on their way up that line.

Note on Sources and Acknowledgements

W hen I started this project nearly a decade ago, I had no idea how important or indeed how famous the Dumbells actually were. In the course
of researching my M.A. thesis, I collaborated with Bill Taylor on an article that
appeared in the *Toronto Star* in November 2001.[1] The article was a lighthearted
overview of the comedy troupe, highlighting their major accomplishments. The
response was overwhelming. Given the number of emails and phone calls I
received, it quickly became apparent that the legacy of the Dumbells was still
very much alive some 70 years after their last official performance. Of course,
the recollections were of family members whose parents or grandparents had
seen the Dumbells in Canada and even a few who had seen the party perform
in France and Belgium during the war. Frances Kerr of Brampton wrote to tell
me that her grandfather, who had been wounded at Passchendaele, "had met
the Dumbells on several occasions ... I wanted to take my mother [to their 1975
reunion show at Lambert Lodge in Toronto] because it was her father that told
us all about the Dumbells and she had gone to one of their concerts."[2]

Likewise, Jim Spencer related that he had grown up hearing his dad's war
songs all the time and that "he got to know quite a few of them along with their
lyrics and probably many or most of these were songs made popular by the
Dumbells. I grew up in Calgary and recall quite clearly going to the theatre with
my Dad, probably some time in the late 1920s, to see the Dumbells—and names
like Red Newman, Al Plunkett always come to mind."[3]

I was thrilled to receive such positive responses to my article and was inspired
to render the Dumbells' story as faithfully and respectively as I could. Of course,
I could not have done it on my own.

First, I am greatly indebted to many historians and researchers for their work
in the social history of Canada, the First World War, and popular culture and

popular music of the late-19th and early-20th centuries. What follows is a brief
list of a few key works that were central to my discussion.

Patrick B. O'Neill's article "The Canadian Concert Party in France," from
Theatre History in Canada, is a thoughtful account of the formation of several
Canadian concert parties during the war. Journalist Andrew Clark devotes a
chapter to the Dumbells in his *Stand and Deliver: Inside Canadian Comedy*,
in which he reviews the importance of the Dumbells to Canadian theatre and
sketch comedy. Niall Ferguson's *Pity of War: Explaining World War One* and
Modris Eksteins' *Rites of Spring* are relatively recent and original works that
survey many facets of the First World War—including humour. Social reviews of
the war, such as Paul Fussel's landmark *The Great War and Modern Memory*, have
aged well and were extremely useful for this study, as was Sandra Gwyn's *Tapestry
of War*, which is still perhaps the most compelling social study of Canadians
during the war. J.G. Fuller's *Troop Morale and Popular Culture in the British
and Dominion Armies: 1914–1918* was an essential source for the study of the
Canadian concert party, examining as it does trench journals and newspapers
of the First World War, including those of the Canadian Corps. John Brophy
and Eric Partridge's hugely important *The Long Trail: What the British Soldier
Sang and Said in the Great War of 1914–1918* presents a review of soldier songs
that were adopted by soldiers and various concert parties of the British Army,
while *Early Stages: Theatre in Ontario, 1800–1914*, edited by Ann Saddlemeyer,
was an essential collection of essays on the development of Canadian theatre
during the study's timeframe.

Official, if brief, records relating to the organization of Canadian concert
parties are found in Colonel G.W.L. Nicholson's *Canadian Expeditionary Force:
1914–1918*; J. Castell Hopkins' *Canada at War: 1914–1918*; Charles Bishop's *The
Canadian YMCA in the Great War*; Ralf Sheldon-Williams' *The Canadian Front
in France and Flanders*; and the official CEF six-volume *Canada and the Great
World War*. Ralph Hodder-Williams' *Princess Patricia's Canadian Light Infantry,
1914–1919* and Jeffrey Williams' *Princess Patricia's Canadian Light Infantry* are
additional sources that provide an outline of the organization of the Canadian
concert party in France.

A wide range of primary sources was available for this study. I am extremely
fortunate to have had access to the private family collections of the following individuals: John McLaren, son of John Wilson (Jack) McLaren; Stephen
Plunkett, grandson of Morley Plunkett; Gail Hannan, granddaughter of Morley
Plunkett; and Annie O'Brien, daughter of Captain Mert Plunkett. Along with
these, collections from the National Archives of Canada, Lorne Brown (Dumbell
memorabilia collector), and the CBC, as well as Jack Ayre's Private Collection at
the Toronto Reference Library, added to the great number of primary sources
obtained. The thoughts and opinions of both the performers and the regular

soldiers help to inform the study and are found in dozens of periodicals and newspaper articles, several concert-party programs, the personal memoirs of Jack McLaren, a biography of Albert Plunkett written by his second wife Patrise Earle, over 30 pieces of Dumbell sheet music, several Dumbell-related recordings from the original 78s, tour itineraries for the Dumbells' cross-Canadian tours that followed the war, and, perhaps most remarkably, the original sketchbook of comedy skits written by Jack McLaren in the trenches.

Some 20 hours of Dumbell-related audiotape were collected for this study. These audiotapes include personal performances of individual Dumbells, several CBC radio interviews with various concert-party performers, several hours of material relating to Jack McLaren, and various recordings of Dumbell reunions. In particular, I am indebted to the work of Grace Lydiatt Shaw and Bill McNeil for their exhaustive research on the Dumbells. Both Shaw and McNeil conducted several interviews in the 1960s and 1970s with many of the surviving members of the famous concert party. There also exists some film footage of the Dumbells from the private collection of Stephen Plunkett, the CBC, London, Ontario's Grand Theatre, and the National Archives of Canada. These sources assist in uncovering the nuances of comedic material so often undetected in the written word.

Although many of the primary sources deal exclusively with the Dumbells, there is still a substantial amount of material related to the PPCLI CC and, to a lesser extent, the other concert parties of the Canadian Corps. As most of the Dumbell performers had already been entertaining with other concert parties prior to joining the Dumbells, it is sometimes uncertain whether, in the course of a radio or print interview, an individual soldier is talking of his experience as a Dumbell, or his concert party experience at large. I have every effort to distinguish between Dumbell experiences and the PPCLI CC, the Y-Emmas, the Maple Leafs, and so forth. When it is not certain in which concert party a particular experience occurred, I used the blanket term of "Canadian concert party," or "concert party of the Canadian Corps."

I am so very grateful to everyone who helped me rescue the Dumbells. My sincere thanks go out to Joyce Beaton, Lorne Brown, Terry Crowley, Gael Hannan, Shawn Henshall, Jim Kennedy, John McLaren, Annie O'Brien, Bob Plunkett, Marion Plunkett, Stephen Plunkett, Richard Reid, Thomas Symons, Kathy Witheridge, and many others who gave me a hand when I was deep in the trenches. This work would not have been possible without the special care and attention it received from first my thesis adviser, Cathy Wilson, who helped me out of the starter's gate, and later from Lisa Quinn, who helped me cross the finish line. I could not have seen this work through to its conclusion without being constantly buoyed by the support of my wife Alana, and by my mom and dad, John and Jessie Wilson. I am happy to report that all three have since been fully indoctrinated in all things Dumbells. Finally, and most importantly, I want to thank Jack McLaren. Tucked away as I was, in a crevice of the National Archives with my headphones plugged into a magical, if outmoded reel-to-reel machine, I was rapt by McLaren's three-dimensional portrayal of Canada's First World War concert parties in a lengthy interview he gave over 45 years after war's end (and six years before I was born). As he spoke to me through the magnetic tape, Jack brought the PPCLI Comedy Company and the Dumbells alive. As we approach the 100th anniversary of the outbreak of Jack's war, I hope that this book goes some way in returning the favour.

Appendix A

Dramatis Personae: Canadian Concert Party Entertainers of WW1

Many Dumbells who performed at the Front did not join the North American version of the concert party. Likewise, many concert-party performers who were not in the Dumbells in France became honorary Dumbells in Canada. Eventually, the Dumbells and the Originals would use actors that had not been in the war. Over 100 performers are listed below.

Entertainer	Concert Party Affiliate	Note
N. Fraser Allan	postwar (pw) Dumbells	Pianist, musical director
Art Allan	pw Dumbells	—
Ben Allen	16th Battalion, Dumbells	Director of the 16th Battalion's concert party
Glen Allen	pw Dumbells	—
Barry Anderson	pw Dumbells	—
Bob Anderson	pw Originals	—
Ivor "Jack" Ayre	116th Battalion, Dumbells	Pianist, musical director, comp. of "Dumbell Rag"
Billie Baker	pw Dumbells	—
Elmer Belding	Dumbells	Original Dumbell tenor from the 3rd Divisional Signals
Stan Bennett	pw Dumbells	Professional singer
Cyril Biddulph	PPCLI CC	Popular independent comedian
Harry Binns	pw Dumbells	Professional tenor
Frank "Jerry" Brayford	10th Field Ambulance, Dumbells	English singer, comedian; settled in Western Canada
Edmund Bullis	Maple Leafs	"Gladys"
Gordon Calder	pw Dumbells	—
Percy Campbell	pw Dumbells	—
Joe Carr	pw Dumbells	—
Nat Castles	pw Dumbells	—
Andre Catranno	Dumbells	Italian-born property manager
Jack Challes	pw Dumbells	—

Entertainer	Concert Party Affiliate	Note
Ted Charter	Dumbells	Assistant manager, comedian; settled in New York
D. Chisholm	pw Dumbells	—
H. Clark	pw Dumbells	—
Norman "Nobby" Clarke	PPCLI CC	Property manager
Louis Crerar	pw Dumbells	—
William I. Cunningham	PPCLI CC	—
Cy Denenny	pw Dumbells	Possibly the most famous hockey star of the era
Jimmy Denson	pw Dumbells	—
Jimmy Devon	pw Dumbells	—
G. Dufresne	pw Dumbells	—
Eddie Duschene	pw Dumbells	—
Fred Emney	pw Dumbells	Comedy partner of Charlie Jeeves
Fred Fenwick	PPCLI CC, Dumbells	Female impersonator
Bob Ferris	5th Canadian Field Ambulance	American-born, known for droll monologues
Bill Filson	PPCLI CC	Baritone
Howard Fogg	pw Dumbells	Violinist, musical director (1925)
Jim Foley	pw Dumbells	
Bob Ford	pw Dumbells	—
Gene Fritsley	pw Dumbells	—
Cameron Geddes	pw Dumbells	Professional bass
Jimmy Goode	pw Dumbells	Blackface comedian
Jack Grace	pw Dumbells	—
Albert Grady	pw Dumbells	—
John Hagan	pw Dumbells	—
C. Hall	Dumbells	—
Percy D. Ham	PPCLI CC	—
Ross Hamilton	9th Field Amb., Maple Leafs, Dumbells	"Marjorie"
Samuel Haslett	13th Battalion	—
Charles Hillman	PPCLI CC	—
Arthur "Jock" Holland	Bow-Bells, Dumbells	Actor, female impersonator
Charlie Jeeves	pw Dumbells	Comedy partner of Fred Emney
Joseph "Al" Johnson	pw Dumbells	—
John Kidd	Dumbells	Property manager
W. Kilpatrick	PPCLI CC	Property manager
Dick Kimberley	pw Dumbells	—
Bertram Langley	Dumbells	Bass baritone
Thomas J. Lilly	PPCLI CC, pw Dumbells	Sketch writer, experienced performer prior to WWI
Roy Locksley	pw Dumbells	—

Entertainer	Concert Party Affiliate	Note
Morris London	pw Dumbells	—
Norman L. Lye	pw Dumbells	—
Don MacLean	pw Dumbells	—
Charlie McLean	Y-Emmas, Dumbells	Singer, actor
Bert Mason	pw Dumbells	—
Charlie Mavor	Dumbells	A Dumbell for three weeks before returning to duty
Jock McCormick	Dumbells	42nd Battalion; settled in Scotland at war's end
John "Jack" W. McLaren	PPCLI CC, Dumbells	Scottish-born influential comedy sketch writer
David L. Michie	Dumbells	
G. Mickey	Dumbells	Property manager
Scotty Morrison	pw Dumbells	—
Stanley Morrison	PPCLI CC	Lost a leg in action; died from wounds in Montreal
Alan Murray	9th Field Ambulance, Dumbells	"Marie"
S. G. Nicholls	PPCLI CC	—
Norman D. Nicholson	PPCLI CC	Pianist
Curley Nixon	pw Dumbells	—
Red Newman	Y-Emmas, Dumbells	English-born singer of "Oh! It's a Lovely War"
Gene Pearson	pw Originals	—
Captain Pembroke	PPCLI CC	—
Al Plunkett	Dumbells	Popular crooner
Merton Plunkett	Dumbells & several other "Y" parties	Captain of the YMCA, entertainment director
Morley Plunkett	Maple Leafs, pw Dumbells	Brother of Al and Merton
Scott Plunkett	pw Dumbells	
Pat Rafferty	Red Patches, Maple Leafs, Dumbells	1st Division; regarded as a "knock-about comedian"
Lt. Archer G. Read	Woodpeckers	PPCLI
Norman "Bill" Redpath	Dumbells (Dec. 1917)	Scottish-born, enlisted 9th Field Art. Signal Comp.
Ted Reve	pw Dumbells	Musical director (1924)
Gitz Rice	Minstrels, PPCLI CC	Immensely popular entertainer
Harold Rich	pw Dumbells	Musical director (1924–25)
Bill Robertson	pw Dumbells	—
Doc Romaine	pw Dumbells	—
Clarence Sawyer	pw Dumbells	
Bobby Scott	pw Dumbells	—
Skinner	Y-Emmas	
Conrad Stephens	PPCLI CC	Chose not to join the Dumbells at Mons
Bill Tennent	10th Field Ambulance, Dumbells	Scottish-born tenor
Bert Thomas	pw Dumbells	—

Entertainer	Concert Party Affiliate	Note
Laurie Thompson	pw Dumbells	Joined 13th edition of the Dumbells in 1929
George Thorne	Dumbells	—
Freddie Treener	pw Dumbells	—
Ernie Watson	pw Dumbells	—
Bert Wilkinson	Dumbells	—
Bert Williams	pw Dumbells	—
Art Witham	pw Dumbells	—
Leonard Young	9th Field Amb., PPCLI CC, Dumbells	Pianist, comedian; lost a leg in duty
Tommy Young	pw Dumbells	Baritone

Appendix B

Notable Concert Parties of the Canadian Corps

Below is a list of the most important Canadian concert parties. Although the Dumbells would become the most famous concert party, between 30 and 40 similar entertainment troupes operated in the Canadian Corps.

The 1st Canadian Field Ambulance (*large minstrel show, the first Canadian concert party formed in the WWI*)

The 5th Canadian Field Ambulance

The 8th Canadian Field Ambulance (*representing Calgary, had an orchestra*)

The 9th Canadian Field Ambulance (*musical comedy, closely associated with the PPCLI*)

The 10th Canadian Field Ambulance (*revue*)

The 13th Canadian Field Ambulance

The 52nd Concert Party

The Canadian Scottish Concert Party of the 16th Battalion

The C2s (a.k.a. The See-Toos) of the Second Division

The Dumbells of the 3rd Division

The Harry Lauders of the 91st Battalion Canadian Militia

The Little Black Devils of the Winnipeg Rifles

The Maple Leafs of the 4th Division

The Princess Patricia's Canadian Light Infantry Comedy Company

The Rouge et Noir of the 1st Division

The Red Patches (*last division to have a concert party; ironically, the first division to arrive in France*)

The Redheckles of the Royal Highlanders of Canada (a.k.a. The Black Watch)

The Volatiles of the 1st Division

The Whizz Bangs of the Canadian Artillery

The Woodpeckers of the 126th Company of the Canadian Forestry Corps

The Y-Emmas of the YMCA

Notable Concert Parties of the British Expedition Forces

The Very Lights
The Fancies of the British 6th Division
The Follies of the British 4th Division
The Bow Bells of the 56th (London) Division
The Gaieties of the Fifth Army
The Jinks
The Ballonatics
The Tangerines
The Goods of the 58th Division
The Crumps of the 41st Division
The Tonics of the 92nd Brigade
The Cheerios of the 2/6th Battalion King's Liverpool Regiment
The Diamond Troupe of the 29th Division
The Whizz Bangs of the 5th Division

Appendix C

Important Canadian Concert Party Casts

PPCLI Comedy Company
Steenvoorde—June 1916
J. McLaren, T.J. Lilly, W.I. Cunningham,
P.D. Ham, S. Morrison, F. Fenwick,
L. Young, Capt. Pembroke, and
Property Manager N. Clarke

Dumbells Original Cast
Gouy-Servins—June 1917
J. Ayre, R. Hamilton, A. Murray,
T. Charter, B. Tennent, E. Belding,
A. Plunkett, and Capt. M. Plunkett

Dumbells
Winter 1917
J. Ayre, R. Hamilton, A. Murray,
T. Charter, B. Tennent, E. Belding,
A. Plunkett, J. Brayford, B. Redpath,
J. McCormick, B. Langley,
Capt. M. Plunkett, with property
managers G. Mickey, L. Kidd, and
A. Catranno

PPCLI Comedy Company
London Performances—1918
J. McLaren, T.J. Lilly, F. Fenwick,
W. Filson, C. Stephens, C. Hillman,
N. Nicholson, and Lt. C. Biddulph

Dumbells Cast of H.M.S. Pinafore
Mons—November 1918
Josephine—R. Hamilton (Marjorie)
Ralph Rackstraw—B. Tennent
Sir Joseph Porter—T. Charter
Captain Corcoran—A. Plunkett
Buttercup—A. Murray (Marie)
Boatswain—B. Langley
Dick-Deadeye—C. Hillman (PPCLI CC)
American Reporter—J. McLaren (PPCLI
 CC)
Cpl. Comedy-Guard—T.J. Lilly
Buttercup's Girlfriend—F. Fenwick
 (PPCLI CC)
with L. Young, G. Thorne, and B. Filson
Musical Director—J. Ayre

Dumbells Biff, Bing, Bang
North American Revue—1919–1920
R. Hamilton, A. Murray, A. Plunkett,
B. Tennent, F. Fenwick, L. Young, J. Ayre,
J. McLaren, B. Allen, C. McLean,
R. Newman, J. Holland, C. Hall,
and B. Langley

Appendix D

Postwar Concert Party Revues

The Dumbells

Biff, Bing, Bang (1921)
[company split in 1922]
The Dumbells Revue of 1922 (1922)
Carry On (1922)
Cheerio (1923)
Ace High (1924)
Oh, Yes (1925)
Lucky Seven (1925)
That's That (1926)
Let 'er Go (1926)
Three Bags Full (1926)
Joy Bombs (1926)
Oo-La-La (1927)
Why Worry (1928) (introduction of women)
[company disbanded in 1932]

The Originals

Full O' Pep (1923) (various recordings for HMV)
Rapid Fire (1924)
Thumbs Up (c. unknown)

Appendix E

North American Tour Itineraries

The Dumbells 1919–1920

Sept. 29, 30, & **Oct.** 1, 1919	London, ON
2	Stratford, ON
3 & 4	Brantford, ON
6–12	Hamilton, ON
13	Brockville, ON
14 & 15	Kingston, ON
16	Pembroke, ON
17	Renfrew, ON
18	Carleton Place, ON
19	Smith Falls, ON
21	Perth, ON
22	Belleville, ON
23	Lindsay, ON
24 & 25	Peterborough, ON
Oct. 27–**Nov.** 3	Toronto, ON
4–10	St. Catharines, ON
13	Guelph, ON
14	Kitchener, ON
15	Brantford, ON
17	Owen Sound, ON
18	Hanover, ON
19 & 20	Galt, ON
21	Simcoe, ON
22	Tillsonburg, ON
25 & 25	St. Thomas, ON
26	Woodstock, ON
Oct. 27, 28 & 29	London, ON
Dec. 1–20	Toronto, ON
22	Oshawa, ON
23	Trenton, ON
24	Cobourg, ON
25	Peterborough, ON
26	Kingston, ON
Dec. 29–**Jan.** 1, 1920	Hamilton, ON
2	Woodstock, ON
3	Paris, ON
5 & 6	Guelph, ON
7	Barrie, ON
8	Midland, ON
9 & 10	Orillia, ON
12 & 13	Cobalt, ON
14 & 15	North Bay, ON
16 & 17	Sudbury, ON
19, 20 & 21	Port Arthur, ON
22, 23 & 24	Fort William, ON
Jan. 26–**Feb.** 1	Winnipeg, MB
2, 3 & 4	Moose Jaw, SK
5, 6 & 7	Prince Albert, SK
9	North Battleford, SK
10	Lloydminster, SK
11	Vermillion, AB
12, 13 & 14	Edmonton, AB
16	Ponoka, AB

Note: Tour itineraries compiled from the diaries of Ivor "Jack" Ayre, who left the Dumbells to join the Originals in 1922. From Ivor "Jack" Ayre's Dumbell Collections at the Metro Toronto Reference Library.

Feb. 17	Lacombe, AB
19	Camrose, AB
20	Drumheller, AB
21	Hanna, AB
23 & 24	Medicine Hat, AB
25	Lethbridge, AB
Feb. 26, 27 & 28	Calgary, AB
Mar. 1	Macleod, AB
2	Pincher Creek, AB
3	Blairmore, AB
4 & 5	Fernie, BC
6	Cranbrook, BC
8 & 9	Nelson, BC
10	Rossland, BC
11	Grand Forks, BC
12 & 15	Vernon, BC
17	Revelstoke, BC
18 & 19	Kamloops, BC
20	Nanaimo, BC
22–27	Vancouver, BC
29–30	Victoria, BC
Apr. 1, 2 & 3	Calgary, AB
5	Medicine Hat, AB
6	Lethbridge, AB
7	Wetaskiwin, AB
8, 9 & 10	Edmonton, AB
12, 13 & 14	Saskatoon, SK
15, 16 & 17	Regina, SK
18–24	Winnipeg, MB
26 & 27	Brandon, MB
28	Estevan, SK
29	Weyburn, SK
Apr. 30–May 1	Swift Current, SK
3, 4 & 5	Moose Jaw, SK
6, 7 & 8	Prince Albert, SK
10, 11 & 12	Saskatoon, SK
13, 14 & 15	Regina, SK
17–22	Winnipeg, MB
24, 25 & 26	Fort William, ON
28	Sudbury, ON
29	North Bay, ON
May 31–June 5	Ottawa, ON
7–26	Montreal, QC

The Dumbells 1920–1921

| Aug. 16–Sept. 11 | Toronto, ON |
| 13, 14 & 15 | St. Catharines, ON |

Sept. 16, 17 & 18	Brantford, ON
20–25	Hamilton, ON
Sept. 27–Oct. 2	London, ON
4 & 5	Woodstock, ON
6 & 7	Sarnia, ON
8 & 9	St. Thomas, ON
11 & 12	Galt, ON
13 & 14	Stratford, ON
15 & 16	Owen Sound, ON
18	Galt, ON
19	Guelph, ON
20 & 21	Kitchener, ON
22 & 23	Peterborough, ON
25–30	Ottawa, ON
Nov. 1 & 2	Sherbrooke, QC
3 & 4	St. John, NB
5	Moncton, NB
6	New Glasgow, NS
8, 9 & 10	Halifax, NS
11	New Glasgow, NS
12 & 13	Sydney, NS
15	Amherst, NS
17	Brockville, ON
18, 19 & 20	Kingston, ON
22–27	Montreal, QC
29–30	Lindsay, ON
Dec. 1	Midland, ON
2	Orillia, ON
3	Collingwood, ON
4	Barrie, ON
6–25	Toronto, ON
27 & 28	Sudbury, ON
Dec. 30, 31 & Jan. 1, 1921	Fort William, ON
3–8	Winnipeg, MB
10 & 11	Moose Jaw, SK
12 & 13	Medicine Hat, AB
14 & 15	Lethbridge, AB
17, 18 & 19	Calgary, AB
20, 21 & 22	Edmonton, AB
24	Revelstoke, BC
25	Kelowna, BC
26 & 27	Vernon, BC
28 & 29	Kamloops, BC
Jan. 31 & Feb. 1	Victoria, BC
2–12	Vancouver, BC

Feb. 14	Penticton, BC
15	Grand Forks, BC
16	Nelson, BC
17	Cranbrook, BC
18	Fernie, BC
19	Lethbridge, AB
21, 22 & 23	Calgary, AB
24, 25 & 26	Edmonton, AB
Feb. 28,	Saskatoon, SK
Mar. 1 & 2	
3, 4 & 5	Regina, SK
7–19	Winnipeg, MB
Mar. 22–Apr. 9	Montreal, QC
11, 12 & 13	Hamilton, ON
14, 15 & 16	London, ON
Apr. 18–	Toronto, ON
May 7	
May 9–Jul. 9	New York, NY

The Dumbells 1922–1923

Aug. 28 –	Toronto, ON
Sept. 9, 1922	
11–16	London, ON
18 & 19	Kitchener, ON
20 & 21	Stratford, ON
22 & 23	Galt, ON
25 & 26	Chatham, ON
27	St. Thomas, ON
28 & 29	Woodstock, ON
30	Niagra Falls, ON
Oct. 9	Brantford, ON
10 & 11	Welland, ON
12, 13 & 14	St. Catharines, ON
16	Barrie, ON
17	Midland, ON
18	Orillia, ON
19	Lindsay, ON
20 & 21	Peterborough, ON
23	Perth, ON
24	Smith Falls, ON
25–28	Ottawa, ON
30	Kingston, ON
Nov. 1	Oshawa, ON
2	Picton, ON
3	Belleville, ON
4	Cornwall, ON
6–11	Montreal, QC
13 & 14	Fredericton, NB

Nov. 15 & 16	St. John, NB
17 & 18	Moncton, NB
20–25	Halifax, NS

The Originals "Full O' Pep" 1923

Jan. 8, 9 &	St. Catharines, ON
10, 1923	
11	St. Thomas, ON
12 & 13	Brantford, ON
15	Kitchener, ON
16	Woodstock, ON
17	Stratford, ON
18, 19 & 20	London, ON
22–27	Hamilton, ON
Jan. 29 –	Toronto, ON
Feb. 17	
19–24	Montreal, QC
26 & 27	Belleville, ON
28	Picton, ON
Mar. 1, 2 & 3	Kingston, ON
5	Lindsay, ON
6	Orillia, ON
7	Barrie, ON
8	Midland, ON
9 & 10	Peterborough, ON
12 & 13	St. John, NB
15, 16 & 17	Sydney, NS
19, 20 & 21	Halifax, NS
22	New Glasgow, NS
23 & 24	Yarmouth, NS
26	Kentville, NS
27 & 28	Halifax, NS
30 & 31	Moncton, NB
Apr. 2	Smiths Falls, ON
3	North Bay, ON
4	Sudbury, ON
6 & 7	Fort William, ON
9	Winnipeg, MB
16, 17 & 18	Regina, SK
19, 20 & 21	Saskatoon, SK
23–28	Edmonton, AB
Apr. 30–	Calgary, AB
May 5	
7, 8 & 9	Victoria, BC
10–19	Vancouver, BC
21	Kamloops, BC
22	Vernon, BC
23	Kelowna, BC

May 24	Penticton, BC
26	Nelson, BC
28	Cranbrook, BC
29	Fernie, BC
31	Lethbridge, AB
June 1	Medicine Hat, AB
2	Swift Current, SK
4, 5 & 6	Moose Jaw, SK
7, 8 & 9	Saskatoon, SK
11, 12 & 13	Regina, SK
14	Virden, MB
15 & 16	Brandon, MB
18–23	Winnipeg, MB
25	Kenora, ON
26 & 27	Fort William, ON
29	Sudbury, ON
30	North Bay, ON

The Originals "Rapid Fire" 1923–1924

Aug. 30 – Sept. 1, 1923	Hamilton, ON
3 & 4	Peterborough, ON
5 & 6	Belleville, ON
7 & 8	Kingston, ON
10 & 11	Ottawa, ON
12	Perth, ON
13	Brockville, ON
14 & 15	Sherbrooke, QC
17–22	Montreal, QC
24	North Bay, ON
25	Sudbury, ON
27, 28 & 29	Fort William, ON
Oct. 1–13	Winnipeg, MB
15, 16 & 17	Saskatoon, SK
18, 19 & 20	Regina, SK
22–27	Edmonton, AB
29 & 30	Vancouver, BC
Oct. 31, Nov. 1 & 2	Victoria, BC
4–10	Seattle, WA
11	Aberdeen, WA
12	Raymond, WA
13 & 14	Tacoma, WA
15, 16 & 17	Portland, WA ?
19 & 20	Spokane, WA
22, 23 & 24	Calgary, AB
26 & 27	Lethbridge, AB
28	Medicine Hat, AB

Nov. 30–Dec. 1	Prince Albert, SK
3, 4 & 5	Saskatoon, SK
6	Estevan, SK
7 & 8	Moose Jaw, SK
10 –15	Winnipeg, MB
17	Kenora, ON
19–22	Sault Ste. Marie, ON
24 & 25	Brantford, ON
26 & 27	Galt, ON
28 & 29	Welland, ON
Dec. 31, Jan. 1 & 2, 1924	Hamilton, ON
3	Oshawa, ON
4 & 5	Peterborough, ON
7, 8 & 9	St. Catharines, ON
10	Niagara Falls, ON
11 & 12	Stratford, ON
14	Woodstock, ON
15 & 16	Sarnia, ON
17, 18 & 19	London, ON
21, 22 & 23	Chatham, ON
25 & 26	Owen Sound, ON
Jan. 28 – Feb. 2, 4–9, 11–16, 18–23	Toronto, ON
25	Barrie, ON
26	Orillia, ON
27	Lindsay, ON
28	Cobourg, ON
29	Picton, ON
Mar. 1	Brockville, ON
3 & 4	Woodstock, NB
5 & 6	St. John, NB
7	Amherst, NS
8	New Glasgow, NS
10–15	Halifax, NS
18, 19 & 20	Sydney, NS
21 & 22	Glace Bay, NS
Mar 24	Sackville, NB
26 & 27	Charlottetown, PE
28 & 29	Moncton, NB
Mar. 31 – Apr. 5, 7–12	Montreal, QC
14–19	Ottawa, ON
21	Perth, ON
22	Pembroke, ON
23	Renfrew, ON
24	Smith Falls, ON

Apr. 25 & 26	Kingston, ON	May 3	Tillsonburg, ON
28 & 29	St. Catharines, ON	5, 6 & 7	Windsor
30	Woodstock, ON		(Walkerville), ON
May 1	St. Thomas, ON	8	Chatham, ON
2	Galt, ON	9 & 10	Guelph, ON

Appendix F

Catalogue of Dumbells Sheet Music

Song Title
Performer
Composer(s)
Featured Revue
Publishing Information

Coal Black Mammy
Al Plunkett
L. Cliff and I. St. Helier
Dumbells Revue of 1922
Leo Feist Company Limited
  Toronto, Ontario

Come Back Old Pal
Mert Plunkett
M. W. Plunkett
Carry On
Leo Feist Company Limited
  Toronto, Ontario

Down Texas Way
Al Plunkett
F. Godfrey, A. Mills, and B. Scott
Biff Bing Bang
Leo Feist Company Limited
  Toronto, Ontario

Dumbell Rag
The Dumbells
Ivor E. Jack Ayre
Biff Bing Bang
Leo Feist Company Limited
  Toronto, Ontario

Everybody Slips a Little
Al Plunkett
R. B. Saxe
Cheerio
Leo Feist Company Limited
  Toronto, Ontario

For No Good Reason at All
Al Plunkett
Abel Baer
Here T' is
Leo Feist Company Limited
  Toronto, Ontario

Gee I Wish I Was a Kid Once More
Plunkett Bros.
Fraser Allen
Ace High
Leo Feist Company Limited
  Toronto, Ontario

Golden Dream Boat
Ross Hamilton
W. David and H. Nicholls
Carry On
Leo Feist Company Limited
  Toronto, Ontario

High Street Africa
Morley Plunkett
C. Clark, H. Trevor, and E. Lynton
Lucky Seven
Leo Feist Company Limited
  Toronto, Ontario

I Know Where the Flies Go
Al Plunkett
S. Mayo and J. Harrington
Biff Bing Bang
Leo Feist Company Limited
  Toronto, Ontario

I Miss My Swiss
Morley Plunkett
W. Gilbert and A. Baer
Lucky Seven
Leo Feist Company Limited
  Toronto, Ontario

I'm a Daddy
Red Newman
A. Newman and C. Althoff
Revue of 1922
Leo Feist Company Limited
  Toronto, Ontario

Keep Your Head Down "Fritzie Boy"
Lt. G. Rice
Lt. G. Rice
Leo Feist Inc., 1918
  New York, New York

K-K-K-Kiss Me Again
Al Plunkett
W. Stanley and A. Allen
Revue of 1922
Leo Feist Company Limited
  Toronto, Ontario

Lil' Old Granny Mine
Al Plunkett
J. P. Long
Cheerio
Leo Feist Company Limited
  Toronto, Ontario

Ma Look at Charlie
Red Newman
Elven Hedges
OO-LA-LA
Leo Feist Company Limited
  Toronto, Ontario

Most Powerful Love
Stan Bennett and Fraser Allen
Fraser Allen
Carry On
Leo Feist Company Limited
  Toronto, Ontario

My Blue Heaven
Al Plunkett
W. Donaldson and G. Whiting
Ind.
Leo Feist Company Limited
  Toronto, Ontario

My Mothers Humming Lullaby
Al Plunkett
D. Terriss and L. Wood
Oh Yes
Leo Feist Company Limited
  Toronto, Ontario

My Ohio Home
Al Plunkett
G. Kahn and W. Donaldson
Ind.
Leo Feist Company Limited
  Toronto, Ontario

Oh It's a Lovely War
Red Newman
J. Long and M. Scott
Biff Bing Bang
Leo Feist Company Limited
  Toronto, Ontario

On the Road to Anywhere
Ben Allen
S. Sanders
Cheerio
Leo Feist Company Limited
  Toronto, Ontario

The Photo of the Girl I Left Behind
Red Newman
W. Merson
Ace High
Leo Feist Company Limited
  Toronto, Ontario

Catalogue of Dumbells Sheet Music 175

Say You'll Not Forget Me
Ross Hamilton
P. Campbell and C. McLean
Revue of 1922
Leo Feist Company Limited
  Toronto, Ontario

Shall I Have It Bobbed or Shingled?
Al Plunkett
R. Weston and B. Lee
Ace High
Leo Feist Company Limited
  Toronto, Ontario

She Must Be a Wonderful Girl
Al Plunkett
J. Malcolm and A. Herbert
Cheerio
Leo Feist Company Limited
  Toronto, Ontario

Shufflin Along
Al Plunkett
R. Stanley and N.D. Ayer
Carry On
Leo Feist Company Limited
  Toronto, Ontario

Snuggled on Your Shoulders
Laurie Thompson
J. Young and C. Lombardo
Ind.
Leo Feist Company Limited
  Toronto, Ontario

Swing Me in the Moonlight
Capt. Plunkett's Maple Leafs
A. Mills and M. Scott
Maple Leafs
Leo Feist Company Limited
  Toronto, Ontario

Take In the Sun Hang Out the Moon
Al Plunkett
Lewis, Young, and H. Wood
Cheerio
Leo Feist Company Limited
  Toronto, Ontario

That's My Mammy
Al Plunkett
H. Please, A. Baer, and E. Nelson
Ind.
Leo Feist Company Limited
  Toronto, Ontario

Too Many Girls
Al Plunkett
R. Weston and B. Lee
Cheerio
Leo Feist Company Limited
  Toronto, Ontario

We're on Our Way
Mert Plunkett
M.W. Plunkett
Ind.
Gordon V. Thompson Ltd.

Winter Will Come
Mert Plunkett
M.W. Plunkett
Cheerio
Leo Feist Company Limited
  Toronto, Ontario

Yum Yum Yum Yum
Al Plunkett
R. Weston and B. Lee
Ace High
Leo Feist Company Limited
  Toronto, Ontario

Note: From the private collection of Stephen Plunkett

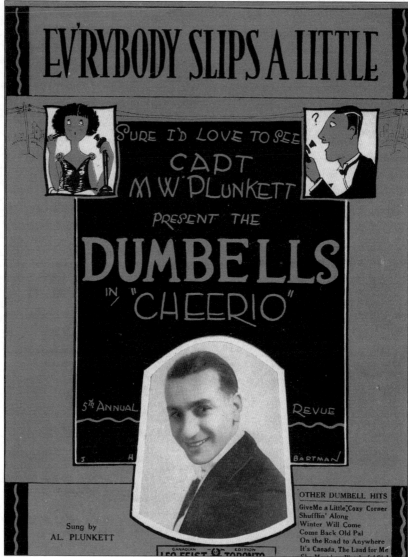

Figure 39   Al Plunkett's matinee-idol looks helped to sell Dumbells-related sheet music, including this example from 1923. (Courtesy Stephen Plunkett)

Appendix G

Catalogue of Dumbells-Related Music

Dumbells-related 78s (original recordings 1922–1932 on His Master's Voice)

Song Title
Performer
Composer
Publishing Information

"And Her Mother Came Too"
Al Plunkett
Written by Ivor Novello and Dion Titheradge
Montreal: Berliner Gram-O-Phone, Issue No. 216390
March 1923

"Archibald"
S. Bennett, piano accompaniment Freddie Treneer
Written by Philip Braham
Montreal: Victor Records, Issue no. 216485
1926

"Asleep in the Deep"
Wilfred Glenn, bass with orchestra
Written by Arthur J. Lamb and Henry W. Petrie
Camden, NJ: Victor Talking Machine Co. 20244-A
1913

"Canada for Canadians: Let's Keep the Money in the Country"
Red Newman
Written by B. Lee and R.P. Weston
Montreal: Berliner Gram-O-Phone, Issue no. 216496
1926

"Capt. Thingamabob"
Red. Newman
unknown
Montreal: Victor Talking Records, Issue no. 217004
1926

"Dear Old Pal of Mine"
John McCormack
Words and Music by Lt. Gitz Rice
Montreal: Berliner, His Master's Voice, Issue no. 64785
1918

"Dirty Work"
Red Newman and Charlie McLean
Written by R.P. Weston and B. Lee
Montreal: Berliner Gram-O-Phone, 216439
December 1923

"Everybody Slips a Little (Now and Then)"
Al Plunkett
Written by D. Meher, and R.B. Saxe
Montreal: Berliner Gram-O-Phone, Issue
No. 216455
1924

"Fun in Flanders—Part Two"
Written by Henry Burr and Lt. Gitz Rice
Montreal: Berliner, His Master's Voice,
Issue no. 18405
March 1918

"I Would If I Could"
Jock Holland
Written by Donovan Parsons, Reginald
Relsie, and Edward Tracey
Montreal: Berliner Gram-O-Phone, Issue
No. 216399
May 1923

*"Keep the Home Fires Burning (Till the
Boys Come Home)"*
Columbia Stellar Quartet
Words by Lena Ford, music by Ivor
Novello
Columbia: Columbia Record 6028
1918

"Medals on My Chest"
Red Newman
Written by Ted Waite
Montreal: Berliner, His Master's Voice,
Issue no. 216398
1923

"My Old Dutch"
Red Newman
Words by A. Chevalier, music by C. Ingle,
c. 1892
Montreal: Berliner Gram-O-Phone, Issue
no. 216398
May 1923

"O Gee! O Gosh! O Golly, I'm in Love"
Al Plunkett
Written by E. Breuer, O. Olsen, and
C. Johnson
Montreal: Berliner Gram-O-Phone, Issue
No. 216432
November 1923

"The Rose of No Man's Land"
Henry Burr
Words by J. Caddigan, music by J. Brennan, c. 1916
Montreal: Berliner Gram-O-Phone, Issue
No. 216039
December 1918

"Take Me Back to the Land of Promise"
Lt. Gitz Rice
Anonymous
Montreal: Berliner, His Master's Voice,
Issue no. 216016
1917

"Yum-Yum-Yum-Yum"
Al Plunkett
Written by R.P. Weston, B. Lee, and
R. Harris-Weston
Montreal: Victor, His Master's Voice,
Issue No. 216479
1926

Appendix H

Miscellaneous Songs

"*The Clock Song*"
Words by C. Grey, music by N. Ayer

"*Conscientious Objector*"
A. Lester
Written by H. Finck and C.M.S. McLellan

"*The Field Postcard* "
Words by R. Roberts, music by H. Montague
1916

"*Hello My Dearie*"
Words by G. Buck, music by D. Stamper
1917

"*I'll Make a Man of You*" a.k.a. "*On Sunday I Walk Out with a Soldier*"
Words by Arthur Wimperis, music by
  Herman Finck
C. unknown

"*Lily of Killarney*" a.k.a. "*The Moon Hath Raised Her Lamp Above*"
F. Kreisler
Written by Sir J. Benedict
London: Matrix, B 14693-1 Victor Cat.
  64440
April 1914

"*Little Grey Home in the West*"
Written by Hermann Lohr and
  D. Eardley-Wilmot, c. 1913
1915

"*The Old Barbed Wire*"
Roosters Concert Party
Traditional
1929

"*On the Staff*"
Words by C. Grey, music by Ivor Novello
1917

"*Pack Up Your Troubles in Your Old Kit Bag*"
Words by George Asaf (a.k.a. G. Powell),
  music by F. Powell
London: Chappell & Co.
1915

"*Roses of Picardy*"
J. McCormack
Words by F.E. Weatherley, music by
  H. Wood, c. 1916
1919

"*Shirts*"
Written by P. Braham, I. Novello, et al.

"*Sure a Little Bit of Heaven*"
Written by S. Graham
1914

"*Take Me Back to Dear Old Blighty*"
Florrie Forde
Written by A.J. Mills, F. Godfrey, and
  B. Scott, c. 1916
1917

"There's a Long, Long Trail A-Winding"
Words by S. King, music by A. Elliott
1915

"365 Days"
Leslie Henson and David Burnaby
Words by Clifford Grey, music by Jerome
   Kern

"Where Did That One Go?"
Lee White
Written by R.P. Weston, C. Smith, and
   B. Lee
c. unknown

Appendix I

Important British Music-Hall Revues

Revue
Main Composers
Venue
Year

Around the Map
H. Finck and C.M.S. McLellan
New Amsterdam Theatre
1915

The Bing Boys Are Here
Words by C. Grey, music by N. Ayer,
P. Braham, I. Novello, et al.
London: The Alhambra
1916

Cheep
Written by R.P. Weston, C. Smith, and B.
  Lee
London: Vaudeville Theatre
1917

Chu Chin Chow
Written by O. Asche, music by F. Norton
London: His Majesty's Theatre
1916

See-Saw
A. Charlot
London: Comedy Theatre
1916

Yes, Uncle,
Written by N. Ayre and C. Grey
London: The Prince of Wales Theatre,
1917

Zig Zag
Words by G. Buck, music by D. Stamper
London: The Hippodrome
1917

Notes

Notes to Chapter I

1 R. O'Connell, *Of Arms and Men* (Oxford: Oxford University Press, 1989), pp. 242, 246; A.F. Duguid, *Official History of the Canadian Forces in the Great War, 1914–1919*, Vol. I (Ottawa: J.O. Patenaude, 1938), pp. 135–36; T. Cook, *No Place to Run: The Canadian Corps and Gas Warfare in the First World War* (Vancouver; Toronto: UBC Press, 1999), p. 12.

2 Cook, *No Place to Run*, p. 6.

3 Norman "Nobby" Clarke was in attendance for the Dumbells' Farewell Concert at Lambert Lodge in 1975. See CBC, "The Dumbells Farewell Concert"; J.W. McLaren, "Mirth and Mud Part Three: In Which the Curtain Is Rung Down on the 'Comic Relief' of the Greatest Drama in History," *Maclean's* (15 May 1929), p. 76.

4 P. Earle, as told by Al Plunkett, *Al Plunkett: The Famous Dumbell* (New York: Pageant Press, 1956), p. 49.

5 Stanley Morrison of the PPCLI Comedy Company lost a leg in the war, a wound that claimed his life a few years later in Montreal. See McLaren, "Mirth and Mud Part Three," p. 76.

6 J.W. McLaren, "Mirth and Mud: The Chronicle of the First Organized Canadian Concert Party to Tour the Trenches during the Great War," *Maclean's* (1 January 1929), p. 14.

7 P. Hawkins, *Chanson: The French Singer-Songwriter from Aristide Bruant to the Present Day* (Aldershot: Ashgate, 2000), p. 11; T. Cook, "The Singing War: Canadian Soldiers' Songs of the Great War," *American Review of Canadian Studies*, 39, 3 (September 2009), p. 224.

8 Hayes' edited work on Vimy remains the standard in Canadian history. See G. Hayes, A. Iarocci, and M. Bechthold (eds.), *Vimy Ridge: A Canadian Reassessment* (Waterloo: Wilfrid Laurier University Press, 2007). Ted Barris's work on Vimy is a vital weapon in the arsenal of the Canadian historian studying the war. See T. Barris, *Victory at Vimy, Canada Comes of Age: April 9–12, 1917* (Toronto: Thomas Allen Publishers, 2007). Some of the best examples from Tim Cook's prolific output include T. Cook, *Shock Troops: Canadian Fighting the Great War, 1917–1918*, Vol. II (Toronto: Viking, 2008); T. Cook, *At the Sharp End: Canadians Fighting the Great War, 1914–1916*, Vol. I (Toronto: Viking, 2007).

Notes to Chapter II

1   F. Cosentino, *The Renfrew Millionaires: The Valley Boys of Winter 1910* (Burnstown, 1990), p. 11; M. Moss, *Manliness and Militarism: Educating Young Boys in Ontario for War* (Toronto, 2001), pp. 23–25.

2   A. Saddlemyer, "Introduction," A. Saddlemyer (ed.), *Early Stages: Theatre in Ontario 1800–1914* (Toronto: Ontario Historical Studies Series for the Government of Ontario, University of Toronto Press, 1990), p. 10.

3   For a superb review of the development of music halls in Britain, see P. Bailey, *Leisure and Class in Victorian England: Rational Recreation and the Contest for Control, 1830–1885* (London: Routledge and Keegan Paul, 1978), pp. 147–68.

4   P. Bailey, "Conspiracies of Meaning: Music-Hall and the Knowingness of Popular Culture," *Past and Present*, 144 (1994), pp. 138–70.

5   G. Lenton-Young, "Variety Theatre," A. Saddlemyer (ed.), *Early Stages: Theatre in Ontario 1800–1914* (Toronto: Ontario Historical Studies Series for the Government of Ontario, University of Toronto Press, 1990), p. 204.

6   Ibid., p. 166.

7   J.W. McLaren, *Dumbells: Arts and Letters Meeting P.P.L.L.I.S.* (Toronto: unknown, from the private collection of John McLaren).

8   Ibid.

9   Rice's character/song "Jim Crowe" gave its name to the infamous segregation laws of the American South. See K.S. Frost, *I've Got a Home in Glory Land: A Lost Tale of the Underground Railroad* (Toronto: Thomas Allen Publishers, 2007), pp. 87–88.

10 R. Davies, "The Nineteenth-Century Repertoire," A. Saddlemyer (ed.), *Early Stages: Theatre in Ontario 1800–1914* (Toronto: Ontario Historical Studies Series for the Government of Ontario, University of Toronto Press, 1990), p. 114.

11 N. LeVasseur, "Musique et musiciens à Québec," *La Musique*, 2 (August 1920).

12 Tommy was popular singer/songwriter and music agent Billy O'Connor's father, see A. Barriss and T. Barriss, *Making Music: Profiles from a Century of Canadian Music* (Toronto: HarperCollins Publishers, 2001).

13 For further discussion, see R.C. Toll, *Blacking Up: The Minstrel Show in Nineteenth-Century America* (New York: Oxford University Press, 1974).

14 CBC, "The Dumbells Farewell Concert at Lambert Lodge"; see also Lenton-Young, "Variety Theatre," p. 184.

15 J. Brophy and E. Partridge, *The Long Trail: What the British Soldier Sang and Said in the Great War of 1914–18* (London: Andre Deutsch, 1965), p. 213.

16 Brophy and Partridge, *The Long Trail*, p. 213.

17 Although the United States do not sign it, the principal international agreement on copyright, also known as the Berne Convention, was signed in 1886. Further changes in copyright law came in 1891 that made it impossible for companies to publish foreign music without payment to the composer or original publisher. For further discussion, see D. Laing, "Berne Convention," as found in J. Shepherd, D. Laing, and D. Horn (eds.), *Continuum Encyclopedia of Popular Music of the World*, five vols. (London: Continuum, 2003), pp. 480–81; D. Horn and D. Sanjek, "Sheet Music," as found in J. Shepherd, D. Laing and D. Horn (eds.), *Continuum Encyclopedia of Popular Music of the World*, five vols. (London: Continuum, 2003), pp. 599–605. For a discussion on how the copyright laws affected Canadian sheet music sales, see P.B. O'Neill, "The Impact of Copyright Legislation upon the Publication of Sheet Music in Canada, Prior to 1924," *Journal of Canadian Studies*, 28, 3 (Fall 1993).

18 J. Shepherd, *Continuum Encyclopedia of Popular Music of the World*, Vol. I: Media, Industry and Society (London: Continuum, 2003), p. 603.

19 For further discussion, see T.E. Scheurer, *American Popular Music: The Nineteenth Century and Tin Pan Alley*, Vol. I (Bowling Green State University, Popular Press, 1989).

20 R. Sanjek, *From Print to Plastic: Publishing and Promoting America's Popular Music (1900–1980)* (Brooklyn: Institute for Studies in American Music, 1983), p. 8; R. Sanjek and D. Sanjek, *American Popular Music Business in the 20th Century* (New York: Oxford University Press, 1991), p. 16.

21 It was also sung by Canadian Henry Burr. R.A. Whiting and R.B. Egan, "Till We Meet Again" (Jerome H. Remick & Co., 1918); Shepherd, *Continuum Encyclopedia of Popular Music of the World*, p. 603.

22 "Geoffrey O'Hara," encyclopaedia entry, as found in H. Kallmann (ed.), *Encyclopedia of Music in Canada*, 2nd ed. (Toronto: University of Toronto Press, 1992); G. O'Hara, "Ontario to Tin Pan Alley," *Maclean's* (1 April 1921), pp. 24, 36–37.

23 By his own calculation, Burr believed that he had recorded some 12,000 songs under his own name and pseudonyms, see "Henry Burr," encyclopaedia entry, as found in H. Kallmann (ed.), *Encyclopedia of Music in Canada*, 2nd ed. (Toronto: University of Toronto Press, 1992)

24 A. Bryan, "I Didn't Raise My Boy to Be a Soldier," Words by A. Bryan, Music by A. Piantadosi (New York: Leo Feist, 1915).

25 Bryan also co-wrote "Come, Josephine, in My Flying Machine" with Fred Fisher. For further discussion, see E.B. Moogk, *Roll Back the Years: History of Canadian Recorded Sound and Its Legacy: Genesis to 1930* (Ottawa: National Library of Canada, 1975).

26 Ibid., 36–38.

27 During one speech, Lauder addressed a crowd of over 100,000 standing outside Wall Street's Sub-Treasury Office. He also penned a song especially for American troops entitled "Marching with the President," which was widely sung across the United States. Sir Harry Lauder, *Roamin' in the Gloamin'* (London: Hutchinson and Co., 1928), 199. Wallace, *Harry Lauder in the Limelight* (Sussex: The Guild, 1988), 50.

28 Ibid.

29 Ibid., pp. 77, 108–9.

30 Lauder wrote "The End of the Road" to commemorate his son. The song was specifically inspired by Captain Lauder's last words: "carry on." H. Lauder, "The End of the Road," words and music by William Dillon and Harry Lauder, *Scotland's Stars on 78 Presents Sir Harry Lauder* (Glasgow: Lismor Recordings, [1926] 1994).

31 For one radio broadcast in 1929, Lauder pocketed $15,000 for singing only three songs. His was a meteoric rise; from working in the flax mills, where he had earned 2/1d a week, Lauder would one day command $3,000 a week during his many performance tours. A. Green, liner notes from *Sir Harry Lauder Favourites, 1926–1928* (Montreal: RCA Victor Immortal Performances, c. unknown).

32 Beginning in 1907, Lauder toured the USA a remarkable twenty two times over the course of forty years. Green, liner notes from, *Sir Harry Lauder Favourites*; H. Lauder, *Scotland's Stars on 78 Presents Sir Harry Lauder*, liner notes by Frank Wappat (Glasgow: Lismor Recordings, 1994).

33 D. Baker and L.F. Kiner, *The Sir Harry Lauder Discography* (Metuchen, NJ, and London: Scarecrow Press, 1990).

34 K.S. Frost, *I've Got a Home in Glory Land: A Lost Tale of the Underground Railroad* (Toronto: Thomas Allen Publishers, 2007), pp. 87–88.

35 P. Maloney, *Scotland and the Music Hall, 1850–1914* (Manchester: Manchester University Press, 2003), p. 159.

36 D. Goldie, "Hugh MacDiarmid, Harry Lauder and Scottish Popular Culture," *International Journal of Scottish Literature*, 1 (Autumn 2006), p. 10.

37 H.V. Morton, *In Search of Scotland* (London: Methuen and Company, 1929), pp. 155–56; Goldie, "Hugh MacDiarmid, Harry Lauder and Scottish Popular Culture," p. 12.

38 J.G. Fuller, *Troop Morale and Popular Culture in the British and Dominion Armies, 1914–18* (Oxford: Oxford University Press, 1990), p. 125; Lauder, *A Minstrel in France*, 19–21; F. Wappat, liner notes for, Sir Harry Lauder, "Waggle o' the Kilt," *Scotland's Stars on 78 Presents Sir Harry Lauder* (Glasgow: Lismor Recordings, 1994).

39 Davies, "The Nineteenth-Century Repertoire," p. 160.

40 Brophy and Partridge, *The Long Trail*, p. 215.

41 M. Bell, "Amusing the Canadian Soldier in Old London," *Maclean's* (1 October 1916), p. 32.

42 Ibid.

43 Ibid., p. 33.

44 Ibid., p. 34.

45 Jack Ayre, from, CBC, *Canadian Theatre Fact and Fancy with Grace Lydiatt Shaw: Parts 4 and 5* (Toronto: 1964, National Archives of Canada, ISN 60431, Shelf no. C09285{1}).

46 The First World War was often referred to as the "Singing War." McLaren, *Dumbells: Arts and Letters Meeting P.P.L.L.I.S.*

47 Cook, "The Singing War: Canadian Soldiers," p. 232.

48 "There's a Long, Long Trail A-Winding," words by S. King, music by A. Elliott, c. 1915. www.firstworldwar.com.

49 H. Burr, "The Rose of No Man's Land," words by J. Caddigan, music by J. Brennan, c. 1916 (Montreal: Berliner Gram-O-Phone, Issue No. 216039, December 1918).

50 J. McCormack, "Roses of Picardy," words by F.E. Weatherley, music by H. Wood, c. 1916 (1919). www.firstworldwar.com.

51 Al Plunkett as quoted in Earle, *Al Plunkett: The Famous Dumbell*, p. 50.

52 Wilfred Glenn, bass with orchestra, "Asleep in the Deep," written by Arthur J. Lamb and Henry W. Petrie (Camden, NJ: Victor Talking Machine Co. 20244-A, 1913); J. Rodgers, "Asleep in the Deep," written by Arthur J. Lamb and Henry W. Petrie (New York: F.A. Mills, 721 Seventh Ave., 1897).

53 Columbia Stellar Quartet, "Keep the Home Fires Burning (Till the Boys Come Home)," words by L. Ford, music by I. Novello (Columbia: Columbia Record 6028, 1918).

54 Brophy and Partridge, *The Long Trail*, p. 20.

55 R. Newman, "My Old Dutch," words by A. Chevalier, music by C. Ingle, c. 1892. (Montreal: Berliner Gram-O-Phone, Issue 216398, May 1923).

56 "Pack Up Your Troubles in Your Old Kit Bag," words by George Asaf (a.k.a. G. Powell), music by F. Powell (London: Chappell & Co., 1915). www.firstworldwar.com.

57 F. Kreisler, "Lily of Killarney," a.k.a. "The Moon Hath Raised Her Lamp Above," written by Sir J. Benedict (London: Matrix, B 14693-1 Victor Cat. 64440, April 1914). www.firstworldwar.com.

58 Tennent was also in charge of packing the company's truck. See CBC, "The Dumbells Press Conference."

59 F. Forde, "Take Me Back to Dear Old Blighty," written by A.J. Mills, F. Godfrey, and B. Scott, c. 1916 (1917). www.firstworldwar.com.

60 The Field Service Post Card, Form A 2042, also known as the "Quick Firer." See N. Ferguson, *The Pity of War: Explaining World War I* (New York: Basic Books, {1998} 1999), p. 351.

61 DCM – Distinguished Conduct Medal; CB – Confined to Barracks.

62 J. McLaren, "The Field Postcard," words by R. Roberts, music by H. Montague, CBC, *Old Sweats and Dumbells* (Toronto: 11 November, 1961 {1916}).

63 See L. MacDonald, "Foreword" in R. Palmer, *"What a Lovely War!": British Soldiers' Songs from the Boer War to the Present Day* (London: Penguin, 1990), pp. 1, 12.

64 Brophy and Partridge, *The Long Trail*, p. 213.

65 F.T. Nettleingham quoted in Palmer, *"What a Lovely War!"* p. 12.

66 "I'll Make a Man of You," a.k.a. "On Sunday I Walk Out with a Soldier," words by A. Wimperis, music by Herman Finck. See McLaren, *Dumbells: Arts and Letters Meeting P.P.L.L.I.S..*

67 *Oh! What a Lovely War* (Paramount Pictures: 1969).

68 A. Lester, "Conscientious Objector," H. Finck and C.M.S. McLellan, *Around the Map* (New Amsterdam Theatre, 1915).

69 McLaren, *Dumbells: Arts and Letters Meeting P.P.L.L.I.S.*

70 CBC, *Old Sweats and Dumbells.*

71 W. Bird, *The Communication Trench* (Ottawa: CEF Books, 2000), pp. 49–50; Cook, "The Singing War: Canadian Soldiers," pp. 232–33.

72 C.H. Savage, "Memoir," c. 1936, as found in *The Canadian Letters and Images Project* (Nanaimo; London; Vancouver Island University; University of Western Ontario, 2003). www.canadianletters.ca.

73 Cook, "The Singing War: Canadian Soldiers," p. 232.

74 Philip Gibbs was awarded a knighthood for his work during the war. See Fussel, *The Great War and Modern Memory*, p. 201.

75 A. Bridle, "Music and Mars," *Maclean's* (15 December 1915), p. 22.

76 J.B. Priestley in Palmer, *"What a Lovely War!"* p. 15.

77 M. Manley, "Good Luck to the Boys of the Allies," written by Morris Manley (Toronto: Morris Manley, 1915).

78 Fuller, *Troop Morale and Popular Culture*, p. 103.

79 Cook, "The Singing War: Canadian Soldiers," p. 237.

80 J.A. Napier, "Letter to Ruthie," 26 September 1915, as found in *The Canadian Letters and Images Project* (Nanaimo; London; Vancouver Island University; University of Western Ontario, 2003), www.canadianletters.ca; Cook, "The Singing War: Canadian Soldiers," p. 237.

81 D. Hoerder, "Ethnic Studies in Canada from the 1880s to 1962: A Historiographical Perspective and Critique," *Canadian Ethnic Studies*, 26, 1 (1994), pp. 1–18; S. Leacock, "Canada and the Immigration Problem," *National and English Review* (April 1911).

82 This recommendation materialized out of the findings of, J.A. Chapleau and J.H. Gray, *Report of the Royal Commission on Chinese Immigration: Report and Evidence* (Ottawa: Printed by Order of the Commission, 1885).

83 For further discussion on the Asian-Canadian experience see P.E. Roy, "Educating the East: British Columbia and the Oriental Question in the Inter-War Years," *B.C. Studies*, 18 (1973), pp. 50–69; P.E. Roy, *The Oriental Question: Consolidating a White Man's Province, 1914–1941* (Vancouver: UBC Press, 2003); W.P. Ward, *White Canada Forever: Popular Attitudes and Public Policy towards Orientals in British Columbia* (Montreal: McGill-Queen's University Press, 1978); J. Morton, *In the Sea of Sterile Mountains: The* Chinese in British Columbia (Vancouver: J.J. Douglas, 1974); M.E. Hallett, "A Governor General's View on Oriental Immigration to B.C.: 1904–1914," *B.C. Studies*, 14 (1972), pp. 51–74; Z. Chen, "Chinese Minority and Everyday Racism in Canadian Towns and Small Cities: An Ethnic Study of the Case of Peterborough, Ontario, 1892–1951," *Canadian Ethnic Studies*, 36, 1 (2004), pp. 71–91.

84 James W. St.G. Walker, *"Race," Rights and the Law in the Supreme Court of Canada: Historical Case Studies* (Waterloo: Osgoode Society for Canadian Legal History and Wilfrid Laurier University Press, 1997).

85 Ibid., pp. 1–26.

86 Ibid., p. 1.

87 General Willoughby Gwatkin, "Memorandum on the Enlistment of Negroes in Canadian Expeditionary Force," 13 April 1916 (Ottawa: National Archives of Canada, RG 24, vol. 1206, file 297-1-21).

88 Walker, "Race and Recruitment in World War I," pp. 1–26; D. Read, "Jane Walters Interview," *The Great War and Canadian Society: An Oral History* (Toronto: New Hogtown Press, 1978), p. 147.

89 A sad example was evidenced in the pervasive anti-Semitic sentiment among Canada's official policy makers and bureaucrats. Comparatively tiny countries like Bolivia and Chile managed to rescue some 20,000 Jews, while by war's end Canada rescued only 4,000 to 5,000 fleeing refugees. With this in mind, it is perhaps less shocking to learn that Hitler's pre-war government looked to Canada for its selective immigration policy. See I. Abella and H. Troper, *None Is Too Many: Canada and the Jews of Europe, 1933–1948* (New York: Random House, 1983).

90 Dumbells Programme, "The Dumbells: Third Canadian Divisional Concert Party, France, Under the Patronage of Maj. Gen. L.J. Lipsett C.M.G." (France: 1917).

91 B. McNeil, *Dumbells Reunion* (National Archives of Canada: 1975), ISN 177078, Shelf no. C10896{1}).

92 For further discussion see P. Roy, *The Chinese in Canada* (Ottawa: Canadian Historical Association, 1985), p. 15; C.F. Lee, "The Road to Enfranchisement: Chinese and Japanese in British Columbia," *BC Studies*, 30 (1976), pp. 57–58; E. Wickberg, *From China to Canada: A History of the Chinese Community in Canada* (Toronto: McClelland and Stewart in association with the Multiculturalism Directorate, Department of the Secretary of State and the Canadian Govt. Pub. Centre, Supply and Services Canada, 1982), p. 200; Walker, "Race and Recruitment in World War I," pp. 1–26.

93 Another Immigration Act introduced in 1923 banned entry of Chinese workers into Canada entirely and lasted for two years. See Roy, *The Oriental Question*.

94 *Chu Chin Chow*, written by O. Asche, music by F. Norton (London: His Majesty's Theatre, 1916).

95 B. Jones and B. Howell, *Popular Arts of the First World War* (London: Studio Vista Blue Star House, 1972), p. 130.

96 F.C. Cousins, "Letter to Mother," 9 March 1918, as found in *The Canadian Letters and Images Project* (Nanaimo; London; Vancouver Island University; University of Western Ontario, 2003). www.canadianletters.ca.

97 Dumbells Programme, *The "Dumbell" Concert Party: Assisted by No. 7 Convalescent Depot Orchestra*, Canadian Red Cross Recreation Hut, No. 3 Canadian General Hospital, Monday 29 July 1918.

98 *The Bing Boys Are Here*, words by C. Grey, music by N. Ayer, P. Braham, I. Novello, et al. (London: The Alhambra, 1916).

99 Cook, "The Singing War: Canadian Soldiers," p. 227.

100 J. McLaren, "The Clock Song," words by C. Grey, music by N. Ayer, originally from *The Bing Boys Are Here*. See McLaren, *Dumbells: Arts and Letters Meeting P.P.L.L.I.S.*

101 A. Plunkett, "Everybody Slips a Little (Now and Then)," written by D. Meher and R.B. Saxe, as performed in the Dumbell revue, *Let'er Go* (Montreal: Berliner Gram-O-Phone, Issue No. 216455, 1924).

102 *Yes, Uncle*, written by N. Ayre and C. Grey (London: Prince of Wales Theatre, 1917).

103 "Hello My Dearie," words by G. Buck, music by D. Stamper, from *Zig Zag* (London: Hippodrome, 1917).

104 Tate's "Motoring Sketch," where two would-be motorists are unable to get started, was extremely popular with both civilian and soldier audiences. Fuller, *Troop Morale and Popular Culture*, p. 123.
105 Brophy and Partridge, *The Long Trail*, p. 219.
106 The Dumbells first show was on 17 August 1917 at Goyeux Servans. CBC, "Interview with Jack Ayre," *Grace Lydiatt Shaw* (Toronto: 14 December 1961, National Archives of Canada, ISN 61338, Shelf no. A19907-0003}).
107 Palmer, *"What a Lovely War!"* p. 14.
108 National Library of Canada, Biography of Al Plunkett, *The Virtual Gramophone: Canadian Historical Sound Recording*. www2.nlc-bnc.ca/gramophone/src/plunketae.htm.
109 Brophy and Partridge, *The Long Trail*, pp. 218–19. "Texas Way" should not be confused with "Texas," another popular American marching song during the war.
110 It is Alicia's version that still survives as Scotland's most famous love song. J.J. Wilson, "Anatomy of a Scottish Woman's Ballad" (Guelph, 2002), pp. 4–8.
111 F.T. Nettleingham, Tommy's Tunes (London: Erskine, MacDonald, 1917); Palmer, *"What a Lovely War!"* p. 12.
112 CBC, "Interview with Ivor Jack Ayre," *In Flanders Fields* (Toronto: 17 May 1963, National Archives of Canada, ISN 117350, Shelf no. C07853{2}).

Notes to Chapter III

1 A. Kellett, *Combat Motivation: The Behaviour of Soldiers in Battle* (Hingham: Kluwer Boston, 1982), p. 3.
2 Ibid., p. 5.
3 Ibid., p. xiii.
4 E.N. Gladden, *Ypres, 1917: A Personal Account* (London: Kimber, 1967), p. 154; J.G. Fuller, *Troop Morale and Popular Culture in the British and Dominion Armies 1914–1918* (Oxford: Clarendon Press, 1990), p. 102.
5 W.H.A. Groom, *Poor Bloody Infantry: A memoir of the First World War* (London: Kimber, 1976), p. 63; Fuller, *Troop Morale and Popular Culture*, p. 108.
6 C.M.W. Moran, *The Anatomy of Courage* (London: Constable, 1945), p. 190; Fuller, *Troop Morale and Popular Culture*, p. 144.
7 For a discussion on American troops and humour in the Second World War, see S.A. Stouffer et al. (ed.), *The American Soldier* (Princeton: Princeton University Press, 1949), p. 190; Fuller, *Troop Morale and Popular Culture*, p. 144.
8 E. MacCallum-Stewart (ed.), *The First World War and Comedy*, University of Sussex. http://www.whatalovelywar.co.uk/.
9 E. Blunden, "Concert Party: Busseboum," as found in P. Fussel, *The Great War and Modern Memory* (London: Oxford University Press, 1975), p. 200.
10 R.F.L. Sheldon-Williams, *The Canadian Front in France and Flanders* (London: A. and C. Black, 1920), pp. 189–91.
11 *Overseas Military Force in Canada 1918*, Report of the Ministry (London: Printed by Authority of the Ministry Overseas Military Forces of Canada, Queen's Printer, {1918} 1919), p. 499.
12 P.B. O'Neill, "The Canadian Concert Party in France," *Theatre History in Canada*, 5 (Fall 1983), p. 193.
13 Ibid., p. 193; C. Bishop, *The Y.M.C.A. in the Great War* (Toronto: 1921), p. 150.
14 The concentration of men gathered at one of Lauder's front-line concerts caught the eye of a passing German plane, which subsequently drew enemy fire from the other side of no man's land. H. Lauder, *Roamin' in the Gloamin'* (London: Hutchinson and Co., 1928), p. 194.

15 H. Lauder, *A Minstrel in France* (Toronto: McClelland Goodchild and Stewart, 1918), pp. 111–12.

16 Ibid., 301.

17 Ibid., 210.

18 O'Neill, "The Canadian Concert Party in France," p. 197.

19 Cook, "The Singing War," p. 224.

20 J.J. Wilson, "Interview with Bob Plunkett' (Toronto, December 2001).

21 Cook, "The Singing War," p. 225.

22 McLaren, "Mirth and Mud: The Chronicle," p. 14.

23 J.A. McArthur, "Letter to Hazel," 9 November 1916, as found in *The Canadian Letters and Images Project* (Nanaimo; London; Vancouver Island University; University of Western Ontario, 2003). www.canadianletters.ca.

24 The Follies were the first concert party of the BEF. Fuller, *Troop Morale and Popular Culture*, p. 186.

25 Al Plunkett as quoted in Earle, *Al Plunkett: The Famous Dumbell*, pp. 53–55.

26 A. Russell, *With the Machine Gun Corps* (London: 1923), p.135; MacCallum-Stewart (ed.), *The First World War and Comedy*.

27 MacCallum-Stewart (ed.), *The First World War and Comedy*.

28 For a further discussion on the Gaities (Leslie Henson, Tolly Brightman, Rob Currie and the female impersonator Bert Errol), see L. Henson, "My Concert Party at the Front— How the 'Gaieties' Cheered the Troops," MacCallum-Stewart (ed.), *The First World War and Comedy*.

29 Fuller, *Troop Morale and Popular Culture*, p. 96; "The Story of The Dumbells, The Famous Concert Party of Third Canadian Division," newspaper clipping (St. John, 26 April 1919, from Ivor Jack Ayre's Dumbell Collection at the Metro Toronto Reference Library).

30 Fuller offered a list of Divisional, Brigade, and Battalion concert parties for the British and Dominion Armies in his work troop morale. Listed are approximately 60 "official" British concert parties, including those from various Scottish, Irish, and Welsh regiments. O'Neill estimates there were somewhere between 30 and 40 concert parties in the Canadian Corps, which is consistent with the estimations of various Dumbell performers. See Fuller, *Troop Morale and Popular Culture*, pp. 181–93; O'Neill, "The Canadian Concert Party in France," p. 195.

31 Al Plunkett as quoted in Earle, *Al Plunkett: The Famous Dumbell*, pp. 53–55.

32 J.D. McLaren, *The Life Story of John Wilson McLaren, 1895–1988* (Toronto: McLaren Press Graphics, c. 2006), p. 15.

33 CBC, "Interview with Sergeant John (Jack) McLaren," *In Flanders Fields* (Toronto, March/ April 1964, National Archives of Canada, Tapes R7728 and R7729).

34 McLaren, *The Life Story of John Wilson McLaren*, p. 15.

35 CBC, "Interview with Sergeant John (Jack) McLaren," *In Flanders Fields*. It is, of course, possible that McLaren may never been attested during his first round of soldiering, which would explain why he never had to explain his hiatus.

36 V. Chertkov, L. Tolstoy, and J. Mavor, *Christian Martyrdom in Russia: An Account of the Members of the Universal Brotherhood or Doukhobortsi, now migrating from the Caucasus to Canada* (Toronto: G.N. Morang, 1899). See also D.A. Signori, *Guide to the Papers of James Mavor* (Toronto: Thomas Fisher Rare Book Library, 1989).

37 McLaren, *The Life Story of John Wilson McLaren*, pp. 14–15.

38 S. Gwyn, *Tapestry of War: A Private View of Canadians in The Great War* (Toronto: Harper Collins Publishers, 1992).

39 Ibid., p. 85.

40 The PPCLI arrived at Bustard Camp on Salisbury Plain on 18 October 1914 as the 80th Brigade of the 27th Division of the British Army. On 8 November 1915, the PPCLI left the British Army and joined the Canadian forces in the 7th Canadian Infantry Brigade. For further discussion on the regiment's history see J. Williams, *First in the Field: Gault of the Patricias* (St. Catharines: Vanwell Publishing, 1995); J. Williams, *Princess Patricia's Canadian Light Infantry* (London: Leo Cooper, 1972); R.W. Hodder-Williams, *Princess Patricia's Canadian Light Infantry, 1914–1919* (London: Hodder and Stoughton, 1923); Sheldon-Williams, *The Canadian Front in France and Flanders*.

41 McLaren, *The Life Story of John Wilson McLaren*, p. 17.

42 Mavor wrote Adamson to let him know that McLaren had had some experience in theatre and that he was a painter. J.W. McLaren, "Jack McLaren, O.S.A., ex-Dumbell," Four Page Overview of His Life (Toronto: unpublished, c. 1927), pp. 2–3; McLaren, *The Life Story of John Wilson McLaren*, p. 17.

43 CBC, "Interview with Sergeant John (Jack) McLaren," *In Flanders Fields*; McLaren, *The Life Story of John Wilson McLaren*, p. 17.

44 CBC, "Interview with Sergeant John (Jack) McLaren," *In Flanders Fields*.

45 McLaren, *The Life Story of John Wilson McLaren*, p. 17.

46 See Capt. F.R. McGuire, "The Great War Concert Parties," *The Sentinel* (April 1967, from Ivor Jack Ayre's Dumbell Collection at the Metro Toronto Reference Library).

47 See McLaren, "Mirth and Mud: The Chronicle," p. 15.

48 Hodder-Williams, *Princess Patricia's Canadian Light Infantry: 1914–1919*, p. 140.

49 CBC, "The Dumbells Farewell Concert at Lambert Lodge," *Between Ourselves*, with Bill McNeil (Toronto: 3 May 1975, National Archives of Canada, ISN 177084, Shelf no. C10900{1}); The hands-on organization of the PPCLI Comedy Company was left to Captain H.E. Pembroke, the company's paymaster.

50 CBC, "Interview with Alan Murray," *Grace Lydiatt Shaw*; The two most famous Canadian concert parties often took in each other's performances whenever possible, see CBC, "Interview with Jack Ayre," *Grace Lydiatt Shaw*.

51 O'Neill, "The Canadian Concert Party in France," p. 196.

52 CBC, "Interview with Conrad Stephens," *Grace Lydiatt Shaw* (Toronto, 1962, National Archives of Canada, ISN 61306, Shelf no. C09407).

53 McLaren confessed that he was not as much disapproving of Clarke as he was impressed with the 9th Field Ambulance's virtuoso Leonard Young. Clarke, as McLaren described, "was an excellent pianist, but was lacking the flair, the necessary theatrical embroidery and flourish to theatricalize his renditions, to accompany a review show such as ours." See CBC, "Interview with Sergeant John (Jack) McLaren," *In Flanders Fields*; McLaren, *The Life Story of John Wilson McLaren*, p. 21.

54 McLaren, *The Life Story of John Wilson McLaren*, p. 21.

55 Ibid., p. 25.

56 Ibid., pp. 14–15.

57 CBC, "Interview with Sergeant John (Jack) McLaren," *In Flanders Fields*.

58 The date McLaren offered for the PPCLI CC's first performance was 28 May 1916, which predates the official date given for the Steenvoorde concert by a couple of weeks. See ibid.

59 McLaren, *The Life Story of John Wilson McLaren*, p. 21.

60 McLaren, "Mirth and Mud: The Chronicle," p. 47.

61 Hodder-Williams, *Princess Patricia's Canadian Light Infantry*, p. 140.

62 J. McLaren as told to S. Franklin, "A Funny Thing Happened on the Way to the Trenches," *Weekend Magazine* (Toronto, 25 November, 1967, No. 47), p. 28.

63 McLaren, *The Life Story of John Wilson McLaren*, p. 25.

64 Ibid., p. 25.

65   Ibid., p. 25.

66   Trench duty, as McLaren illustrated, most often consisted of three of four trips to the front lines, lasting approximately six weeks. CBC, "Interview with Sergeant John (Jack) McLaren," *In Flanders Fields*.

67   Ibid.

68   In the Kinmel Park Camp Riots of 1919, approximately 1,000 Canadian soldiers were involved in a riot in Bodelwyddan in northeast Wales. The soldiers, mostly from the Forestry Troops and Railway Corpsmen who had not seen actual combat, had been suffering poor conditions in the Welsh camp and their passage home was being continuously postponed in favour of combat soldiers. Some of the rioters looted the local YMCA and the Navy and Army Canteen Board, who had raised the price of goods while soldiers were desperately waiting to go home. Interestingly, the rioters chose to spare the Salvation Army. In the end, five Canadians were killed and another 28 wounded in the riot and related skirmishes. For further discussion on the riot see J. Putkowski, *The Kinmel Park Camp Riots 1919* (England: Flintshire Historical Society, 1989); D. Morton, Desmond, "Kicking and Complaining: Demobilization Riots in the Canadian Expeditionary Force, 1918–1919," *Canadian Historical Review*, 61, 3 (September 1980). For a firsthand account, see M. Acheson, "Facts about Kinmel Park Made Public," *Calgary Daily Herald* (17 June 1919).

69   *Overseas Military Force in Canada 1918*, pp. 498–99.

70   Ibid., p. 497.

71   Ibid., pp. 502–3.

72   Annie O'Brien, as quoted in J.J. Wilson, "Interviews with Annie O'Brien" (Toronto: December 2001; December 2008; 11 March 2010).

73   Merton Plunkett as quoted in F. Claridge, "YMCA's Aid to Dumbells Recalled by Plunkett," *Globe and Mail* (Toronto, 13 June 1956), p. 8.

74   Plunkett later organized amateur shows for the 35th Battalion at Bramshott Camp in England. F. Claridge, "YMCA's Aid to Dumbells Recalled by Plunkett," *Globe and Mail* (13 June 1956).

75   Al Plunkett as quoted in Earle, *Al Plunkett: The Famous Dumbell*, pp. 53–55.

76   By example, Captain Plunkett discovered Dumbells' pianist Jack Ayre this way and had him transferred from the 116th Battalion to the YMCA. See CBC, "Interview with Ivor Jack Ayre," *In Flanders Fields*.

77   Earle, *Al Plunkett: The Famous Dumbell*, p. 50.

78   O'Neill, "The Canadian Concert Party in France," p. 197.

79   CBC, "Interview with William Redpath," *Grace Lydiatt Shaw* (Toronto, 1962, National Archives of Canada, ISN 61324, Shelf no. C09407{6}).

80   CBC, "The Dumbells Press Conference," *Fresh Air*, with Bill McNeil, interview includes Jack Ayre, Jerry Brayford, Jack McLaren, and William Redpath (1 May 1975).

81   M. Plunkett, quoted in R. Allen, "Famed Hoofers and Players of 1917 May Answer Canada's 'Fall In,'" *Globe and Mail* (19 October 1939), cover page.

82   The tins were so named after the manufacturer of the stew. See CBC, *Camera Canada: The Dumbells with Affection* (Toronto: 1965, Tape No. B-07510).

83   McLaren, "Mirth and Mud: The Chronicle," p. 15; McLaren, "Mirth and Mud Part Two: Orphans Are Orphans," p. 16.

84   McLaren, *The Life Story of John Wilson McLaren*, p. 31.

85   Ibid., pp. 25–27.

86   Ibid., pp. 25–26.

87   It was at Warloy that Jack McLaren believed the PPCLI Comedy Company had done their "best work." McLaren, "Mirth and Mud Part Two: Orphans Are Orphans," p. 16.

88 Ibid.

89 McLaren, *The Life Story of John Wilson McLaren*, p. 27.

90 Hodder-Williams, *Princess Patricia's Canadian Light Infantry*, p. 140.

91 C.D. Richardson, "Letter to Mother," 31 December 1916, as found in *The Canadian Letters and Images Project* (Nanaimo; London; Vancouver Island University; University of Western Ontario, 2003). www.canadianletters.ca.

92 McLaren, *The Life Story of John Wilson McLaren*, p. 29.

93 Captain M. Plunkett, "We'll Make 'Em Laugh Again," *Toronto Star* (Toronto: 13 January 1940), section cover page.

94 O'Neill, "The Canadian Concert Party in France," p. 197.

95 Ibid., p. 198.

96 Earle, *Al Plunkett*, p. 55. It was the Maple Leaf on the 4th Division patch that inspired that division's concert party name. Similarly, a "C" with two strokes through it gave the Canadian 2nd Division their C2s. See CBC, "Interview with Ivor Jack Ayre," *In Flanders Fields*; Murray, "The Dumbells: Nostalgic Memories of World War I's Great Soldier Entertainers," *The Legionary* (January 1965), p. 7.

97 Murray, "The Dumbells: Nostalgic Memories," p. 9.

98 Captain Plunkett recollected one tongue-lashing he received from a Colonel, not pleased, but abiding by Gault and Lipsett's recommendation to release his men, "'Blankety-blank you, Plunkett, you never did intend to return those men to me in the first place.' Plunkett, 'We'll Make 'Em Laugh Again,'" section cover page.

99 Y-Emmas Programme (12 and 13 September 1918, the Imperial War Museum, London); O'Neill, "The Canadian Concert Party in France," pp. 198, 206.

100 H.H. Simpson, "Letter to Mother," 2 February 1918, as found in *The Canadian Letters and Images Project* (Nanaimo; London; Vancouver Island University; University of Western Ontario, 2003). www.canadianletters.ca.

101 O'Neill, "The Canadian Concert Party in France," p. 195.

102 Plunkett, "We'll Make 'Em Laugh Again," section cover page.

103 *The Canadian Daily Record* (Issued by the Canadian War Records Office to All Units of the Overseas Military Forces of Canada, 8 February 1918); O' Neill, "The Canadian Concert Party in France," p. 206.

104 9th Canadian Field Ambulance, *Official War Diary* (31 December 1916). www.collections canada.ca.

105 See CBC, "Interview with Alan Murray," *Grace Lydiatt Shaw*.

106 See Col. G.W.L. Nicholson, *Canadian Expeditionary Force 1914–1919: Official History of the Canadian Army in the First World War* (Ottawa: Queen's Printer and Controller of Stationery, 1962), p. 384.

107 O'Neill, "The Canadian Concert Party in France," p. 198.

108 CBC, *Camera Canada: The Dumbells with Affection*.

109 For example, the war diary for the 116th Battalion, who were with the 3rd Division at Gouy-Servins in June 1917, recorded that the battalion attended a concert at the YMCA in the evening of 22 June 1917. See *The Logistical Summary for the 116th (Ontario County) Canadian Infantry Battalion's Sojourn in France.* (Transcribed 2004-05). www .ontrmuseum.ca.

110 CBC, *Camera Canada: The Dumbells with Affection*.

111 W.J. McLellan, "Letter Home," 26 May 1917, as found in *The Canadian Letters and Images Project*. Nanaimo; London; Vancouver Island University; University of Western Ontario, 2003. www.canadianletters.ca.

112 Foster has mistakenly put the sports day Tincques show down as occurring on 1 July 1917. There was no show at Tincques on that date, and the big event at Tincques happened

precisely one year later to the day. K.W. Foster, "Memoir," date not specified, as found in *The Canadian Letters and Images Project* (Nanaimo; London; Vancouver Island University; University of Western Ontario, 2003), www.canadianletters.ca.

113 "SCORED BIG HIT: Third Division Concert Party Play to Packed Houses," *The Canadian Daily Record* (Issued by the Canadian War Records Office to All Units of the Overseas Military Forces of Canada, 6 September 1918), 511, pp. 1, 6.

114 CBC, "Interview with Archie Wills," *Voice of the Pioneer*, with B. McNeil (Toronto: 1981, National Archives of Canada, ISN 169473, Shelf no. C10917).

115 Various regimental bands included the Royal Canadian Regiment (RCR), the 49th Battalion, the 43rd Battalion, the Canadian Mounted Rifles (CMR), the 116th Battalion and Billet 13, and the 83rd Queen's Own Rifles Regiment, featuring violinist and vocalist Jack Slack. See J. Beaton, *Memories of and by Marjorie* (Baysville: Joyce Beaton Communications, December 2001, from the private collection of Joyce Beaton), pp. 2–3; Murray, "The Dumbells: Nostalgic Memories," p. 7.

116 CBC, "Interview with Jack Ayre," *Voice of the Pioneer*, with B. McNeil (Toronto, 1975, National Archives of Canada, ISN 177083, Shelf no. A1 2002-09-0019).

117 McLaren, *The Life Story of John Wilson McLaren*, p. 27.

118 Ibid., p. 37.

119 Ibid.

120 Ibid., p. 41.

121 A.M. Ashley, "Bill Redpath: From Flanders to Dumbells," *Ottawa Citizen* (6 September 1977), p. 78.

122 McNeil, *Dumbells Reunion*.

123 CBC, *Camera Canada: The Dumbells with Affection*.

124 Ibid.

125 Earle, *Al Plunkett: The Famous Dumbell*, p. 60.

126 CBC, "Interview with Ross Hamilton," *Grace Lydiatt Shaw* (Toronto, 1962, National Archives of Canada, ISN 61429, Shelf no. C09417{4}).

127 F. Rasky, "When Shells Fell in World War I, He Played On," *The Toronto Star* (9 November, 1974), p. G3.

128 I.C. Maharg, "Diary Entry," 9 July 1918, as found in *The Canadian Letters and Images Project* (Nanaimo; London; Vancouver Island University; University of Western Ontario, 2003). www.canadianletters.ca.

129 McLaren, *The Life Story of John Wilson McLaren*, p. 27.

130 McLaren, "Mirth and Mud Part Two: Orphans Are Orphans," p. 66; McLaren, *The Life Story of John Wilson McLaren*, p. 29.

131 O'Neill, "The Canadian Concert Party in France," pp. 198–99.

132 CBC, "'The Dumbells Farewell Concert at Lambert Lodge, Toronto: Out-Takes," with Bill McNeil (Toronto, 3 May 1975, National Archives of Canada, ISN 177082, Shelf no. A4 2002-09-0019{2}); See J.W. McLaren, "Mirth and Mud Part Three," p. 76.

133 McLaren, *The Life Story of John Wilson McLaren*, pp. 25–27.

134 Fuller, *Troop Morale and Popular Culture*, p. 98. Also see CBC, "Interview with Ivor Jack Ayre," *In Flanders Fields*; Nicholson, *Canadian Expeditionary Force 1914–1919*, p. 384.

135 Murray, "The Dumbells: Nostalgic Memories," p. 7.

136 The venue was inaugurated by the Dumbells on 17 October 1917. See "The Pavilion," *'Tchun 1* (5 December 1917), p. 13; O'Neill, "The Canadian Concert Party in France," p. 195.

137 O'Neill, "The Canadian Concert Party in France," p. 195.

138 Murray, "The Dumbells: Nostalgic Memories," p. 9.

139 Ibid.

140 Murray, "The Dumbells: Nostalgic Memories," p. 8.

141 McLaren, *The Life Story of John Wilson McLaren*, p. 35.

142 CBC, "Interview with Sergeant John (Jack) McLaren," *In Flanders Fields*; McLaren, *The Life Story of John Wilson McLaren, 1895–1988*, p. 35.

143 Franklin, "A Funny Thing Happened on the Way to the Trenches," p. 28.

144 McLaren, *The Life Story of John Wilson McLaren*, p. 37.

145 Ibid., p. 35.

146 "SCORED BIG HIT," p. 6.

147 Ibid.

148 See "The Story of The Dumbells, The Famous Concert Party of Third Canadian Division," newspaper clipping from Ivor Jack Ayre's Dumbell Collection at the Metro Toronto Reference Library; CBC, "Interview with Ross Hamilton," *Grace Lydiatt Shaw*; Earle, *Al Plunkett: The Famous Dumbell*, p. 63.

149 CBC, "The Dumbells Press Conference."

150 Lopakova later went to see the Dumbells on Broadway while she was performing in New York. See "The Story of The Dumbells, The Famous Concert Party of Third Canadian Division" (newspaper clipping from Ivor Jack Ayre's Dumbell Collection at the Metro Toronto Reference Library).

151 O'Neill, "The Canadian Concert Party in France," p. 202.

152 In 1934 the Comedy Company reassembled for a PPCLI reunion in Toronto. McNeil, *Dumbells Reunion*.

153 O'Neill, "The Canadian Concert Party in France," p. 201.

154 The show was scheduled for 11 November but was moved to the following day because the Germans had cut the electrical wires of the theatre before leaving. Three days after the Armistice, the Dumbells performed at a gala reception at the Hôtel de Ville. Hodder-Williams, *Princess Patricia's Canadian Light Infantry*, p. 403; McNeil, *Dumbells Reunion*.

155 See Allen, "Famed Hoofers and Players of 1917," cover page.

156 CBC, "Interview with Sergeant John (Jack) McLaren," *In Flanders Fields*. The Bow Bells, however, were still performing as late as 20 June 1918, when they performed for the 116th Battalion. Likewise, the 16th Battalion were performing as late as 20 October 1918. See *The Logistical Summary for the 116th*.

157 McLaren, *The Life Story of John Wilson McLaren*, p. 41.

158 *Pinafore* ran for 32 days, with two performances a day. See M. Braithwaite, "The Rise and Fall of the Dumbells," *Maclean's* (1 January 1952), p. 38.

159 CBC, "Interview with Sergeant John (Jack) McLaren," *In Flanders Fields*.

160 CBC, "The Dumbells Press Conference."

161 CBC, *Camera Canada: The Dumbells with Affection*.

162 See McLaren, "Mirth and Mud Part Three," pp. 20, 76, 78, 81; CBC, "Interview with Conrad Stephens."

163 C.R. Gass, "Letter to Lillian," 10 October 1918, as found in *The Canadian Letters and Images Project* (Nanaimo; London; Vancouver Island University; University of Western Ontario).

164 Hodder-Williams, *Princess Patricia's Canadian Light Infantry*, p. 140.

165 McLaren, *The Life Story of John Wilson McLaren*, p. 41.

166 Ibid., p. 43.

167 H.W. Lovell, "Some Memories of 'Our Days in France' 1916–1919," c. 1931, as found in *The Canadian Letters and Images Project* (Nanaimo; London; Vancouver Island University; University of Western Ontario, 2003). www.canadianletters.ca.

168 The supergroup was supposed to perform on 11 November, but the Germans had cut the electrical wires in the theatre and the hall had no lights. McLaren, *The Life Story of John Wilson McLaren*, p. 43.

169 On 19 November 1918, the 116th War Diary records that "in the afternoon 225 other ranks marched to the theatre in Mons, and witnessed the play H.M.S. Pinafore, put on by the Dumbells performance commenced at 6:00 p.m." See *The Logistical Summary for the 116th.*

170 McLaren, *The Life Story of John Wilson McLaren,* p. 43.

171 National Library of Canada, "The Dumbells: Part One—The Canadian Army Third Division Concert Part (1917–1919)," *The Virtual Gramophone.* www2.nlc-bnc.ca/gramophone/src/dumbellse.htm.

172 F. James, "PERFORMED FOR ROYALTY: Canadian 'Dumbells' Have Great Success on Brussels and London Stage," *Toronto Daily Star* (4 January 1919), p. 5.

173 Plunkett, "We'll Make 'Em Laugh Again," section cover page.

174 The 116th took in one Dumbell performance at Le Havre on 9 February 1919. See *The Logistical Summary for the 116th.*

175 Murray, "The Dumbells: Nostalgic Memories," p. 8.

176 McLaren, *The Life Story of John Wilson McLaren,* p. 45.

177 A. Wilson, "'Diary Entry," 25 March 1918, as found in *The Canadian Letters and Images Project* (Nanaimo; London; Vancouver Island University; University of Western Ontario, 2003). www.canadianletters.ca.

178 G.L. Scherer, "Letter to Catherine Crawford," 25 March 1918, as found in *The Canadian Letters and Images Project* (Nanaimo; London; Vancouver Island University; University of Western Ontario, 2003). www.canadianletters.ca.

179 Shortreed would have seen a later incarnation of the C2s, the official concert party of the Second Division, as the show he saw was on 23 January 1919, when the Second Division was in Bonn. See R. Shortreed, "Letter to Sister," 28 January 1919, as found in *The Canadian Letters and Images Project* (Nanaimo; London; Vancouver Island University; University of Western Ontario, 2003). www.canadianletters.ca.

180 O'Neill, "The Canadian Concert Party in France," p. 205.

Notes to Chapter IV

1 McLaren, "Mirth and Mud: The Chronicle," p. 47.

2 Brophy and Partridge, *The Long Trail,* p. 16.

3 L. O'Dell, "Amateurs of the Regiment, 1815–1870," A. Saddlemyer (ed.), *Early Stages: Theatre in Ontario 1800–1914* (Toronto: Ontario Historical Studies Series for the Government of Ontario, University of Toronto Press, 1990), p. 52.

4 Ibid., p. 84.

5 Ibid., p. 60.

6 Sheldon-Williams, *The Canadian Front in France and Flanders,* pp. 190–91.

7 This liberty taking became a point of contention for the D'Oyly Carte Opera Company, who had lent the score to Captain Plunkett in the first place. Ayre remembered, "Carte wrote a stern letter to Plunkett warning him to stick to the original or else he would take back the score, but they carried on." CBC, "Interview with Jack Ayre," *Grace Lydiatt Shaw.*

8 P. Summerfield, "The Effingham Arms and the Empire: Deliberate Selection in the evolution of the Music Hall in London," E. Yeo and S. Yeo (eds.), *Popular Culture and Class Conflict 1590–1914* (Brighton: Harvester Press, 1981), p. 235; Fuller, *Troop Morale and Popular Culture,* p. 124.

9 M. Eksteins, *The Rites of Spring: The Great War and the Birth of the Modern Age* (Toronto: Lester & Orpen Dennys, 1989), p. 220.

10 A. Clark, *Stand and Deliver: Inside Canadian Comedy* (Toronto: Doubleday Canada, 1997), p. 12.

11 Rasky, "When Shells Fell in World War I," p. G3.

12 CBC, "Interview with Ivor Jack Ayre," *In Flanders Fields.*
13 *The Wipers Times* was printed under various titles, including *The New Church Times, The Kemmel Times, The Somme Times, The B. E. F. Times,* and finally at war's end, *The Better Times.* "Wipers" referred to the peculiar pronunciation of Ypres.
14 *The Somme Times* (31 July 1916); Eksteins, *The Rites of Spring,* p. 221.
15 E.H. Armstrong, *The Crisis of Quebec, 1914–1918* (New York: Columbia University Press, 1937), p. 248; Fuller, *Troop Morale and Popular Culture,* p. 124.
16 Fuller, *Troop Morale and Popular Culture,* pp. 9, 181–83; *The Listening Post,* 19 (London: Canadian Military Headquarters, October 1916), p. 118.
17 "Don't Pull the Little Glass Ball," *The Listening Post,* 29, published by the 7th Battalion (1 December 1917), p. 32.
18 For an excellent overview of over 200 Canadian trench newspapers, see M. Cinq-Mars, *L'Écho du Front: Journaux de Tranchées, 1915–1919* (Outremont, QC: Athéna, 2008). Also see J. Keshen, *Propaganda and Censorship during Canada's Great War* (Edmonton: University of Alberta Press, 1996).
19 S. Audoin-Rouzeau, *Men at War 1914–1918: National Sentiment and Trench Journalism in France during the First World War,* translated from the French by Helen McPhail, Legacy of the Great War, Volume 1 (Providence: Berg Publishers, 1992).
20 Ibid., p. 188.
21 J. McLaren, "Where Did That One Go?," Written by R.P. Weston, C. Smith and B. Lee, originally performed by L. White in *Cheep* (London: Vaudeville Theatre, 1917). See McLaren, *Dumbells: Arts and Letters Meeting P.P.L.L.I.S.*
22 MacCallum-Stewart (ed.), *The First World War and Comedy.*
23 Brophy and Partridge, *The Long Trail,* p. 15.
24 Captain T. Papineau of the PPCLI, "Letter to Beatrice Fox," as found in Gwyn, *Tapestry of War,* p. 221.
25 Eksteins, *The Rites of Spring,* p. 229.
26 C.R. Innes, *With Paget's Horse to the Front* (1901), pp. 97–98; Fuller, *Troop Morale and Popular Culture,* pp. 119–21.
27 CBC, *Camera Canada: The Dumbells with Affection.*
28 Cook, "The Singing War," p. 238.
29 Murray, "The Dumbells: Nostalgic Memories," p. 9.
30 A. O'Connor, "Letter to the Editor," *The Toronto Star* (3 December 1974).
31 For one soldier's opinion see Bird, *The Communication Trench;* Cook, "The Singing War: Canadian Soldiers," p. 228.
32 Brophy and Partridge, *The Long Trail,* p. 18.
33 Cecil Lewis, as quoted in Fussel, *The Great War and Modern Memory,* p. 201.
34 S. Graham, "Sure a Little Bit of Heaven," 1914.
35 CBC, "The Dumbells Farewell Concert at Lambert Lodge, Toronto: Out-Takes"; CBC, *Camera Canada: The Dumbells with Affection.*
36 J.P. Long, M. Scott and B. Felman, "Oh, It's a Lovely War," 1917.
37 Clark, *Stand and Deliver,* p. 17.
38 P.W. Lewis, *Blasting and Bombardiering* (London: Calder & Boyars, {1937} 1967), pp. 37–38; Fuller, *Troop Morale and Popular Culture,* p. 147.
39 R. Newman, "Medals on My Chest," words and music by Waite (Montreal: Berliner, His Master's Voice, Issue no. 216398, 1923).
40 Fuller, *Troop Morale and Popular Culture,* p. 48.
41 MacDonald, "Foreword," Palmer, *"What a Lovely War!"* p. 2.
42 McLaren, *Dumbells: Arts and Letters Meeting P.P.L.L.I.S..*
43 Excerpt from "Kit Inspection," author unknown, Palmer, *"What a Lovely War!"* p. 20.

44   CBC, "Interview with Jack Ayre," *Voice of the Pioneer*.

45   Kit Inspection was a hit in the Second World War, when Jack Ayre performed it with the Lifebuoy Follies. "The Kit Inspection," *Dumbell Sketches* (Ivor Jack Ayre's Dumbell Collection at the Metro Toronto Reference Library), pp. 26–38; CBC, *Camera Canada: The Dumbells with Affection*; CBC, "The Dumbells Farewell Concert at Lambert Lodge."

46   Monty Python, *Monty Python and the Holy Grail* (Python [Monty] Pictures; Michael White Productions; National Film Trustee Company; Twickenham Film Studios, 1975).

47   Cook, "The Singing War: Canadian Soldiers," p. 237.

48   J. McLaren, "Shirts," written by P. Braham and I. Novello et al., A. Charlot, *See-Saw* (London: Comedy Theatre, 1916).

49   MacDonald, "Foreword," Palmer, *"What a Lovely War!"* p. 24.

50   Cook, *Shock Troops*.

51   Savage, "Memoir."

52   J. McLaren, "On the Staff," Words by C. Grey, Music by I. Novello, 1917, McLaren, *Dumbells: Arts and Letters Meeting P.P.L.L.I.S.*

53   McLaren and company may have built on an existing sketch with the devil as a main character. CBC, "Interview with Jack McLaren," *In Flanders Fields*.

54   McLaren, "Mirth and Mud Part Two: Orphans Are Orphans," p. 16.

55   Nicholson, *Canadian Expeditionary Force 1914–1919*, p. 529.

56   Hodder-Williams, *Princess Patricia's Canadian Light Infantry*, p. 140.

57   Murray, "The Dumbells: Nostalgic Memories," p. 7.

58   Fuller, *Troop Morale and Popular Culture*, pp. 96, 102.

59   CBC, "Interview with Jack McLaren," *In Flanders Fields*.

60   A. Adamson, "Letter to wife Mabel' (October 1916), S. Gwyn, *Tapestry of War: A Private View of Canadians in the Great War* (Toronto: HarperCollins Publishers, 1992), pp. 311–12.

61   W. Churchill as quoted in M. Gilbert, *Churchill and Canada* (delivered at the Annual Meetings of the Sir Winston S. Churchill Society, Edmonton, Calgary, and Vancouver, Canada, May 1987).

62   Murray, "The Dumbells: Nostalgic Memories," p. 8.

63   Eksteins, *The Rites of Spring*, p. 177.

64   S. Bennett, "Archibald," written by Philip Braham, piano accompaniment Freddie Treneer (Montreal: Victor Records, Issue no. 216485, 1926).

65   "Archibald," for example, takes a German trench all by himself. Ibid.

66   J. Laffin, *British Butchers and Bunglers of World War One* (London: 1988), *passim*.

67   T.E. Lawrence, *Seven Pillars of Wisdom* (Harmondsworth, {1927} 1962), p. 395.

68   J.W. McLaren, *Personal Memoirs* (c. 1927, from the private collection of John McLaren).

Notes to Chapter V

1   German trenches, however, were generally more comfortable than Allied ones. See G. Coppard, *With a Machine Gun to Cambrai: The Tale of a Young Tommy in Kitchener's Army, 1914–1918* (London: 1969), p. 80.

2   Also see C.R.M.F. Cruttwell, *A History of the Great War, 1914–18* (Oxford: Oxford University Press, 1964).

3   D. Morton and J.L. Granatstein, *Marching to Armageddon: Canadians and the Great War 1914–1919* (Toronto: Lester & Orpen Dennys Limited, 1989), p. 8.

4   D. Morton, *A Peculiar Kind of Politics: Canada's Overseas Ministry in the First World War*, (Toronto: University of Toronto, 1982), p. 12.

5   Ibid. The rifle's weaknesses were documented at its first trial in 1902 despite the efforts of Sir Charles Ross to sabotage the tests. When the Ross was being tested for its durability

in sandy conditions, Sir Charles Ross was caught pouring oil on the rival Lee-Enfield. See Morton, *A Peculiar Kind of Politics*, pp. 12–13.

6 Earle, *Al Plunkett: The Famous Dumbell*, p. 45.

7 Alderson sent the test results along with a letter to General Willoughby Gwatkin, Chief of Staff in Ottawa. In his letter, Alderson added that even these poor results flattered the Ross, because the official report did not state that during the test, "the hands of the men using the Ross were cut and bleeding, owing to the difficulty they had in knocking back the bolt." Sir Edwin Alderson in a letter to General Willoughby Gwatkin, as found in Gwyn, *Tapestry of War*, pp. 276–78.

8 Morton, *A Peculiar Kind of Politics*, p. 60.

9 Canadian boots, Bain wagons, and MacAdam shovels were "gratefully abandoned" at Salisbury Plain. See Morton and Granatstein, *Marching to Armageddon*, pp. 48–49.

10 Lieutenant Colonel Francis Farquhar quoted in an official CEF memo, as found in Gwyn, *Tapestry of War*, p. 100.

11 Quote from an anonymous colonel, as found in Morton and Granatstein, *Marching to Armageddon*, pp. 109–10.

12 Gwyn, *Tapestry of War*, pp. 280–82.

13 McLaren, *The Life Story of John Wilson McLaren*, p. 15.

14 Sir Harry Lauder, "Roaming in the Gloaming," *Scotland's Stars on 78 Presents Sir Harry Lauder* (Glasgow: Lismor Recordings, 1994), liner notes by Frank Wappat.

15 Liner notes by Frank Wappat from, Sir Harry Lauder, *Scotland's Stars on 78 Presents*.

16 CBC, "Interview with Jack McLaren," *In Flanders Fields*.

17 G.R. Stevens, *A City Goes to War* (Brampton: Charters Publishing Co., 1964), p. 35; Cook, "The Singing War: Canadian Soldiers," p. 236.

18 CBC, "Interview with Jack McLaren," *In Flanders Fields*.

19 J.S. Williams as quoted in Cook, "The Singing War: Canadian Soldiers," *American Review of Canadian Studies*, *39*, *3* (September 2009), p. 233.

20 E. Kirkland, *Lady Julia Drummond*, Biographical Entry (Montreal: September 2002). www.rootsweb.ancestry.com.

21 Ibid.

22 Excerpt from *The Bedfordshire Times and Independent*, as found in L. MacDonald, *1914–18, Voices and Images of the Great War* (London: Penguin Books, 1989); MacCallum-Stewart, *The First World War and Comedy*.

23 MacCallum-Stewart, *The First World War and Comedy*.

24 "Entertaining the Fighters," *Echoes*, No. 66 (December 1916), pp. 43–46.

25 O'Neill, "The Canadian Concert Party in France," p. 194.

26 CBC, "The Dumbells Press Conference."

27 Earle, *Al Plunkett: The Famous Dumbell*, p. 63.

28 Sheldon-Williams, *The Canadian Front in France and Flanders*, p. 190.

29 Lauder, *A Minstrel in France*, p. 66.

30 Although McLaren wrote the bulk of both the Dumbells and the PPCLI Comedy Company's comedy sketches, Leonard Young also contributed some sketches to both concert parties. Several sources confirm McLaren as the author of the "Duchess" sketch; however, Dumbell Alan Murray claimed that Young wrote the sketch in an interview with *The Legionary* in 1965. It is possible that Murray have been mistaken in giving Young credit for writing the sketch because Young performed as the "Duchess" with the Dumbells after the war. See Murray, "The Dumbells: Nostalgic Memories," p. 9.

31 CBC, *Camera Canada: The Dumbells with Affection*.

32 CBC, "Interview with Jack McLaren," *In Flanders Fields*.

33 In some cases, the sketch was performed with only two wounded soldiers. "The Duchess Entertains," *Dumbell Sketches* (Ivor Jack Ayre's Dumbell Collection at the Metro Toronto Reference Library), pp. 11–14.

34 Alternatively, the Duchess replied, "Oh that's marvellous, wonderful, of all things I love above anything else is cleanliness." Ibid. Also see CBC, "The Dumbells Farewell Concert."

35 C.S. Peel, *How We Lived Then* (London: 1929); Gwyn, *Tapestry of War*, pp. 219–21.

36 CBC, "Interview with Ross Hamilton."

37 CBC, *Camera Canada: The Dumbells with Affection.*

38 "Dumbells Score Immense Success: Clever Soldier Entertainers Delight Capacity Avenue Audience" (Vancouver: c. 1921). See *Scrapbook of Reviews* (Ivor Jack Ayre's Dumbell Collection at the Metro Toronto Reference Library).

39 The real Duchess returned to see the show on at least two more occasions. Jack McLaren as quoted in S. Handman, "The Dumbells Are Back," *Toronto Telegram: Weekend Magazine* (16 April 1955), p. 59. Alan Murray in an interview suggested that it was the Duchess of Devonshire who had paid the Dumbells a visit; Jack Ayre, however, was from Devonshire, England, and perhaps Murray had gotten the event confused with this. See CBC, *Camera Canada: The Dumbells with Affection.*

40 McLaren may have dismissed Thalberg because the latter was only 14 when he offered McLaren the screen test. Franklin, "A Funny Thing Happened on the Way to the Trenches," p. 32.

41 W. Owen, "Dulce Et Decorum Est," J. Silkin (ed.), *The Penguin Book of First World War Poetry* (London: Penguin, 1981), p. 183.

42 "The Contracting Powers agree to abstain from the use of projectiles the object of which is the diffusion of asphyxiating or deleterious gases." See James Brown Scott, *The Hague Peace Conferences of 1899 and 1907*, A Series of Lectures Delivered before the Johns Hopkins University in the Year 1908, Volume II (Baltimore, MD: Johns Hopkins Press, 1909).

43 L. MacDonald, *1915: The Death of Innocence* (London: Penguin Books {1993} 1997), p. 187.

44 Eksteins, *The Rites of Spring*, p. 162; B.H. Liddell Hart, *History of the First World War* (London: 1972), p. 145; P.G. Kielmansegg, *Deutschland und der Erste Weltkrieg* (Frankfurt am Main: 1968), p. 91.

45 V.M. Fergusson, "Letter dated 5 May 1915" (Imperial War Museum); as found in Eksteins, *The Rites of Spring*, p. 162.

46 Cook, *No Place to Run*, p. 213.

47 L.H. Addington, *Patterns of War since the Eighteenth Century* (Indiana: Indiana University Press {1984} 1994), p. 148.

48 For a provocative Canadian-centric discussion on the effects of gas and soldiers, see Cook, *No Place to Run*, p. 6.

49 F.R. Sidell, J.S. Urbanetti, W.J. Smith, and C.G. Hurst, "Chapter 7: Vesicants," as found in Sidell, Frederick R., Ernest T. Takafuji and David R. Franz (eds.), *Medical Aspects of Chemical and Biological Warfare*. Office of the Surgeon General, Department of the Army, USA: 1997.

50 See C.E. Heller, "The Peril of Unpreparedness: The American Expeditionary Force and Chemical Warfare," *Military Review*, 65, 1 (1985), p. 24; Cook, *No Place to Run*, pp. 233, 283.

51 Lance-Corporal J.D. Keddie, H. Coy., 48th Highlanders of Canada, memoir from, MacDonald, *1915*, p. 194.

52 Morton and Granatstein, *Marching to Armageddon*, pp. 59–60. Some soldiers found relief by urinating on their bandoliers, as urine went some way in neutralizing the gas.

53 Ibid., p. 62. Following action at Frezenberg Ridge on 8 May, only 150 of the Princess Pats' initial 550 soldiers remained. It was at this Second Battle of Ypres where Lieutenant Colonel John McCrae penned his famous "In Flanders Fields" before he was killed.

54 Cook, *No Place to Run*, p. 217.

55 McLaren, *The Life Story of John Wilson McLaren*, p. 27.

56 CBC, *Camera Canada: The Dumbells with Affection*.

57 B. Norman, "Music on the Home Front," *Sheet Music from Canada's Past*, National Library of Canada, www.nlc-bnc.ca/sheetmusic/m5-170-e.html. For a further review of Rice's part in the song, see National Library of Canada, "Lieutenant Gitz Rice," *The Virtual Gramophone*, www2.nlc-bnc.ca/gramophone/src/ricee.htm.

58 This might be a case of romance lusting after fact, as Gitz, a soldier in the 5th Battery, Canadian Field Artillery, was in all likelihood still in England for Christmas 1914. Still, the "legend" endures; see Eksteins, *Rites of Spring*, pp. 96–98; MacDonald, *1915*, pp. 3–5; Helmut Kallmann (ed.), "Gitz Rice," *Encyclopedia of Music in Canada*, 2nd ed. (Toronto: University of Toronto Press, 1992), p. xxxii.

59 The piano was "rescued" from an old house that was being shelled by Rice and some of his comrades in the autumn of 1915. "The Story of Gitz Rice," *New York Times* (16 June 1918). The song was recorded several times by different artists and given various treatments and was also released in sheet-music form. See J. McCormack, "Dear Old Pal of Mine," words and music by Lt. G. Rice (Montreal: Berliner, His Master's Voice, Issue no. 64785, 1918). See also "Lieutenant Gitz Rice," *The Virtual Gramophone*, National Library of Canada. www2.nlc-bnc.ca/gramophone/src/ricee.htm.

60 "Keep Your Head Down 'Fritzie Boy,'" was inspired by a brave Tommy and written at the Battle of Ypres in 1915. See Lt. G. Rice, "Keep Your Head Down 'Fritzie Boy'" (New York: Leo Feist, 1918).

61 While on tour with the Dumbells during one of their cross-Canada tours following the war, Newman contracted food-poisoning which the other member mistook for a "gas flashback." CBC, "Interview with Laurie Thompson," *Grace Lydiatt Shaw* (Toronto: 1962, National Archives of Canada, ISN 61304, Shelf no. C09407).

62 CBC, "Interview with Alan Murray."

63 The topic of gas was used in the Dumbells' *Real Estate* sketch, but only as a passing inference supporting the punchline of selling no man's land to an unaware prospective buyer on the strength of its, "spacious property being well serviced with gas and water." J. McLaren, "Real Estate," CBC, *The Dumbells* (Toronto: 1978, National Archives of Canada, ISN 107627, Shelf no. 8901-0026).

64 For further discussion, see G. Browne, "Soldiers' Songs of the Great War," The Western Front Association (22 May 2008). www.westernfrontassociation.com.

65 B. Bairnsfather, "The Candid Friend," as found in B. Bairnsfather, *Fragments from France* (New York and London: G.P. Putnam's Sons, Knickerbocker Press, 1917), p. 115. For further discussion on how gas was represented in Britain's popular press, see chapter five of M. Girard, *A Strange and Formidable Weapon: British Responses to World War I Poison Gas* (Lincoln: University of Nebraska Press, 2008), pp. 126–56.

66 CBC, "Interview with Jack McLaren," *In Flanders Fields*.

67 McLaren, *The Life Story of John Wilson McLaren*, p. 41.

68 C. Biddulph, "My Motta," as found in McLaren, *The Life Story of John Wilson McLaren*, p. 41.

69 Ibid.

70 Monty Python, *The Meaning of Life* (Monty Python Partnership, March 1982).

71 Ferguson, *The Pity of War*, pp. 350–54.

72 Ibid., p. 351.

73 For an excellent discussion on the vital usages of rum, see T. Cook, "'More a Medicine Than a Beverage': 'Demon Rum' and the Canadian Trench Soldier of the First World War," *Canadian Military History*, 9, 1 (2000), pp. 6–22.

74 H. Burr and G. Rice, "Fun in Flanders—Part Two" (Montreal: Berliner, His Master's Voice, Issue no. 18405, March 1918).

75 Cook, "Rum in the Trenches," p. 54.

76 Ibid., pp. 54–56.

77 Roosters Concert Party, "The Old Barbed Wire," *Traditional* (1929). www.firstworldwar .com.

78 B. Bairnsfather, "The Spirit of Our Troops Is Excellent," *The Bystander* (London, c. 1916), as found in *The Great War: The Virtual History Collection* (England: Castle Multi Media, 1995).

79 Cook, "More a Medicine Than a Beverage," pp. 6–22.

80 H.H. Simpson, "Letter to Mother," 21 April 1918, as found in *The Canadian Letters and Images Project* (Nanaimo; London; Vancouver Island University; University of Western Ontario, 2003). www.canadianletters.ca.

81 CBC, "Interview with Jack Ayre," *Voice of the Pioneer.*

82 Burr and Rice's "Fun in Flanders" series is seemingly recorded in front of a live audience, who voice their wild appreciation when the rum rations are mentioned. Burr and Rice, "Fun in Flanders—Part Two."

83 R. Newman, "Capt. Thingamabob," songwriter unknown (Montreal: Victor Talking Records, Issue no. 217004, 1926).

84 McLaren, *The Life Story of John Wilson McLaren*, p. 25.

85 Ibid., p. 33.

86 I.E. Ayre, "The Dumbell Rag," handwritten by the composer, souvenir copy (from Ivor Jack Ayre's Dumbell Collection at the Metro Toronto Reference Library, c. 1921).

87 Lt. G. Rice, "Take Me Back to the Land of Promise" (Montreal: Berliner, His Master's Voice, Issue no. 216016, 1917). "Little Grey Home in the West" was a music-hall hit that had caught on among British soldiers in 1915, and was written by Hermann Lohr and D. Eardley-Wilmot in 1913.

88 See B. McNeil with J. Ayre, "The Last Tune They'll Ever Whistle," B. McNeil, *Voice of the Pioneer* (Toronto: Macmillan Company of Canada, 1978), pp. 143–48; CBC, *Camera Canada: The Dumbells with Affection.*

89 Rasky, "When Shells Fell in World War I," p. G3.

90 Brophy and Partridge, *The Long Trail*, p. 21.

91 Palmer, *"What a Lovely War!"* p. 1.

92 MacCallum-Stewart, *The First World War and Comedy.*

93 The lyrics may have been inspired by one of the better-known German atrocities in Belgium; a rape featured in the Bryce Treaty paper of 1914. Ibid.

94 McLaren, "Mirth and Mud: The Chronicle," p. 14.

95 Brophy and Partridge, *The Long Trail*, p. 24.

96 CBC, "The Dumbells Press Conference."

97 Advance publicity for Dumbell performance of *H.M.S. Pinafore* at the Old Russell Theatre in Ottawa in 1919. E.J. Donovan, "Percy Campbell Talks to Edward J. Donovan: Remember the Dumbells?" *Ottawa Journal* (30 November 1963).

98 Franklin, "A Funny Thing Happened," p. 31.

99 Ibid., p. 27.

100 I. Drysdale, "'Dumbells Marjorie Now Man Again, but Gave War Troops Good Times," *Owen Sound Sun-Times* (19 May 1961), p. 6.

101 M. Meyer, "Unveiling the Word: Science and Narrative in Transsexual Striptease," L. Senelick (ed.), *Gender in Performance: The Presentation of Difference in the Performing Arts* (Hanover: University Press of New England, 1992), pp. 68–85.

102 Homosexuality was officially criminalized in Britain with the Labouchère Amendment of 1881. See D.A. Boxwell, "The Follies of War: Cross-Dressing and Popular Theatre on the British Front Line, 1914–1918," *Modernism/Modernity*, 9, 1 (Johns Hopkins University Press, 2002), pp. 1–22.

103 Clark, *Stand and Deliver*, p. 9.

104 V. Turner, *From Ritual to Theatre: The Human Seriousness of Play* (New York: Harper Collins, 1993), pp. 10–11; Boxwell, "The Follies of War," p. 3.

105 Boxwell, "The Follies of War," p.10. In rare examples, like the bizarre circumstances of the German POW camps along the Eastern Front, such behaviour did manage to transcend the stage and a few greatly admired "divas" were freely able (and indeed encouraged) to continue their impersonation around the clock. For an insightful discussion on the over 40 theatrical groups made up exclusively of German prisoners of war along the Eastern Front, see A. Rachamimov, "The Disruptive Comforts of Drag: (Trans)Gender Performances among Prisoners of War in Russia, 1914–1920," *American Historical Review*, 11, 2 (April 2006), pp. 362–82.

106 N.Z. Davis, "Women on Top," N.Z. Davis, *Society and Culture in Early Modern France: Eight Essays* (Stanford: Stanford University Press, 1965), pp. 129–31.

107 Rachamimov, "The Disruptive Comforts of Drag," p. 364.

108 J. Butler, *Gender Trouble: Feminism and the Subversion of Identity* (New York: Routledge, 1990), *passim*.

109 Perhaps Dame Edna is the archetypal example of this form of drag.

110 L. Senelick, "Boys and Girls Together: Subcultural Origins of Glamour Drag and Male Impersonation," Lesley Ferris (ed.), *Crossing the Stage: Controversies on Cross-Dressing* (New York: Routledge, 1993), p. 80.

111 Ibid.

112 Boxwell, "The Follies of War," p. 13.

113 Fuller, *Troop Morale and Popular Culture*, p. 105.

114 McNeil, *Dumbells Reunion*.

115 Drysdale, "Dumbells Marjorie Now Man Again," p. 6.

116 K.C. Gibson, "Sex and Soldiering in France and Flanders: The British Expeditionary Force along the Western Front, 1914–1919," *International History Review*, 23, 3 (2001), pp. 535–79.

117 Niall Ferguson observed that the cases of venereal disease among British soldiers numbered 48,000 in 1917 alone—60,000 in 1918, when Dominion troops were included in the total. It was thought that one out of every five soldiers had syphilis, but the actual annual rate for the British army was 4.83 percent, which was really an improvement on pre-war figures, though the rates for Dominion troops, as Ferguson confirms, were higher. See Ferguson, *Pity of War*, p. 353; I. Beckett, "The Nation in Arms, 1914–1918," in I. Beckett and K. Simpson (eds.), *A Nation in Arms: A Social Study of the British Army in the First World War* (Manchester: 1985), p. 19.

118 Ferguson, *Pity of War*, p. 353.

119 C. Smythe with S. Young, *Conn Smythe: If You Can't Beat 'Em in the Alley* (Toronto: PaperJacks, 1982), p. 42.

120 Clark, *Stand and Deliver*, pp. 9–10.

121 E. Minton, "P.S. on The Dumbells," *Ottawa Journal* (2 December 1972).

122 Tragically, Evans was killed in action on 1 September 1918, less than 10 weeks shy of the signing of the armistice. See J.L. Evans, "Letter to Wife," 20 June 1918, as found in *The*

Canadian Letters and Images Project (Nanaimo; London; Vancouver Island University; University of Western Ontario, 2003). www.canadianletters.ca.

123 Franklin, "A Funny Thing Happened," p. 27.

124 McLaren, "Mirth and Mud: The Chronicle," p. 15.

125 Franklin, "A Funny Thing Happened," p. 27; Gwyn, *Tapestry of War*, pp. 311–12.

126 CBC, *Camera Canada: The Dumbells with Affection*. Court dressmakers made clothes for those members of the public who would be attending a Royal event. They did not necessarily provide clothes for the Royals themselves.

127 Simpson, "Letter to Mother," 2 February 1918.

128 Review from Dumbell performance at the Australian YMCA at the Aldwych Theatre in London, England, c. 1918. See *Scrapbook of Reviews* (Ivor Jack Ayre's Dumbell Collection at the Metro Toronto Reference Library).

129 Franklin, "A Funny Thing Happened," p. 30.

130 *Behind the Footlights*, "Review of Biff, Bing, Bang!" (9 April 1920). From Ayre, "Scrapbook of Reviews" (Ivor Jack Ayre's Dumbell Collection at the Metro Toronto Reference Library).

131 CBC, *Camera Canada: The Dumbells with Affection*.

132 CBC, "Interview with Basil Donn," *Grace Lydiatt Shaw* (Toronto, 1961, National Archives of Canada, ISN 62482, Shelf no. C09445{1}). The Trinity Theatre in Montreal had been the longest-surviving amateur theatre in Canada before its closure in the early 1960s.

133 Drysdale, "Dumbells Marjorie Now Man Again," p. 6.

134 Leonard Young would eventually tour with the Dumbells in North America, but instead became attached to the PPCLI Comedy Company before he was officially put out of the war at Vimy, when he lost a leg.

135 CBC, "Interview with Ross Hamilton," *Grace Lydiatt Shaw*.

136 Braithwaite, "The Rise and Fall of the Dumbells," p. 38.

137 E. Minton, "The Dumbells: Flashback," *Ottawa Journal* (11 November 1972), p. 35.

138 H. Whittaker, "Dumbells' Rag: From Vimy to Broadway," *Globe and Mail* (27 June 1977), p. 17.

139 CBC, *Canadian Theatre Fact and Fancy: Parts 4 and 5*.

140 McLellan, "Letter Home," 26 May 1917.

141 "Dumbells Score Big in Griffins Here Last Night" (Fort William, 1920). See *Scrapbook of Reviews* (Ivor Jack Ayre's Dumbell Collection at the Metro Toronto Reference Library).

142 Franklin, "A Funny Thing Happened," p. 30.

143 *Toronto Telegram*, 10 May 1921. See *Scrapbook of Reviews* (Ivor Jack Ayre's Dumbell Collection at the Metro Toronto Reference Library).

144 Ibid.

145 CBC, "Interview with Conrad Stephens."

146 Hamilton had vowed never to play in a show with girls in it, and he never did, confessing that, "I knew I couldn't compete with a beautiful girl." CBC, *Canadian Theatre Fact and Fancy: Parts 4 and 5*; Drysdale, "Dumbells Marjorie Now Man Again," p. 6.

147 Plunkett, "We'll Make 'Em Laugh Again," section cover page.

148 Drysdale, "'Dumbells Marjorie Now Man Again," p. 6.

149 CBC, *Camera Canada: The Dumbells with Affection*.

150 J. McLaren, "'Interview with unknown journalist," perhaps a CBC work tape (Toronto: 6 May 1983), from the private collection of John McLaren.

151 "The Duchess Entertains," "The Estaminet," "'The Estaminet Coffee House," "Untitled Sketch (Boarding the Train Home to Canada)," and "The Dug-Out" are among Dumbell

and PPCLI Comedy Company sketches that have strong Canadian content. See *Dumbell Sketches* (Ivor Jack Ayre's Dumbell Collection at the Metro Toronto Reference Library), pp. 1–43; McLaren, "Sketchbook of Comedy Sketches" (France: c. 1915–18, from the private collection of John McLaren); CBC, "Interview with William Redpath," *Grace Lydiatt Shaw*.

152 M. De La Roche, *Jalna* (New York: Grosset and Dunlap, 1927); F.P. Grove, *Settlers of the Marsh* (Toronto: Ryerson Press, 1925); M. Ostenso, *Wild Geese* (New York: Dodd, Mead and Co., 1925).

153 For further discussion see G. Davies, *Myth and Milieu: Atlantic Literature and Culture, 1918–1939* (Fredericton: Acadiensis Press, 1993); I. McKay, *The Quest of the Folk: Antimodernism and Cultural Selection in Twentieth-Century Nova Scotia* (Montreal; Kingston: McGill-Queen's University Press, 1994).

154 See above.

155 J.J. Wilson, "Skating to Armageddon: Of Canada, Hockey and the First World War," *The International Journal of the History of Sport*, 22, 3 (Oxford: Routledge, May 2005), pp. 315–43.

156 M. Bliss, *Banting: A Biography* (Toronto: University of Toronto Press, 1992); M. Bliss, *The Discovery of Insulin* (Chicago: University of Chicago, 1982); F.G. Banting and H.S. Clark, *Banting as an Artist: A Collection of Sketches by Sir Frederick Banting* (Toronto: Academy of Medicine reproduced 1971); A.Y. Jackson, *Banting as an Artist*, with a Memoir by Frederick W.W. Hipwell (Toronto: Ryerson Press, Canadian Art Series, 1943).

157 C.C. Hill, *The Group of Seven: Art for a Nation* (Ottawa: National Gallery of Canada, 1995); A. Davis, *The Logic of Ecstasy: Canadian Mystical Painting, 1920–1940* (Toronto: University of Toronto Press, 1992); D. Reid, *A Concise History of Canadian Painting* (Toronto: Oxford University Press, 1988); J.R. Harper, *Painting in Canada: A History* (Toronto: University of Toronto Press, 1977); P. Mellen, *The Group of Seven* (Toronto: McClelland & Stewart, 1970).

158 J.W. McLaren, "The Group of Seven," from the Private Collection of John McLaren (Toronto: unpublished, c. 1978), p. 2A.

159 J.W. McLaren, "Sir Frederick Banting," from the Private Collection of John McLaren (Toronto: unpublished, c. 1978), p. 4A.

160 Ibid.

161 CBC, "Interview with Sergeant John (Jack) McLaren," *In Flanders Fields*.

162 "Hear 'Dumbells' Artists by Radio," newspaper advertisement, *Toronto Daily Star* (c. 1922), from Ivor Jack Ayre's Dumbell Collection at the Metro Toronto Reference Library. See also M. Vipond, *Listening In: The First Decade of Canadian Broadcasting, 1922–1932* (Montreal; Kingston: McGill-Queen's University Press, 1992); G.A. Proctor, *Canadian Music of the Twentieth Century* (Toronto: University of Toronto Press, 1980).

163 M. Vipond, *The Mass Media in Canada* (Toronto: James Lorimer & Co., 1989), p. 24.

164 Vipond, *Listening In*, pp. 78–89.

165 R. Newman, "Canada for Canadians," written by B. Lee and R.P. Weston (Montreal: Berliner Gram-O-Phone, Issue no. 216496, 1926).

166 See CBC, "Interview with Jack Ayre," *Voice of the Pioneer*.

167 "Obituary: Albert Edward Newman," *Boxoffice* (11 October 1952), p. 96.

Notes to Chapter VI

1   McNeil, *Dumbells Reunion*; CBC, *Camera Canada: The Dumbells with Affection*.
2   "The Story of The Dumbells, The Famous Concert Party of Third Canadian Division," newspaper clipping (from Ivor Jack Ayre's Dumbell Collection at the Metro Toronto Reference Library).
3   Earle, *Al Plunkett: The Famous Dumbell*, p. 77.
4   Review of Dumbells, "Biff, Bing, Bang," *New York Times* (10 May 1921).
5   A. Dale, "Review of Dumbells' 'Biff, Bing, Bang,'" *New York American*, as cited in *The Toronto Telegram*, 10 May 1921. See *Scrapbook of Reviews* (Ivor Jack Ayre's Dumbell Collection at the Metro Toronto Reference Library).
6   As quoted in "The Story of The Dumbells, The Famous Concert Party of Third Canadian Division," newspaper clipping (from Ivor Jack Ayre's Dumbell Collection at the Metro Toronto Reference Library).
7   Frank Willis, as quoted in CBC, *Camera Canada: The Dumbells with Affection*.
8   The Dumbells were performing at Toronto's Grand Theatre when Small disappeared. It had been thought that a man named Dougherty, treasurer of the theatre and Small's right-hand man, may have been responsible for his disappearance, but the crime was never solved and Small's body never found. See Jack McLaren quoted in D. Kucherawy, "Artist Remembers Dumbells, Group of 7," *London Free Press* (11 February 1978, from Ivor Jack Ayre's Dumbell Collection at the Metro Toronto Reference Library).
9   McLaren, *The Life Story of John Wilson McLaren*, p. 27.
10 Journalist Max Braithwaite suggested in his *Maclean's* article that the show made a profit of $80,000 in its first year. All told, Braithwaite suggested that Captain Plunkett made $500,000 from the Dumbells in North America. Braithwaite, "The Rise and Fall of the Dumbells," p. 39.
11 McLaren, *The Life Story of John Wilson McLaren*, p. 49.
12 Ibid.
13 Ibid., p. 51.
14 Ibid.
15 Ibid., p. 53.
16 Murray, "The Dumbells: Nostalgic Memories," p. 9.
17 J.J. Wilson, 'Interviews with Gael Hannan' (Toronto: December 2001; December 2008; 11 March 2010).
18 Annie O'Brien, as quoted in Wilson, "Interviews with Annie O'Brien."
19 Al Plunkett as quoted in Earle, *Al Plunkett: The Famous Dumbell*, p. 91.
20 Ibid., p. 104.
21 Bob Plunkett, as quoted in Wilson, "Interview with Bob Plunkett."
22 D. Braithwaite, "Dumbells Gave Us Hicks the Greatest Show on Earth," *On and Off the Air: The Toronto Star* (7 March 1978), section cover page.
23 McLaren, *The Life Story of John Wilson McLaren*, p. 53.
24 CBC, "Interview with Jack Ayre," *Voice of the Pioneer*.
25 CBC, "The Dumbells Press Conference."
26 Ibid.
27 W. Dickinson, "Dumbells Review," *New York Evening Telegraph*, as found in McLaren, *The Life Story of John Wilson McLaren*, p. 55.
28 F.V. Stade, as quoted in A. Anderson, "The Grocer's Boy Who Became a Big Theatrical Success," *The New Magazine* (c. 1922), from Ivor Jack Ayre's Dumbell Collection at the Metro Toronto Reference Library.
29 "'Dumbells' to Become Canadian Institution," *Daily Times-Journal* (c. spring 1920), from Ivor Jack Ayre's Dumbell Collection at the Metro Toronto Reference Library.

30 CBC, "The Dumbells Press Conference."

31 "'Dumbells' Show Responsible for Sale of Several Feist Hits—Sale of Capt. Plunkett's 'Come Back Old Pal' Away Up in Five Figures," *Canadian Music Trades Journal*, 24, 8 (January 1924), pp. 71–72.

32 "Dumbells Featuring Feist Songs," *Canadian Music Trades Journal*, 23, 1 (June 1922), p. 66.

33 Braithwaite, "The Rise and Fall of the Dumbells," p. 39.

34 Morley and his wife Joan were married in Peterborough and later moved to Halifax. Morley Plunkett died April 1953. Wilson, "Interviews with Gael Hannan."

35 "'Dumbells' Show Responsible for Sale of Several Feist hits," *Canadian Music Trades Journal*, pp. 71–72.

36 Red Newman later rejoined the Dumbells.

37 See Appendices D and E.

38 "The Originals Score Heavily in 'Rapid Fire,'" *Edmonton Bulletin* (23 October 1923).

39 "At the Grand: Rapid Fire," *Peterborough Examiner* (4 September 1923).

40 CBC, *Camera Canada: The Dumbells with Affection*. Toronto, 1965. Tape No. B-07510. Video.

41 For example, the article suggested that the Originals had folded within a year of their formation, whereas the truth of the matter is that the splinter group toured with several revues until 1928. The Braithwaite article is full of references to the Dumbells' financial affairs, and these two must be viewed with some suspicion. See Braithwaite, "The Rise and Fall of the Dumbells," p. 39; CBC, "Interview with Alan Murray," *Grace Lydiatt Shaw*; "Interview with Jerry Brayford," *Grace Lydiatt Shaw* (Toronto, 1962, National Archives of Canada, ISN 61334, Shelf no. C09408{6}).

42 Brayford claimed that the men were owed approximately $15,000 each. CBC, "Interview with Jerry Brayford," *Grace Lydiatt Shaw* (Toronto, 1962, National Archives of Canada, ISN. 61334, Shelf no. C09408{6}).

43 Braithwaite, "The Rise and Fall of the Dumbells," p. 39.

44 "Plunketts Forego Pay," *Toronto Daily Star* (23 April 1930).

45 Loose newspaper clipping (c. 1936), from Ivor Jack Ayre's Dumbell Collection at the Metro Toronto Reference Library.

46 CBC, *Canadian Theatre Fact and Fancy: Parts 4 and 5*; Drysdale, "Dumbells Marjorie Now Man Again," p. 6.; Drysdale, "Dumbells Marjorie Now Man Again," p. 6.

47 Jim Kennedy, son-in-law of Morley Plunkett, as quoted in J.J. Wilson, "Interview with Jim Kennedy" (Tilsonburg, 11 March 2010).

48 "Ross Hamilton, World War I Dumbell, Dies," *Montreal Gazette* (30 September 1965), p. 20.

49 From 29 September 1919 through until 25 November 1922, the Dumbells performed an incredible 250 shows that ranged from one-night stands to eight-week runs.

50 The Grand Theatre was torn down in 1930. S. Handman, "The Dumbells Are Back," *Weekend Magazine, The Toronto Telegram* (16 April 1959), p. 59.

51 National Library of Canada, "The Dumbells: Part Two—The North American Tour (1919–1932)," *The Virtual Gramophone*: www2.nlc-bnc.ca/gramophone/src/dumbells2e .htm. See also "Plunketts Forego Pay," p. 8.

52 J.D. McLaren, "Short Chronological Biography of his Father Jack" (Toronto: c. unknown, from the private collection of John McLaren).

53 CBC, "Interview with Jack Ayre," *Grace Lydiatt Shaw*.

54 G. Salverson, "Email letter to Kathy Witheridge," 7 April 2001 (from the collection of Kathy Witheridge).

55   Plunkett, "We'll Make 'Em Laugh Again," cover page. Also see "Soldier-Concert Parties Are Being Organized in Every Military Camp under Capt. M. Plunkett of Dumbells Fame: Legion Offers Study Courses to C.A.S.F. Units," *Globe and Mail* (28 November 1939).

56   L. Halladay, "*Ladies and Gentlemen, Soldiers and Artists": Canadian Military Entertainers, 1939–1946*, M.A. thesis (Calgary: University of Calgary, 2000), p. 13.

57   Ibid., p. 14.

58   L. Henson, *Yours Faithfully* (London: Long, 1948). Some soldiers were, however, less impressed with ENSA's quality. For these soldiers, the ENSA acronym became colloquially known as Every Night Something Awful.

59   D. Behan, *Milligan: The Life and Times of Spike Milligan* (London: Methuen, 1988).

60   H. Carpenter, *Spike Milligan: The Biography* (London: Hodder & Stoughton, 2003).

61   S. Milligan, *Adolf Hitler: My Part in His Downfall* (London: Penguin Books, 1971); Biography of Spike Milligan, www.telegoons.org.

62   Milligan, *Adolf Hitler: My Part in His Downfall*, preface.

63   *Royal Variety Performance*: Held in the presence of Her Majesty Queen Elizabeth II and His Royal Highness The Duke of Edinburgh K.G., K.T; presented by Val Parnell; musical director: Eric Rogers; stage director: Charles Henry. London: Palladium Theatre, 1 November 1954. Concert.

64   Morrison, Richard, "Music Lifts the Mood of War: A fascinating exhibition reveals how wartime entertainment inspired the country and had a lasting cultural impression," *The Times* (15 April 2003).

65   John Cleese, as quoted in M. Ventham, *Spike Milligan: His Part in Our Lives* (London: Robson, 2002), p. 150.

66   Monty Python, *The Pythons: Autobiography by the Pythons* (New York: Thomas Dunne Books, 2003).

67   L. Halladay, "'It Made Them Forget about the War for a Minute': Canadian Army, Navy and Air Force Entertainment Units during the Second World War," *Canadian Military History*, 11, 4 (Autumn 2002), p. 22. For further discussion on several Second World War Canadian entertainment troupes including the Bluebell Bullets and the Halifax Concert Party, see P.B. O'Neill, "The Halifax Concert Party in World War II," *Theatre Research in Canada*, 20, 2 (Fall 1999).

68   V.S. Purdy, *As Luck Would Have It: Adventures in the Canadian Army Show, 1938–1946* (St. Catharines: Vanwell, 2003).

69   L. Halladay, "Canada's Military Planted Seeds for Flourishing Arts Scene," *In the News* (University of Calgary, 4 November 2004).

70   Palmer, "*What a Lovely War!*" pp. 16–17.

71   Ibid.

72   A. Barris, "Goodbye, Farewell, Adieu, Frank Shuster," *Toronto Star* (21 January 2002).

73   D. Hill and J. Weingrad, *Saturday Night* (New York: Vintage Books, 1986), p. 37. See also T. Shales and James Andrew Miller, *Live from New York: An Uncensored History of Saturday Night Live* (Boston: Little, Brown, 2002).

74   For a discussion on SCTV, its Canadian roots and its cast's relationship with *Saturday Night Live*, see D. Thomas with Robert Crane and Susan Carney, *SCTV: Behind the Scenes* (Toronto: M&S, 1996).

75   For an excellent overview of the reunion and its significance, see J. Vance, "'Today They Were Alive Again': The Canadian Corps Reunion of 1934," *Ontario History*, 87, 4 (December 1995), pp. 327–44.

76   Vance, "'Today They Were Alive Again,'" p. 327.

77   For the veterans' role in the development of Social Welfare in Canada, see L. Campbell, "We Who Have Wallowed in the Mud of Flanders: First World War Veterans, Unemployment,

and the Development of Social Welfare in Canada, 1929–1939," *Journal of the Canadian Historical Association*, 11 (2000), pp. 125–49.

78 The Canadian Legion of the British Empire Service League, "Report of the Ontario Provincial Command," Annual Convention (1933).

79 Canon Scott's sermon on 6 August 1934, as reprinted in T.C. Lapp (ed.), *The Story of the Canadian Corps, 1914–1934* (Toronto: Canadian Veteran Associates, 1934), pp. 35–36; Vance, "'Today They Were Alive Again,'" pp. 336–37, 343.

80 Vance, "'Today They Were Alive Again,'" p. 334.

81 Vance, "'Today They Were Alive Again,'" pp. 333–34.

82 G. Anglin, "Direct Hit: Old Soldier Shows Never Die," *The Canadian* (25 February 1978), p. 20.

83 G.R. Stevens, *Princess Patricia's Canadian Light Infantry: 1914–1964 – In Proud Memory of a Cherished Fellowship in a Rare Company* (Calgary: PPCLI, 1964), pp. 1–2.

84 *Globe* (7 August 1934), edition cover page; *Brantford Expositor* (3 August 1934), p. 3; Vance, "'Today They Were Alive Again,'" pp. 338, 343.

85 Mrs. T.J. Lilly, "Letter to J.W. McLaren," as found in McLaren, *The Life Story of John Wilson McLaren*, p. 33.

86 The Originals' reunion was featured on a rare coast-to-coast radio performance on the CBC on 28 August 1937. See "Told to 'Put Show Over' or Go Back into Trenches," *Toronto Star* (21 August 1937).

87 CBC, "The Dumbells Press Conference."

88 The singer continued his musical studies with Dr. Albert Hamm, the then head of the Canadian Academy of Music and conductor of the Toronto Choral Union. Even at 86 years of age, Redpath was still a member of the Scarborough Art Guild and with the Singers Over Sixty choral group. A.M. Ashley, "Bill Redpath: From Flanders to Dumbells," *Ottawa Citizen* (6 September 1977), p. 78.

89 McLaren, *The Life Story of John Wilson McLaren*, p. 61.

90 V. Ross, "One More Flight of the Canada Goose." *Maclean's* (24 March 1980); D. Harron, "Remembering Spring Thaw," *Toronto Life* (April 1979); T. Frayne, "They Kid Canada for Fun and Profit," *Toronto Star Weekly* (14 April 1962).

91 Ibid., p. 63.

92 He was asked by Lismer.

93 J. Champagne, "The Charlottetown Festival brings back The Dumbells," *Canadian Composer* (September 1977, No. 123), p. 26.

94 "The Legend of The Dumbells," Artistic Director Duncan McIntosh (Charlottetown, 11 June–29 August 2002, Confederation Centre of the Arts).

95 Frank Willis as quoted in CBC, *Camera Canada: The Dumbells with Affection*.

96 CBC, *The Observer* (Toronto, 23 January 1964, No. 17, National Archives of Canada, ISN 287842, Shelf no. V1 8205-0064).

97 Annie O'Brien, as quoted in Wilson, "Interviews with Annie O'Brien."

98 CBC, "Interview with Laurie Thompson," *Grace Lydiatt Shaw*.

99 Ibid.

100 CBC, "Interview with Hugh Mill," *Grace Lydiatt Shaw* (Toronto: 1962, National Archives of Canada, ISN 62722, Shelf no. C09475{2}).

101 Wilson, "Interview with Bob Plunkett."

102 L. Brown, *Father and Me and The Dumbells* (Toronto: unpublished, c. 1990s), p. 2.

103 Ibid.

104 Ibid., pp. 2–6.

105 W.B. Davis, "Official Proclamation Presented to the Four Surviving Dumbell Members, McLaren, Redpath, Bradford and Ayre" (Parliament Buildings Toronto, 2 May 1975, from the private collection of John McLaren).

106 E.B. Moogk, "Liner Notes," *The Dumbells: The Original Dumbells Music*, Head of the
     Recorded Sound Section, National Library of Canada (Canada: CBS, 1977).
107 Franklin, "A Funny Thing Happened on the Way to the Trenches," p. 28.

Notes on Sources

1 B. Taylor, with files from J.J. Wilson, "Daredevils in Drag: The Dumbells," *Toronto Star*
   (6 November 2001).
2 J.J. Wilson, "Email Correspondence from Frances Kerr," November 2001.
3 J.J. Wilson, "Email Correspondence from Jim Spencer," November 2001.

Bibliography

Primary Sources

Art, Photographs, and Miscellaneous

3 photographs of 13 Billet's John H R. (Jack) Slack. From the private collection of Joyce Beaton.

30 pieces of Dumbells' sheet music. From the private collection of Stephen Plunkett. (*See Appendix F.*)

36 black-and-white slides of the Dumbells. From the private collection of Stephen Plunkett.

Archives of Ontario, *Toronto Centennial Celebrations*, Toronto Centennial Collection. Toronto: MU2989, 1934. <*program*>

Bairnsfather, Bruce, "Fragments from France," *The Bystander*. London: Tallis House, Whitefriars, c. 1916.

Davis, W.B., Premier, "Official Proclamation Presented to the Four Surviving Dumbell Members, McLaren, Redpath, Braford and Ayre." Parliament Buildings Toronto, 2 May 1975. From the private collection of John McLaren.

Dumbells. http://www.playbill.on.ca/dumbells.htm.

Dumbells. *Program for the Lambert Lodge Reunion Special*, CBC: 3 May 1975. From the private collection of Stephen Plunkett.

———. Dumbells, *Grand Theatre Programs*, 1923. University of Guelph. <*programs*>

———. *Program for "Carry On": Russel Theatre*, Dumbells Company. Modern Press: 31 May–1 June 1923. <*program*>

———. *Program for The "Dumbell" Concert Party*, France: 29 July 1918. From the private collection of Stephen Plunkett. <*program*>

———. *The "Dumbell" Concert Party: Assisted by No. 7 Convalescent Depot Orchestra*, Canadian Red Cross Recreation Hut, No. 3 Canadian General Hospital. 29 July 1918. <*program*>

———. *Program for Third Divisional Concert Party* France: 1917. From the private collection of Stephen Plunkett.

———. *Programme for The Dumbells: Third Canadian Divisional Concert Party, France, Under the Patronage of Maj. Gen. L. J. Lipsett C.M.G.* France: 1917. <*program*>

"The Legend of the Dumbells," Artistic Director Duncan McIntosh. Charlottetown: 11 June–29 August 2002, Confederation Centre of the Arts. *<program>*
———. Tapestry Music Theatre Production. *<program>*
McLaren, J.W., 101 black-and-white slides of the Dumbells and the Princess Patricia's Canadian Light Infantry. From the private collection of John McLaren.
———."Sketchbook of Comedy Sketches." c. 1915–18. From the private collection of John McLaren.
———. "Self-Portrait," Steenvoorde: 1916. From the private collection of John McLaren.
Royal Variety Performance: Held in the presence of Her Majesty Queen Elizabeth II and His Royal Highness, The Duke of Edinburgh K.G., K.T, presented by Val Parnell; musical director, Eric Rogers; stage director: Charles Henry. London: Palladium Theatre, 1 November 1954. *<concert>*
Y-Emmas Programme, London: The Imperial War Museum, 12 and 13 September 1918. *<program>*

Audio, Film, Oral Interviews, Sheet Music, and Video
Bryan, Alfred. "I Didn't Raise My Boy to Be a Soldier." Words by A. Bryan, music by A. Piantadosi. New York: Leo Feist Inc. 1915. *<sheet music>*
CBC. *Between Ourselves: The Dumbells Reunion*, with host Bill McNeil. 7 November 1975. *<audio>*
———. "The Dumbells Farewell Concert at Lambert Lodge." *Between Ourselves*, with Bill McNeil. Toronto: 3 May 1975. National Archives of Canada, ISN 177084, Shelf no. C10900{1}. *<audio>*
———. "Blyth Festival: The Life That Jack Built," *Sunday Morning*. 10 August 1980. *<audio>*
———. *Camera Canada: The Dumbells with Affection*. Toronto: 1965. Tape No. B-07510. *<video>*
———. *The Dumbells*. Toronto: 1978. National Archives of Canada, ISN 107627, Shelf no. 8901-0026. *<television program>*
———. *The Dumbells Farewell Concert at Lambert Lodge, Toronto: Out-Takes*, with Bill McNeil. Toronto: 3 May 1975. National Archives of Canada, ISN 177082, Shelf no. A4 2002-09-0019{2}. *<audio>*
———. "The Dumbells Press Conference," *Fresh Air*, with Bill McNeil, interview includes Jack Ayre, Jerry Brayford, Jack McLaren, and William Redpath. 1 May 1975. *<audio>*
———. "The Dumbells Reunion," *Fresh Air*, with Bill McNeil. 2 May 1975. *<audio>*
———. "Interview with Jack Ayre," *Grace Lydiatt Shaw*. Toronto: 14 December 1961. National Archives of Canada, ISN 61338, Shelf no. A19907-0003}. *<audio>*
———."Interview with Jerry Brayford," *Grace Lydiatt Shaw*. Toronto: 1962. National Archives of Canada, ISN 61334, Shelf no. C09408{6}. *<audio>*
———. *Canadian Theatre Fact and Fancy with Grace Lydiatt Shaw: Parts 4 and 5*. Toronto: 1964. National Archives of Canada, ISN 60431, Shelf no. C09285{1}.
———."Interview with Basil Donn," *Grace Lydiatt Shaw*. Toronto: 1961. National Archives of Canada, ISN 62482, Shelf no. C09445{1}. *<audio>*

———. "Interview with Ross Hamilton," *Grace Lydiatt Shaw*. Toronto: 1962. National Archives of Canada, ISN 61429, Shelf no. C09417(4). <*audio*>

———. "Interview with Hugh Mill" *Grace Lydiatt Shaw*. Toronto: 1962. National Archives of Canada, ISN 62722, Shelf no. C09475(2). <*audio*>

———. "Interview with Alan Murray," *Grace Lydiatt Shaw*. Toronto: 1961. National Archives of Canada, ISN 61426, Shelf no. C09417{3}. <*audio*>

———."Interview with William Redpath," *Grace Lydiatt Shaw*. Toronto: 1962. National Archives of Canada, ISN 61324, Shelf no. C09407(6). <*audio*>

———."Interview with Conrad Stephens," *Grace Lydiatt Shaw*. Toronto: 1962. National Archives of Canada, ISN 61306, Shelf no. C09407. <*audio*>

———."Interview with Laurie Thompson," *Grace Lydiatt Shaw*. Toronto: 1962. National Archives of Canada, ISN 61304, Shelf no. C09407. <*audio*>

———. "Interview with Ivor Jack Ayre," *In Flanders Fields*. Toronto: 17 May 1963. National Archives of Canada, ISN 117350, Shelf no. C07853(2). <*audio*>

———. "Interview with Sergeant John (Jack) McLaren," *In Flanders Fields*. Toronto: March/April 1964. National Archives of Canada, Tapes R7728 and R7729. <*audio*>

———. *Old Sweats and Dumbells*. Toronto: 11 November 1961. <*audio*>

———. *The Observer*. Toronto: 23 January 1964, No. 17. National Archives of Canada, ISN 287842, Shelf no. V1 8205-0064. <*video*>

———. "Interview with Jack Ayre," *Voice of the Pioneer*, with B. McNeil. Toronto: 1975. National Archives of Canada, ISN 177083, Shelf no. A1 2002-09-0019. <*audio*>

———. "Interview with Archie Wills," *Voice of the Pioneer*, with B. McNeil. Toronto: 1981. National Archives of Canada, ISN 169473, Shelf no. C10917. <*audio*>

———. "Interview with Captain Mert Plunkett." Journalist unknown. Date unknown. <*audio*>

———. "Interview with Jack McLaren." Journalist unknown. Toronto: 6 May 1983. <*audio*>

Dumbells. "Shall I Have It Bobbed or Shingled?" Toronto: Leo Feist, 1924. From the private collection of Helen C. Armitage. <*sheet music*>

Feinstein, Michael. *Over There*. Hayes: Middlesex/EMI, 1989. <*audio*>

The Great War: The Virtual History Collection. England: Castle Multi Media, 1995. <*CD-ROM*>

Lauder, Harry. *Scotland's Stars on 78 Presents Sir Harry Lauder*. Liner notes by Frank Wappat. Glasgow: Lismor Recordings, 1994. <*audio*>

———. *Sir Harry Lauder Favourites, 1926–1928*. Liner notes by Abel Green. Montreal: RCA Victor, Treasury of Immortal Performances, n.d. <*audio*>

———. "The Road to the Isles," from *The Scottish Songbook*, The Balladeer Series. Moidart Music Group, 1994. <*audio*>

Manley, Morris, and Mildred Manley. "Good Luck to the Boys of the Allies." Written by Morris Manley. Toronto: Morris Manley, 1915. <*sheet music*>

McLaren, Jack. *Pension Meeting*, 23 January 1981. From the private collection of John McLaren. <*audio*>

———. *Dumbells: Arts and Letters Meeting P.P.L.L.I.S.*. Toronto: n.d. From the private collection of John McLaren. <*audio*>

McLaren, Jack, and Ed Stiles. "Live Performance," 14 November 1984. From the private collection of John McLaren. <audio>

McNeil, Bill. Dumbells Reunion, National Archives of Canada: 1975, ISN 177078, Shelf no. C10896{1}. <audio>

Molloy, Bruce. Bruce Molloy. <phono LP>

Monty Python. The Meaning of Life. The Monty Python Partnership, March 1982. <film>

———. Monty Python and the Holy Grail. Python (Monty) Pictures; Michael White Productions; National Film Trustee Company; Twickenham Film Studios, 1975. <film>

Moogk, E.B. Liner notes, The Dumbells: The Original Dumbells Music. Head of the Recorded Sound Section, National Library of Canada, CBS, 1977. <phono>

National Film Board of Canada. Good Bright Days. 29 minutes. 1960. <film>

National Library of Canada. "Albert Edward (Red) Newman: 1887–1952." The Virtual Gramophone: Canadian Historical Sound Recordings. www.2.nlc-bnc.ca/gramo phone/src/newmane.htm

———. "Albert Plunkett: 1899–1957." The Virtual Gramophone: Canadian Historical Sound Recordings. www.2.nlc-bnc.ca/gramophone/src/plunketae.htm

———. "Captain Merton (Mert) Wesley Plunkett: 1888–1966," The Virtual Gramo-phone: Canadian Historical Sound Recordings. www.2.nlc-bnc.ca/gramophone/src/ plunketme.htm

———. "Ivor (Jack) Ayre: 1894–1977," The Virtual Gramophone: Canadian Historical Sound Recordings. www.2.nlc-bnc.ca/gramophone/src/ayree.htm

———. "Lieutenant Gitz Rice," The Virtual Gramophone: Canadian Historical Sound Recordings. www.2.nlc-bnc.ca/gramophone/src/ricee.htm

———. "Ross Hamilton: 1889–1965," The Virtual Gramophone: Canadian Historical Sound Recordings. www.2.nlc-bnc.ca/gramophone/src/hamiltone.htm

———. "The Dumbells Part One: The Canadian Army Third Division Concert Party (1917–1919)." The Virtual Gramophone: Canadian Historical Sound Recordings. www.2.nlc-bnc.ca/gramophone/src/dumbells1e.htm

———. "The Dumbells Part Two: The North American Tour (1919–1932)," The Virtual Gramophone: Canadian Historical Sound Recordings. www.2.nlc-bnc.ca/gramophone/ src/dumbells2e.htm

———. "The Dumbells," The Virtual Gramophone: Canadian Historical Sound Record-ings. www.2.nlc-bnc.ca/gramophone/src/dumbellse.htm

Newman, Red. "Oh! It's a Lovely War," written by J. Long, M. Scott, & B. Felman. The Dumbells, Biff Bing Bang, Toronto: Leo Feist Inc., 1920. <sheet music>

Norman, B. "Music on the Home Front." Sheet Music from Canada's Past, National Library of Canada. www.nlc-bnc.ca/sheetmusic/m5-170-e.html

Oh, What a Lovely War. 1983. <phono LP>

Rutherford, George. "Home Movie." Simcoe County Archives, National Archives of Can-ada. <film>

Soldier Songs of Canada. Toronto: G.V. Thomson/London: Studio Vista.

Turner, M.E. "The Dumbells." From a collection of 33 × 35 mm films and 46 × 16 mm films, 1951–1954, National Archives of Canada. <*film*>

Whiting, Richard A., and Raymond B. Egan. "Till We Meet Again." Jerome H. Remick & Co., 1918. <*sheet music*>

Wilson, John Jason. "Interviews with John D. McLaren." Toronto, December 2001; December 2009.

————. "Interviews with Annie O'Brien." Toronto, December 2001; December 2008; 11 March 2010. <*video*>

————. "Interview with Jim Kennedy." Tilsonburg, 11 March 2010.

————. "Interviews with Gael Hannan." Toronto, December 2001; December 2008; 11 March 2010. <*video*>

————. "Interview with Stephen Plunkett." Peterborough, December 2001. <*video*>

————. "Interview with Bob Plunkett." Toronto, December 2001. <*video*>

————. "Interview with Marion Plunkett." Toronto, December 2001. <*video*>

Books

Banting, Sir Frederick Grant, and Herbert Spencer Clark. *Banting as an Artist: A Collection of Sketches by Sir Frederick Banting.* Toronto: Academy of Medicine, reproduced 1971.

Bird, Will. *The Communication Trench.* Ottawa: CEF Books, 2000.

Bishop, Charles. *The YMCA in the Great War.* Toronto, 1921.

Brophy, John, and Eric Partridge. *Songs and Slang of the British Soldier, 1914–1918.* London: Eric Partridge Ltd., 1931.

Canada in the Great War. Six vols. Toronto: Canadian Annual Review Ltd., 1921.

Canadian Annual Review of Public Affairs, 1934. Toronto: Canadian Review Co. 1935.

Castell Hopkins, J., *Canada at War: 1914–1918.* New York: Canadian Annual Review Ltd., 1919.

Chapleau, J.A., and J.H. Gray, *Report of the Royal Commission on Chinese Immigration: Report and Evidence.* Ottawa: Printed by Order of the Commission, 1885.

Chertkov, Vladimir, Leo Tolstoy, and James Mavor. *Christian Martyrdom in Russia: An Account of the Members of the Universal Brotherhood or Doukhobortsi, now migrating from the Caucasus to Canada.* Toronto: G.N. Morang, 1899.

Duguid, A.F. *Official History of the Canadian Forces in the Great War, 1914–1919,* Vol. I. Ottawa: J.O. Patenaude, 1938.

Earle, Patrise, as told by Al Plunkett. *Al Plunkett: The Famous Dumbell.* New York: Pageant Press, 1956.

Gladden, E.N. *Ypres, 1917: A Personal Account.* London: Kimber, 1967.

Henson, Leslie. *Yours Faithfully.* London: Long, 1948.

Hodder-Williams, Ralph Wilfred. *Princess Patricia's Canadian Light Infantry, 1914–1919.* London: Hodder and Stoughton, 1923.

Innes, C.R. *With Paget's Horse to the Front.* London: 1901.

Lapp, T.C. (ed.). *The Story of the Canadian Corps, 1914–1934.* Toronto: Canadian Veteran Associates, 1934.

Lauder, Harry. *A Minstrel in France.* Toronto: McClelland, Goodchild and Stewart, 1918.

McLaren, John D. *The Life Story of John Wilson McLaren, 1895–1988.* Toronto: McLaren Press Graphics Limited, c. 2006.

Middleton, J.E. *Sea Dogs and Men at Arms: A Canadian Book of Songs.* Toronto: McClelland, Goodchild and Stewart, 1918.

Nettleingham, F.T. *Tommy's Tunes.* London: Erskine, MacDonald, 1917.

Oh, Canada. London: Simpkin, Marshall; Kent and Co. Ltd., 1916.

Overseas Military Force in Canada 1918. Report of the Ministry. London: Printed by Authority of the Ministry Overseas Military Forces of Canada, Queen's Printer, {1918} 1919.

Peel, C.S. *How We Lived Then.* London: 1929.

Russell, A. *With the Machine Gun Corps.* London: 1923.

Scott, James Brown. *The Hague Peace Conferences of 1899 and 1907,* A Series of Lectures Delivered before the Johns Hopkins University in the Year 1908, Vol. II. Baltimore: Johns Hopkins Press, 1909.

Sheldon-Williams, Ralf Frederic Lardy. *The Canadian Front in France and Flanders.* London: A. and C. Black, 1920.

Periodicals

The B.E.F. Times
The Better Times
Brantford Expositor
The Canadian Daily Herald
Canadian Historical Review
Canadian Music Trade Journal
Canadian Press
Daily Mail and Empire (Toronto)
The Daily Times-Journal
Echoes
The Edmonton Bulletin
The Globe (Toronto)
The Globe and Mail
The Guardian
The Guardian (Charlottetown)
The Hamilton Spectator
The Kemmel Times
Kitchener Daily Record
The Legionary
Listening Post
London Free Press
Maclean's Magazine
Maple Leaf Magazine
Montreal Gazette
The National Post
The New Church Times
The New Magazine

The New York Evening Telegraph
The New York Times
The Ottawa Citizen
The Ottawa Journal
The Owen Sound Sun-Times
The Peterborough Examiner
The Somme Times
'Tchun
The Toronto Daily Star
The Toronto Star
Toronto Telegram
Weekend Magazine

Acheson, Maurice. "Facts about Kinmel Park Made Public," *Calgary Daily Herald.* 17 June 1919.

Allen, Ralph. "Famed Hoofers and Players of 1917 May Answer Canada's 'Fall In.'" *Globe and Mail. 19* October 1939.

Anderson, A. "The Grocer's Boy who Became a Big Theatrical Success." *New Magazine.* c. 1922. From Ivor Jack Ayre's Dumbell Collection at the Metro Toronto Reference Library.

Ashley, Audrey M. "Bill Redpath: From Flanders to Dumbells." *Ottawa Citizen.* 6 September 1977.

Anglin, Gerald. "Direct Hit: Old Soldier Shows Never Die." *The Canadian.* 25 February 1978.

"At the Grand: Rapid Fire." *Peterborough Examiner.* 4 September 1923.

Ayre, I. Jack. *Several Newspaper Clippings, Scrapbooks, Sheet Music and Tour Itineraries.* From Ivor Jack Ayre's Dumbell Collection at the Metro Toronto Reference Library.

Barris, Ted. "Soldiers, Snipers and Comedians," *National Post.* 5 April 2007.

Bell, Margaret. "Amusing the Canadian Soldier in Old London." *Maclean's.* October 1916.

"Biff, Bing, Bang." Review of Dumbells Revue. *New York Times.* 10 May 1921.

Braithwaite, Dennis. "Dumbells Gave Us Hicks the Greatest Show on Earth." *Toronto Star.* 7 March 1978.

———. "Remembering Captain Plunkett." *Globe and Mail.* Toronto: 22 June 1965.

Braithwaite, Max. "A *Maclean's* Flashback: The Rise and Fall of The Dumbells." *Maclean's.* 1 January 1952.

Brantford Expositor. 3 August 1934.

Bridle, Augustus. "Music and Mars." *Maclean's.* December 1915.

Brown, Dave. "They're Big Dumbells, but What a Show!" *Ottawa Journal.* 7 September 1977.

Canadian Daily Record. Issued by the Canadian War Records Office to All Units of the Overseas Military Forces of Canada. 8 February 1918.

———. "Third Division Concert Party Scored Big Hit in London," Issued by the Canadian War Records Office to All Units of the Overseas Military Forces of Canada, No. 511. France: 6 September 1918.

Canadian Music Trade Journal. "New Dumbell Revue, 'Ace-High' Will Cover Canada,"
    25. Toronto: Fullerton Publishing, September 1924.

———. "'Dumbells' Show Responsible for Sale of Several Feist Hits," 24. Toronto: Ful-
    lerton Publishing, January 1924.

———. "Dumbells Featuring Feist Songs" 23. Toronto: Fullerton Publishing, June 1922.

Charlesworth, Hector. "A Popular Memory—The Dumbells." *The Legionary.* April 1937.

Chevrons to Stars. "Pierrot Notes," Canadian Training School, England, c. Unknown.

Claridge, Fred. "YMCA's Aid to Dumbells Recalled by Plunkett." *Globe and Mail.*
    Toronto: 13 June 1956.

Daily Mail and Empire. 7 August 1934.

Dale, A. "Biff, Bing, Bang." Review of Dumbells Revue. *The New York American.* 10 May
    1921.

The Dead Horse Corner Gazette, 1. Published by the 4th Batt. First Canadian Contingent,
    B.E.F. October 1915.

Donovan, Edward J. "Percy Campbell Talks to Edward J. Donovan: Remember the
    Dumbells?" *Ottawa Journal.* 30 November 1963.

Drysdale, Ira. "Dumbells Marjorie Now Man Again, but Gave War Troops Good Times."
    Owen Sound Sun-Times. 19 May 1961.

"'Dumbells' to Become Canadian Institution." *Daily Times-Journal.* c. Spring 1920.
    From Ivor Jack Ayre's Dumbell Collection at the Metro Toronto Reference Library.

"Dumbells Together Again." *Canadian Press.* July 1975.

"Entertaining the Fighters." *Echoes, 66.* December 1916.

Franklin, Stephen. "A Funny Thing Happened on the Way to the Trenches: Jack McLaren
    as told to Stephen Franklin." *Weekend Magazine, 47.* 25 November 1967.

Frayne, Trent. "They Kid Canada for Fun and Profit," *Toronto Star Weekly.* 14 April 1962.

Globe. 7 August 1934.

———. 6 August 1934.

———. 4 August 1934.

Handman, S. "The Dumbells Are Back." *Toronto Telegram: Weekend Magazine.* 16 April
    1955.

Harron, Don. "Remembering Spring Thaw." *Toronto Life.* April 1979.

"Hear 'Dumbells' Artists by Radio." Newspaper advertisement, *Toronto Daily Star.*
    c. 1922. From Ivor Jack Ayre's Dumbell Collection at the Metro Toronto Reference
    Library.

James, Fred. "Performed for Royalty: Canadian 'Dumbells' Have Great Success on Brus-
    sels and London Stage," *Toronto Daily Star.* 4 January 1919.

Jeffrey, J. "Dumbells Gives Show Top Marks." *The Guardian.* Charlottetown: 28 June
    1977.

Keen, F.J. "Dumbells of First World War Fame Recalled." *Hamilton Spectator.* 5 February
    1965.

Kitchener Daily Record. 4 August 1934.

Kucherawy, D. "Artist Remembers Dumbells, Group of 7." *London Free Press.* 11 Febru-
    ary 1978.

Leacock, S. "Canada and the Immigration Problem." *National and English Review*. April 1911.

LeVasseur, Nazaire. "Musique et musiciens à Québec." *La Musique*, 2. August 1920.

The Listening Post, 29. Published by the 7th Battalion. London: Canadian Military Headquarters. 1 December 1917.

————, 19. Published by the 7th Battalion. London: Canadian Military Headquarters. October 1916.

————, 5. Published by the 7th Battalion. London: Canadian Military Headquarters. October 1915.

————, 3. Published by the 7th Battalion. London: Canadian Military Headquarters. September 1915.

Maple Leaf Magazine, II. "Singing to Canadians." 5 October 1916.

McLaren, John "Jack" Wilson. "Mirth and Mud Part III—In Which the Curtain Is Rung Down on the 'Comic Relief' of the Greatest Drama in History." *Maclean's*. 15 May 1929.

————. "Mirth and Mud Part II—Being Another Chapter from the Tragically Comic Experiences of the PPCLI Concert Party, Entitled: Orphans and Orphans." *Maclean's*. 1 March 1929.

————. "Mirth and Mud: The Chronicle of the First Organized Canadian Concert Party to Tour the Trenches during the Great War." *Maclean's*. 1 January 1929.

Minton, E. "PS on 'The Dumbells.'" *Ottawa Journal*. 2 December 1972.

————. "The Dumbells." *Ottawa Journal*. 11 November 1972.

Murray, Alan. "The Dumbells—Nostalgic Memories of World War One's Great Soldier Entertainers." *The Legionary*, 39. January 1965.

Musgrove, M.J. "Dumbells Blend Past with Present." *The Guardian*. Charlottetown, 28 June 1977.

"Obituary: Albert Edward Newman." *Boxoffice*. 11 October 1952.

O'Connor, Albert. "Letter to the Editor," *Toronto Star*. 3 December 1974.

O' Hara, Geoffrey. "Ontario to Tin Pan Alley." *Maclean's*, 34. 1 April 1921.

"Old Soldiers Never Die." *Toronto Daily Star*. 7 August 1934.

"The Originals Score Heavily in "Rapid Fire."" *Edmonton Bulletin*. 23 October 1923.

"The Pavilion." *'Tchun*, 1. 5 December 1917.

Plunkett, Merton. "We'll Make 'Em Laugh Again." *Toronto Star*. 13 January 1940.

————. "Merton Plunkett Recalls Gay Days Dumbell Troupe." *Peterborough Examiner*. 1 April 1953.

"Plunketts Forego Pay." *Toronto Daily Star*. 23 April 1930.

Rasky, Frank. "When Shells Fell in World War One, He Played On." *Toronto Star*. 9 November 1974.

"Ross Hamilton, World War I Dumbell, Dies." *Montreal Gazette*. 30 September 1965.

Ross, Val. "One More Flight of the Canada Goose." *Maclean's*. 24 March 1980.

"Soldier-Concert Parties Are Being Organized in Every Military Camp under Capt. M. Plunkett of Dumbells Fame: Legion Offers Study Courses to C.A.S.F. Units." *Globe and Mail*. 28 November 1939.

The Somme Times. 31 July 1916.

Taylor, Bill, with files from John Jason Wilson. "Daredevils in Drag: The Dumbells."
    Toronto Star. 6 November 2001.
"Told to 'Put Show Over' or Go Back into Trenches." Toronto Star. 21 August 1937.
Toronto Daily Star. 7 August 1934.
Toronto Telegram, 10 May 1921.
Whittaker, Herbert. "Dumbells' Rag: From Vimy to Broadway." Globe and Mail. Toronto,
    27 June 1977.

War Diaries, Letters, Memoirs, and Military Records
9th Canadian Field Ambulance. Official War Diary. www.collectionscanada.ca.
116th Battalion. The Logistical Summary for the 116th (Ontario County) Canadian
    Infantry Battalion's Sojourn in France. Transcribed 2004–05. www.ontrmuseum.ca
Adamson, Agar. The Letters of Agar Adamson from the Great War. Ottawa: National
    Archives of Canada, Box MG30 E149.
Beaton, Joyce. Memories of and by Marjorie. Joyce Beaton Communications, December
    2001. From the private collection of Joyce Beaton.
Brown, Lorne. Father and Me and the Dumbells. Toronto: unpublished.
Canadian Legion of the British Empire Service League. "Report of the Ontario Provin-
    cial Command," Annual Convention. 1933.
Charles, Jack, "'Letter Addressed to Mert Plunkett." St. Catharines, 10 March 1958. From
    the private collection of Stephen Plunkett.
Cousins, Frank C. "Letter to Mother." 9 March 1918, as found in The Canadian Letters
    and Images Project. Nanaimo: Vancouver Island University; London: University of
    Western Ontario, 2003. www.canadianletters.ca
Cowley, Deborah (ed.). Georges Vanier, Soldier: The Wartime Letter and Diaries, 1915–
    1919. Toronto: Dundurn Press, 2000.
Dumbells, fan mail. From the private collection of Stephen Plunkett.
Evans, James Lloyd. "'Letter to Wife." 20 June 1918, as found in The Canadian Letters
    and Images Project. Nanaimo: Vancouver Island University; London: University of
    Western Ontario, 2003. www.canadianletters.ca
Fergusson, V.M. "Letter dated 5 May 1915." Imperial War Museum.
Foster, Kenneth Walter. "Memoir." Date not specified, as found in The Canadian Letters
    and Images Project. Nanaimo: Vancouver Island University; London: University of
    Western Ontario, 2003. www.canadianletters.ca
Gass, Clarence Reginald. "Letter to Lillian." 10 October 1918, as found in The Canadian
    Lettersand Images Project. Nanaimo: Vancouver Island University; London: Univer-
    sity of Western Ontario, 2003. www.canadianletters.ca
Gwatkin, Willoughby. "Memorandum on the Enlistment of Negroes in Canadian Expe-
    ditionary Force." 13 April 1916. Ottawa: National Archives of Canada, RG 24, vol.
    1206, file 297-1-21.
Henson, Leslie. "My Concert Party at the Front—How the 'Gaieties' Cheered the Troops."
    Esther MacCallum-Stewart (ed.), The First World War and Comedy. University of
    Sussex. www.whatalovelywar.co.uk

Lovell, Hubert William. "Some Memories of 'Our Days in France' 1916–1919." c. 1931, as found in *The Canadian Letters and Images Project*. Nanaimo: Vancouver Island University; London: University of Western Ontario, 2003. www.canadianletters.ca

Maharg, Ivan Clark. "Diary Entry." 9 July 1918, as found in *The Canadian Letters and Images Project*. Nanaimo: Vancouver Island University; London: University of Western Ontario, 2003. www.canadianletters.ca

McArthur, John Alexander. "Letter to Hazel." 9 November 1916, as found in *The Canadian Letters and Images Project*. Nanaimo: Vancouver Island University; London: University of Western Ontario, 2003. www.canadianletters.ca

McLaren, John D. "Short Chronological Biography of his Father Jack." n.d. From the private collection of John McLaren.

McLaren, John "Jack" Wilson. "Sir Frederick Banting." Toronto: unpublished, c. 1978. From the private collection of John McLaren.

———. "The Group of Seven." Toronto: unpublished, c. 1978. From the private collection of John McLaren.

———. *Personal Memoirs*. Toronto: unpublished, c. 1927. From the private collection of John McLaren.

———. "Jack McLaren, O.S.A., ex-Dumbell. Four Page Overview of His Life." Toronto: unpublished, c. 1927. From the private collection of John McLaren.

McLellan, William John. "Letter Home." 26 May 1917. As found in *The Canadian Letters and Images Project*. Nanaimo: Vancouver Island University; London: University of Western Ontario, 2003. www.canadianletters.ca

Milligan, Spike. *Monty, His Part in My Victory*. Edited by Jack Hobbs. London: Joseph, 1976.

———. *Adolf Hitler: My Part in His Downfall*. London: Penguin Books, 1971.

Napier, Andrew John "Jack." "Letter to Ruthie." 26 September 1915, as found in *The Canadian Letters and Images Project*. Nanaimo: Vancouver Island University; London: University of Western Ontario, 2003. www.canadianletters.ca

National Archives of Canada. *CEF Military Records: Albert Plunkett*, Ottawa.

Princess Patricia's Canadian Light Infantry. *War Diaries: 1914–1919*. Transcribed by Michael Thierens, 2008. www.cefresearch.com

Read, Daphne. *The Great War and Canadian Society: An Oral History*. Toronto: New Hogtown Press, 1978.

Richardson, Charles Douglas. "Letter to Mother." 31 December 1916, as found in *The Canadian Letters and Images Project*. Nanaimo: Vancouver Island University; London: University of Western Ontario, 2003. www.canadianletters.ca

Salverson, George. "Email letter to Kathy Witheridge." 7 April 2001. From the collection of Kathy Witheridge.

Savage, Charles Henry. "Memoir." c. 1936, as found in *The Canadian Letters and Images Project*. Nanaimo: Vancouver Island University; London: University of Western Ontario, 2003. www.canadianletters.ca

Scherer, George Leslie. "Letter to Catherine Crawford." 25 March 1918, as found in *The Canadian Letters and Images Project*. Nanaimo: Vancouver Island University; London: University of Western Ontario, 2003. www.canadianletters.ca

Shortreed, Robert. "Letter to Sister." 28 January 1919, as found in *The Canadian Letters and Images Project.* Nanaimo: Vancouver Island University; London: University of Western Ontario, 2003. www.canadianletters.ca

Simpson, Harold Henry. "Letter to Mother." 21 April 1918, as found in *The Canadian Letters and Images Project.* Nanaimo: Vancouver Island University; London: University of Western Ontario, 2003. www.canadianletters.ca

———. "Letter to Mother." 2 February 1918, as found in *The Canadian Letters and Images Project.* Nanaimo: Vancouver Island University; London: University of Western Ontario, 2003. www.canadianletters.ca

Slack. J.H.R. *Three Little Mice.* Joyce Beaton Communications. 1998. From the Private Collection of Joyce Beaton.

Royal Canadian Regiment. *The First World War Diary of the Royal Canadian Regiment.* http://regimentalrogue.tripod.com

Wilson, Andrew. "Diary Entry." 25 March 1918, as found in *The Canadian Letters and Images Project.* Nanaimo: Vancouver Island University; London: University of Western Ontario, 2003. www.canadianletters.ca

Secondary Sources

Books

Abella, Irving, and Harold Troper. *None Is Too Many: Canada and the Jews of Europe, 1933–1948.* New York: Random House, 1983.

Addington, L.H. *Patterns of War since the Eighteenth Century,* Indiana: Indiana University Press {1984} 1994.

Armstrong, E.H. *The Crisis of Quebec, 1914–1918.* New York: Columbia University Press, 1937.

Audoin-Rouzeau, Stéphane. *Men at War 1914–1918: National Sentiment and Trench Journalism in France during the First World War.* Translated from the French by Helen McPhail, Legacy of the Great War, Vol. 1. Providence: Berg Publishers, 1992.

Bailey, Peter. *Leisure and Class in Victorian England: Rational Recreation and the Contest for Control, 1830–1855.* London: Routledge and Keegan Paul, 1978.

Baker, Darrell, and Larry F. Kiner. *The Sir Harry Lauder Discography.* Metuchen, NJ, and London: Scarecrow Press, 1990.

Barriss, Alex, and Ted Barriss. *Making Music: Profiles from a Century of Canadian Music.* Toronto: HarperCollins Publishers, 2001.

Barris, Ted. *Victory at Vimy, Canada Comes of Age: April 9–12, 1917.* Toronto: Thomas Allen Publishers, 2007.

Beckett, I., and K. Simpson (eds.). *A Nation in Arms: A Social Study of the British Army in the First World War.* Manchester: 1985.

Behan, Dominic. *Milligan: The Life and Times of Spike Milligan.* London: Methuen, 1988.

Bliss, Michael. *Banting: A Biography.* Toronto: University of Toronto Press, 1992.

———. *The Discovery of Insulin.* Chicago: University of Chicago, 1982.

Bowering, Clifford H. *Service: The Story of the Canadian Legion, 1925–1960.* Ottawa: Canadian Legion, 1960.

Brophy, John. *The Long Trail: What the British Soldier Sang and Said in the Great War of 1914–1918*. London: Deutsch, 1965.

Brown, James D., and Stratton, Stephen S. *British Musical Biography*. New York: De Capo Press, 1971.

Butler, Judith. *Gender Trouble: Feminism and the Subversion of Identity*. New York: Routledge, 1990.

Carpenter, Humphrey. *Spike Milligan: The Biography*. London: Hodder & Stoughton, 2003.

Cinq-Mars, Marcelle. *L'Écho du Front: Journaux de Tranchées, 1915–1919*. Outremont, QC: Athéna, 2008.

Clark, Andrew (Beatty). *Stand and Deliver: Inside Canadian Comedy*. Toronto: University of Toronto Press, 1998.

Cook, Tim. *Shock Troops: Canadian Fighting the Great War, 1917–1918*, Vol. II. Toronto: Viking, 2008.

———. *At the Sharp End: Canadians Fighting the Great War, 1914–1916*, Vol. I. Toronto: Viking, 2007.

———. *No Place to Run: The Canadian Corps and Gas Warfare in the First World War*. Vancouver; Toronto: UBC Press, 1999.

Coppard, G., *With a Machine Gun to Cambrai: The Tale of a Young Tommy in Kitchener's Army, 1914–1918*. London: 1969.

Cosentino, Frank. *The Renfrew Millionaires: The Valley Boys of Winter 1910*. Burnstown: 1990.

Cruttwell, C.R.M.F. *A History of the Great War, 1914–18*. Oxford: Oxford University Press, 1964.

Davies, Gwendolyn. *Myth and Milieu: Atlantic Literature and Culture, 1918–1939*. Fredericton: Acadiensis Press, 1993.

Davis, Ann. *The Logic of Ecstasy: Canadian Mystical Painting, 1920–1940*. Toronto: University of Toronto Press, 1992.

Davis, Natalie Z. "Women on Top." *Society and Culture in Early Modern France: Eight Essays*. N.Z. Davis (ed.). Stanford: Stanford University Press, 1965.

De La Roche, Mazo. *Jalna*. New York: Grosset and Dunlap, 1927.

Dunaway, David K. "The Interdisciplinarity of Oral History." *Oral History: An Interdisciplinary Anthology*. 2nd ed. David K. Dunaway and Willa K. Baum (eds.). Waco, TX: Altamira Press, *(1984)* 1996.

Eksteins, Modris. *Rites of Spring: The Great War and the Birth of the Modern Age*. Toronto: Lester and Orpen Dennys, 1986.

Faulk, Barry. *Music Hall and Modernity: The Late-Victorian Discovery of Popular Culture*. Athens: Ohio University Press, 2004.

Featherstone, Simon. "Vestal Flirtations: The Performance of the Feminine in Late-Nineteenth-Century British Music Hall." *Nineteenth-Century Studies*, 19, 2005.

Ferguson, Niall. *The Pity of War: Explaining World War One*. New York: Penguin Press, 1998.

Friedlander, Peter. "Theory, Method and Oral History." *Oral History: An Interdisciplinary Anthology*. 2nd ed. David K. Dunaway and Willa K. Baum (eds.). Waco, TX: Altamira Press, *(1984)* 1996.

Frisch, Michael. *A Shared Authority: Essays on the Craft and Meaning of Oral and Public History.* Albany: State University of New York Press, 1990.

Frost, Karolyn S. *I've Got a Home in Glory Land: A Lost Tale of the Underground Railroad.* Toronto: Thomas Allen Publishers, 2007.

Fuller, J.G. *Troop Morale and Popular Culture in the British and Dominion Armies, 1914–18.* Oxford: Oxford University Press, 1990.

Fussel, Paul. *The Great War and Modern Memory.* Oxford: Oxford University Press, 1975.

Giesler, Patricia. *Valour Remembered: Canada and The First World War.* Ottawa: Department of Veterans Affairs, 1982.

Gilbert, Martin. *Churchill and Canada,* Delivered at the Annual Meetings of the Sir Winston S. Churchill Society Edmonton, Calgary, and Vancouver, Canada, May 1987.

Girard, Marion. *A Strange and Formidable Weapon: British Responses to World War I Poison Gas.* Lincoln: University of Nebraska Press, 2008.

Gray, John, and Eric Peterson. *Billy Bishop Goes to War: A Play by John Gray with Eric Peterson.* Vancouver: Talonbooks, 1981.

Groom, W.H.A. *Poor Bloody Infantry: A Memoir of the First World War.* London: Kimber, 1976.

Grove, Frederick Philip. *Settlers of the Marsh.* Toronto: Ryerson Press, 1925.

Gwyn, Sandra. *Tapestry of War: A Private View of Canadians in the Great War.* Toronto: HarperCollins Publishers, 1992.

Hall, Stuart. *Representation: Cultural Representation and Signifying Practices.* London: Open University, 1997.

Harper, J. Russell. *Painting in Canada: A History.* Toronto: University of Toronto Press, 1977.

Hawkins, Peter. *Chanson: The French Singer-Songwriter from Aristide Bruant to the Present Day.* Aldershot: Ashgate, 2000.

Hayes, Geoffrey, Andrew Iarocci and Mike Bechthold (eds.). *Vimy Ridge: A Canadian Reassessment.* Waterloo: Wilfrid Laurier University Press, 2007.

Henige, David. *Oral Historiography.* New York: Longman, 1982.

Hill, Charles C. *The Group of Seven: Art for a Nation.* Ottawa: National Gallery of Canada, 1995.

Hill, Doug, and Jeff Weingrad. *Saturday Night.* New York: Vintage Books, 1986.

Holmes, Richard. *Tommy: The British Soldier on the Western Front, 1914–1918.* London: HarperCollins, 2004.

Jackson, A.Y. *Banting as an Artist,* with a Memoir by Frederick W.W. Hipwell. Toronto: Ryerson Press, Canadian Art Series, 1943.

Jones, B., and B. Howell. *Popular Arts of the First World War.* London: Studio Vista Blue Star House, 1972.

Keegan, J. *The Face of Battle.* London, Penguin Group, 1976.

Kellett, A. *Combat Motivation: The Behaviour of Soldiers in Battle.* Hingham: Kluwer Boston, 1982.

Keshen, Jeffrey A. *Propaganda and Censorship during Canada's Great War.* Edmonton: University of Alberta Press, 1996.

Keshen, Jeffrey A., and Serge Marc Durflinger (eds.). *War and Society in Post-Confederation Canada*. Toronto: Thomson Nelson, 2007.

Kielmansegg, P.G. *Deutschland und der Erste Weltkrieg*. Frankfurt am Main: 1968.

Kallmann, Helmut (ed.). *Encyclopedia of Music in Canada*. 2nd ed. Toronto: University of Toronto Press, 1992.

Laffin, J. *British Butchers and Bunglers of World War One*. London, 1988.

Lawrence, T.E. *Seven Pillars of Wisdom*. London: Harmondsworth *(1927)* 1962.

Lewis, P.W. *Blasting and Bombardiering*. London: Calder & Boyars *(1937)* 1967.

Liddell Hart, B.H. *History of the First World War*. London, 1972.

Littlejohn, J.H. *The Scottish Music Hall, 1880–1990*. Wigtown: G.C. Book Publishers, 1990.

Lynch, J.W. *Princess Patricia's Canadian Light Infantry, 1917–1919*. Hicksville: Exposition Press, 1976.

MacDonald, L. *1914–18, Voices and Images of the Great War*. London: Penguin Books, 1989.

———. *1915: The Death of Innocence*. London: Penguin Books *(1993)* 1997.

Maloney, Paul. *Scotland and the Music Hall, 1850–1914*. Manchester: Manchester University Press, 2003.

Mander, R., and J. Mitchenson. *British Music Hall*. London: Gentry Books, 1974.

Marks, Lynne. *Revivals and Roller Rinks: Religion, Leisure and Identity in Late-Nineteenth-Century Small-Town Ontario*. Toronto: University of Toronto Press, 1996.

McCaffery, D. *Billy Bishop: Canadian Hero*. Halifax: Formac Publishing, 1990.

McGuire, Capt. F.R. "The Great War Concert Parties." *The Sentinel*. April 1967.

McKay, Ian. *The Quest of the Folk: Antimodernism and Cultural Selection in Twentieth-Century Nova Scotia*. Montreal; Kingston: McGill-Queen's University Press, 1994.

McLaren, John "Jack" Wilson. *Let's All Hate Toronto*. Toronto: Kingswood House, 1956.

McNeil, Bill. *Voice of the Pioneer*. Toronto: Macmillan Company of Canada, 1978.

Mellen, Peter. *The Group of Seven*. Toronto: McClelland & Stewart, 1970.

Mickleborough, Roy. *Keep the Home Fires Burning*. Wotton-Under-Edge: Saydisc, 1986.

Milligan, Spike. *Spike Milligan's Transports of Delight*. Photographs by Popperfoto. London: Sidgwick and Jackson, 1974.

Monty Python. *The Pythons: Autobiography by the Pythons*. New York: Thomas Dunne Books, 2003.

Moogk, Edward B. *Roll Back the Years: History of Canadian Recorded Sound and Its Legacy: Genesis to 1930*. Ottawa: National Library of Canada, 1975.

Moran, C.M.W. *The Anatomy of Courage*. London: Constable, 1945.

Morton, Desmond. *When Your Number's Up: The Canadian Soldier in the First World War*. Toronto: Random House of Canada, 1993.

———. *A Peculiar Kind of Politics: Canada's Overseas Ministry in the First World War*. Toronto: University of Toronto, 1982.

Morton, Desmond, and J.L. Granatstein. *Marching to Armageddon: Canadians and the Great War 1914–1919*. Toronto: Lester & Orpen Dennys, 1989.

Morton, Desmond, and Glenn Wright. *Winning the Second Battle: Canadian Veterans and the Return to Civilian Life, 1915–1930*. Toronto: University of Toronto Press, 1987.

Morton, J. *In the Sea of Sterile Mountains: The Chinese in British Columbia.* Vancouver: J.J. Douglas, 1974.

Morton, H.V. *In Search of Scotland.* London: Methuen and Company, 1929.

Moss, Mark. *Manliness and Militarism: Educating Young Boys in Ontario for War.* Toronto: University of Toronto Press, 2001.

Mosse, George L. *Fallen Soldiers: Reshaping the Memory of the World Wars.* New York; Oxford: Oxford University Press, 1990.

Musgrove, M.J. "Dumbells Blend Past with Present." *The Guardian,* Charlottetown: 28 June 1977.

National Library of Canada. *Roll Back the Years: History of Canadian Recorded Sound and Its Legacy (Genesis to 1930).* Ottawa: National Library of Canada, 1975.

Nicholson, Col. G.W.L. *Canadian Expeditionary Force 1914–1918.* Ottawa: Queen's Printer, 1962.

O'Connell, Robert. *Of Arms and Men.* Oxford: Oxford University Press, 1989.

Ostenso, Martha. *Wild Geese.* New York: Dodd, Mead and Co., 1925.

Owen, Wilfrid. "*Dulce Et Decorum Est.*" J. Silkin (ed.). *The Penguin Book of First World War Poetry.* London: Penguin, 1981. <poem>

Palmer, R. "*What a Lovely War!*": *British Soldiers' Songs from the Boer War to the Present Day.* Foreword by Lyn MacDonald. London: Penguin, 1990.

Princess Patricia's Canadian Light Infantry. *Princess Patricia's Canadian Light Infantry: The First Seventy-Five Years.* Calgary: Published under the authority of Regimental Headquarters, PPCLI, Currie Barracks, 1988.

Proctor, George A. *Canadian Music of the Twentieth Century.* Toronto: University of Toronto Press, 1980.

Purdy, Verity Sweeny. *As Luck Would Have it: Adventures in the Canadian Army Show, 1938–1946.* St. Catharines: Vanwell, 2003.

Putkowski, Julian. *The Kinmel Park Camp Riots 1919.* England: Flintshire Historical Society, 1989.

Rachamimov, Alon. "The Disruptive Comforts of Drag: (Trans)Gender Performances among Prisoners of War in Russia, 1914–1920." *American Historical Review,* 11, 2. April 2006.

Reid, Denis. *A Concise History of Canadian Painting.* Toronto: Oxford University Press, 1988.

Rickman, John (ed.). *Civilization, War and Death.* London: 1939.

Robbins, Jeff. *Second City Television: A History and Episode Guide.* Foreword by Sheldon Patinkin. Jefferson, NC: McFarland, 2008.

Roy, Patricia E. *The Oriental Question: Consolidating a White Man's Province, 1914–1941.* Vancouver: UBC Press, 2003.

———. *The Chinese in Canada.* Ottawa: Canadian Historical Association, 1985.

Saddlemeyer, Ann (ed.). *Early Stages: Theatre in Ontario, 1800–1914.* Toronto: University of Toronto Press, 1990.

Sanjek, Russell. *From Print to Plastic: Publishing and Promoting America's Popular Music (1900–1980).* Brooklyn: Institute for Studies in American Music, 1983.

Sanjek, Russell, and David Sanjek. *American Popular Music Business in the 20th Century.* New York: Oxford University Press, 1991.

Scheurer, Timothy E. *American Popular Music: The Nineteenth Century and Tin Pan Alley,* Vol. I. Bowling Green State University, Popular Press, 1989.

Senelick, Laurence. "Boys and Girls Together: Subcultural Origins of Glamor Drag and Male Impersonation." Lesley Ferris (ed.), *Crossing the Stage: Controversies on Cross-Dressing.* New York: Routledge, 1993.

Senelick, Laurence. *The Changing Room: Sex, Drag and Theatre.* New York: Routledge, 2000.

———. *British Music Hall. 1840–1923.* Hamden: Archon Books, 1981.

Shales, Tom, and James Andrew Miller. *Live from New York: An Uncensored History of Saturday Night Live.* Boston: Little, Brown, 2002.

Shepherd, John, Dave Laing, and David Horn (eds.). *Continuum Encyclopedia of Popular Music of the World.* 5 vols. London: Continuum, 2003.

Signori, Dolores A. *Guide to the Papers of James Mavor.* Toronto: Thomas Fisher Rare Book Library, 1989.

Sidell, Frederick R., Ernest T. Takafuji and David R. Franz (eds.). *Medical Aspects of Chemical and Biological Warfare.* Office of the Surgeon General, Department of the Army, USA: 1997.

Silverman, Jeffrey. *Songs of the British Music Hall.* London: London Music Sales, 1971.

Smith, Leonard V. Stéphane Audoin-Rouzeau, Annette Becker; French sections translated by Helen McPhail, *France and the Great War: 1914–1918.* Cambridge, UK; New York: Cambridge University Press, 2003.

Smythe, Conn, with Scott Young. *Conn Smythe: If You Can't Beat 'Em in the Alley.* Toronto: PaperJacks, 1982.

Stephens, William Ray. *The Harps of War.* Oakville: Harris Music Co., 1985.

Stevens, G.R. *Princess Patricia's Canadian Light Infantry: 1914–1964: In Proud Memory of a Cherished Fellowship in a Rare Company.* Calgary: PPCLI, 1964.

———. *A City Goes to War.* Brampton: Charters Publishing Company, 1964.

Stouffer, Samuel A. *The American Soldier: Combat and Its Aftermath.* Princeton: Princeton University Press, 1949.

Thomas, Dave, with Robert Crane and Susan Carney. *SCTV: Behind the Scenes.* Toronto: M&S, 1996.

Thomas, Mike. *The Second City Unscripted: Revolution and Revelation at the World-Famous Comedy Theater.* New York: Villard, 2009.

Toll, Robert C. *Blacking Up: The Minstrel Show in Nineteenth-Century America.* New York: Oxford University Press, 1974.

Turner, Victor. *From Ritual to Theatre: The Human Seriousness of Play.* New York: Harper-Collins, 1993.

Vance, Jonathan. *A History of Canadian Culture.* Don Mills, ON: Oxford University Press, 2009.

———. *Death So Noble: Memory, Meaning and the First World War.* Vancouver: UBC Press, 1997.

Ventham, Maxine. *Spike Milligan: His Part in Our Lives.* London: Robson, 2002.

Vipond, Mary. *Listening In: The First Decade of Canadian Broadcasting, 1922–1932.* Montreal; Kingston: McGill-Queen's University Press, 1992.

———. *The Mass Media in Canada.* Toronto: James Lorimer & Co., 1989.

Wagner, Anton (ed.). "New World Visions." *Contemporary Canadian Theatre.* Toronto: Simon and Pierre, 1985.

Walden, Keith. *Becoming Modern in Toronto: The Industrial Exhibition and the Shaping of a Late Victorian Culture.* Themes in Canadian Social History. Toronto: University of Toronto Press, 1997.

Walker, James W. St.G. *"Race," Rights and the Law in the Supreme Court of Canada: Historical Case Studies.* Waterloo: Osgoode Society for Canadian Legal History and Wilfrid Laurier University Press, 1997.

Wallace, William. *Harry Lauder in the Limelight.* Sussex: The Guild, 1988.

Walsh, Colin. *Mud, Songs and Blighty.* London: Hutchinson, 1975.

Ward, W.P. *White Canada Forever: Popular Attitudes and Public Policy towards Orientals in British Columbia.* Montreal: McGill-Queen's Press, 1978.

Watkins, Glenn. *Proof through the Night: Music and the Great War.* Berkley: University of California Press, 2003.

Wickberg, Edgar. *From China to Canada: A History of the Chinese Community in Canada.* Toronto: McClelland and Stewart in association with the Multiculturalism Directorate, Department of the Secretary of State and the Canadian Govt. Pub. Centre, Supply and Services Canada, 1982.

Williams, Jeffrey. *First in the Field: Gault of the Patricias.* St. Catharines: Vanwell Publishing, 1995.

———. *Princess Patricia's Canadian Light Infantry.* London: Leo Cooper, 1972.

Wilmut, Roger. *The Goon Show Companion: A History and Goonography.* With a personal memoir by Jimmy Grafton. London: Robson, 1976.

Worthington, Larry. *Amid the Guns Below.* Toronto: 1965.

Yeo, E., and S. Yeo (eds.). *Popular Culture and Class Conflict 1590–1914.* Brighton: Harvester Press, 1981.

Zuehlke, Mark, and Stewart C. Daniel. *The Canadian Military Atlas: The Nation's Battlefields from the French and Indian Wars to Kosovo.* Toronto: Stoddart, 2001.

Journal Articles, Chapters, Theses, and Websites

Bailey, Peter. "Conspiracies of Meaning: Music-Hall and the Knowingness of Popular Culture." *Past and Present,* 144. 1994.

Barris, Alex. "Goodbye, Farewell, Adieu, Frank Shuster." *Toronto Star,* 21 January 2002.

Beckett, I. "The Nation in Arms, 1914–1918." I. Beckett and K. Simpson (eds.), *A Nation in Arms: A Social Study of the British Army in the First World War.* Manchester: 1985.

Boxwell, David A. "The Follies of War: Cross-Dressing and Popular Theatre on the British Front Line, 1914–1918," *Modernism/Modernity,* 9, 1. Johns Hopkins University Press, 2002.

Browne, Gerald. "Soldiers' Songs of the Great War." Western Front Association. 22 May 2008. www.westernfrontassociation.com

Campbell, Lara. "We Who Have Wallowed in the Mud of Flanders: First World War Veterans, Unemployment, and the Development of Social Welfare in Canada, 1929–1939." Journal of the Canadian Historical Association, 11. 2000.

Champagne, Jane. "The Charlottetown Festival Brings Back the Dumbells." *Le Compositeur Canadien, 123.* September 1977.

Chen, Z. "Chinese Minority and Everyday Racism in Canadian Towns and Small Cities: An Ethnic Study of the Case of Peterborough, Ontario, 1892–1951." *Canadian Ethnic Studies,* 36, 1. 2004.

Cook, Tim. "Rum in the Trenches." *Legion Magazine.* Ottawa: September/October 2002.

———. "The Singing War: Canadian Soldiers' Songs of the Great War." *American Review of Canadian Studies,* 39, 3. September 2009.

———. "Wet Canteens and Worrying Mothers: Soldiers and Temperance Groups in the Great War." *Social History/histoire sociale,* 35, 70. 2003.

———. "'More a Medicine Than a Beverage': 'Demon Rum' and the Canadian Trench Soldier of the First World War." *Canadian Military History,* 9, 1. 2000.

Davies, Robertson. "The Nineteenth-Century Repertoire," A. Saddlemyer (ed.). *Early Stages: Theatre in Ontario 1800–1914.* Toronto: A project of the Ontario Historical Studies Series for the Government of Ontario, University of Toronto Press, 1990.

Frisch, Michael. "Oral History, Documentary and the Mystification of Power: A Case Study Critique of Public Methodology." *International Journal of Oral History.* Westport: Meckler Publishing, June 1985.

Gibson, Kenneth Craig. "Sex and Soldiering in France and Flanders: The British Expeditionary Force along the Western Front, 1914–1919." *International History Review,* 23, 3. 2001.

Goldie, David. "Hugh MacDiarmid, Harry Lauder and Scottish Popular Culture." *International Journal of Scottish Literature,* 1. Autumn 2006.

Halladay, Laurel. "Canada's Military Planted Seeds for Flourishing Arts Scene." *In the News.* University of Calgary, 4 November 2004.

———. "'It Made Them Forget about the War for a Minute': Canadian Army, Navy and Air Force Entertainment Units during the Second World War." *Canadian Military History,* 11, 4. Autumn 2002.

———. "'Ladies and Gentlemen, Soldiers and Artists': Canadian Military Entertainers, 1939–1946." M.A. thesis. Calgary: University of Calgary, 2000.

Hallett, M.E, "A Governor General's View on Oriental Immigration to B.C.: 1904–1914." *B.C. Studies,* 14. 1972.

Heller, Charles E. "The Peril of Unpreparedness: The American Expeditionary Force and Chemical Warfare." *Military Review,* 65, 1. 1985.

Hoerder, Dick. "Ethnic Studies in Canada from the 1880s to 1962: A Historiographical Perspective and Critique." *Canadian Ethnic Studies,* 26, 1. 1994.

Kirkland, Elizabeth. *Lady Julia Drummond,* Biographical Entry. Montreal: September 2002. www.rootsweb.ancestry.com

Lee, Carol F. "The Road to Enfranchisement: Chinese and Japanese in British Columbia." *BC Studies,* 30. 1976.

Lenton-Young, G. "Variety Theatre," A. Saddlemyer (ed.), *Early Stages: Theatre in Ontario 1800–1914.* Toronto: A project of the Ontario Historical Studies Series for the Government of Ontario, University of Toronto Press, 1990.

MacCallum-Stewart, Esther, (ed.). *The First World War and Comedy.* University of Sussex. www.whatalovelywar.co.uk/

McGuire, Capt. F.R. "The Great War Concert Parties." *The Sentinel.* April 1967.

Meyer, Moe. "Unveiling the Word: Science and Narrative in Transsexual Striptease," L. Senelick (ed.). *Gender in Performance: The Presentation of Difference in the Performing Arts.* Hanover: University Press of New England, 1992.

Morrison, Richard. "Music Lifts the Mood of War: A Fascinating Exhibition Reveals How Wartime Entertainment Inspired the Country and Had a Lasting Cultural Impression." *The Times.* 15 April 2003.

Morton, Desmond "Kicking and Complaining: Demobilization Riots in the Canadian Expeditionary Force, 1918–1919." *Canadian Historical Review,* 61, 3. September 1980.

O'Dell, Leslie. "Amateurs of the Regiment, 1815–1870." A. Saddlemyer (ed.), *Early Stages: Theatre in Ontario 1800–1914.* Toronto: Ontario Historical Studies Series for the Government of Ontario, University of Toronto Press, 1990.

O' Neill, Patrick B. "The Halifax Concert Party in World War II." *Theatre Research in Canada,* 20, 2. Fall 1999.

———. "The Impact of Copyright Legislation upon the Publication of Sheet Music in Canada, Prior to 1924." *Journal of Canadian Studies,* 28, 3. Fall 1993.

———. "The Canadian Concert in France." *Theatre History in Canada,* 5. Fall 1983.

———. "The Dumbells." H. Kallman, G. Potrin, K. Winters (eds.). *Encyclopaedia of Music in Canada.* 2nd ed. Toronto: Univeristy of Toronto Press, 1992.

Rachamimov, Alon. "The Disruptive Comforts of Drag: (Trans)Gender Performances among Prisoners of War in Russia, 1914–1920." *American Historical Review,* 11, 2. April 2006.

Roy, Patricia E. "Educating the East: British Columbia and the Oriental Question in the Inter-War Years." *B.C. Studies,* 18. 1973.

Summerfield, P. "The Effingham Arms and the Empire: Deliberate Selection in the Evolution of the Music Hall in London," E. Yeo and S. Yeo (eds.), *Popular Culture and Class Conflict 1590–1914. Brighton:* Harvester Press, 1981.

Vance, Jonathan. "'Today They Were Alive Again': The Canadian Corps Reunion of 1934." *Ontario History,* 87, 4. December 1995.

Walker, James W. St.G. "Race and Recruitment in World War I: Enlistment of Visible Minorities in the Canadian Expeditionary Force." *Canadian Historical Review,* 70, 1. 1989.

Wilson, John Jason. "Skating to Armageddon: Of Canada, Hockey and the First World War." *International Journal of the History of Sport,* 22, 3. Oxford: Routledge, May 2005.

———. "Anatomy of a Scottish Woman's Ballad." Paper. University of Guelph: 2002.

Withrow, John B. "Wartime Memories: Patriotic Events in Massey Hall Kept the Home Fires Burning." *Bravo,* 2. Roy Thomson Hall/Massey Hall: December 1989.

Index

Page numbers in italics refer to figures.

4th Division Maple Leafs. *See* Maple Leafs
9th Canadian Field Ambulance, 55
10th Field Ambulance, cast, 56
49th Battalion, 60

Adamson, Captain Agar, 43, 68, 92
Albert, King of Belgium, 71
alcohol, 110–12; rum, 111, 112, 202n82.
    See also morale
alienation, 99
Alladin, 54. *See also* Maple Leafs
Ancre Heights (1916), 51
"Annie Laurie," 33
"Another Little Drink," 29
anti-authoritarian songs, 86
Apollo Theatre (London), 63, 64
"Archibald," 92–93. *See also* parody
Armistice, 68, 70, 71
army: criticism of, 75, 88. *See also* Ross
    Rifle; sarcasm; satire; soldier humour,
    vaudeville
Around the Map, 24, 29
Arts and Letters Club (Toronto), 127, 148.
    See also Jack McLaren
Ashwell, Lena, 100
"Asleep in the Deep" (Arthur J. Lamb and
    Henry W. Petrie, 1987), 19
Atholl, Duchess of, 103, 200n39
Attenborough, Richard, 24

Ayre, Jack, *3*, 17, 32, 33, 85, 148; 10th Field
    Ambulance show, 56; dangers of war,
    60, 77; death, 142–43; discovery of,
    192n76; "Kit Inspection," 198n45;
    Lifebuoy Follies, 142; memories, 58,
    87, 112, 132; with Originals, 139; piano
    work, 13, 137; on radio, 128; touring,
    136; as working musician, 142. *See also*
    Dumbells; "Dumbell Rag"; "Kit Inspec-
    tion"; Second World War

Babcock, John, 4
Bairnsfather, Bruce, 79, 80, 85; cartoon,
    108, 112
bawdy songs, 118
Beaver Hut, 48–49
Bell, Margaret, 17
Biddulph, Cyril "Biddy," 108; killed in
    action, 4, 59, 109; "worried soldier"
    routine, 44, 108
Biff, Bing, Bang (revue), 132, 133, 138; on
    Broadway, 7, 124, 136
The Bing Boys Are Here (revue, 1916),
    29–30
The Bing Boys on Broadway (revue, 1918),
    29
The Bing Girls Are There (revue, 1917), 29
Black Adder, 110
Black Canadians, 27
blackface. *See* minstrel shows
black humour, 1, 4, 78, 108; boundaries,
    109–10; evolution, 77, 81; future, 109;

surreal nature, 143. *See also* comedy; *Monty Python's Flying Circus*; soldier humour; trench newspapers
Black Watch concert party, 73
"Bombed Last Night," 108
Bow Bells of the 56th Division, 121
Brayford, Jerry, 56, 60, 66. *See also* Dumbells; Captain Merton Plunkett
British 5th Army, 63
Broadway, 7, 58, 124–25, 136; critics on, 132; success of Canadian female impersonators on, 117
Brown, Lorne, 151
Bullis, Edmund ("Gladys"), 121
Burr, Henry, 14, 15, 18, 20, 111; prolific songwriting, 185n23

C2s, 58, 73, 196n199
Canadian Army Show, 144
Canadian Corps Reunion (1934), 145–48; Dumbells at CNE, 147; wild affair, 147
Canadian Corps Training School, 54, 62
Canadian Corps, 1, 40, 46, 56, 106; armistice rumours, 68; battles, 51; General Arthur Currie, 56; entertainers in, 16; first concert party in, 44; formation of entertainment groups, 2, 9, 10, 11, 40; last 100 days, 67; rum rations, 112; singalongs, 38; soldiers, 17, 24; theatre training school for, 54; YMCA officers in, 47. *See also* concert parties; Ross Rifle
Canadian Daily Record, 58
Canadian Westerners of the 49th Battalion, 98
Carey, Sergeant, 54
cartoons, 79, 112
censorship: lack of, 91
Charter, Ted, 56, 87, *87*
Chevalier, Albert, 19, 20
Christie, Sergeant, 43
Chu Chin Chow (revue, 1916), 29
civilian audiences, 2, 4, 23, 73, 82–83, 141; Bairnsfather, 80; disconnect with soldiers' tastes, 4, 25, 34, 82; idealism of, 86; material not meant for, 82, 113; music hall, 17, 29; patriotic anthems, 23; perception of war, 26, 34, 81; popular songs for, 18–20, 22; romantic

apprehensions, 83. *See also* drag; soldier humour
Clarke, Norman "Nobby," 3, 45, 59, 148
class gap, 100
"The Clock Song," 30
"The Cobbler's Song," 29
Cochran, Charles, 11
Coliseum (London), 65, 66
comedy, 1, 83, 75, 108, 143; darker, 79; effective, 92; military influence on evolution, 75; good comedy, 101, 108; personal and exclusive quality, 77; postwar development, 143–45; troupes, 143, 148; war experience and, 126; writers, 109, 114, 149. *See also* black humour; concert parties; Jack McLaren; parody; satire; sketch comedy; soldier humour
Comedy Company. *See* PPCLI CC
concert party, 2, 3, 40, 73, 143; British concert parties and, 40; coded dialogue in, 10; as comedy pioneers, 1; development of, 35–73, 92; disbanding, 67; divisional concert parties, 39, 43; film of, 5; first Canadian concert party, 44; history of, 1, 2, 37–40; influence of, 143, 145; number of, 54, 190n30; profound influence of British music hall, 6, 9, 16, 17, 32, 50; organization, of, 2, 6; other influences on, 11–15, 33, 34; permanent parties, 37, 40, 44, 52; positive influence, 121; postwar, 143; purpose, 1, 2, 6, 35, 36, 126; racism in, 27, 28; records of, 153–56; as safety valve, 77, 117; as soldiers' town meeting, 88; theatre school for, 54; wide appeal, 36; writers for, 83, 89; YMCA and, 47–50. *See also* comedy; Dumbells; female impersonators; morale; music hall; Captain Merton Plunkett; PPCLI CC; soldier-entertainers; theatre school at Mons
concert party performers. *See* soldier-entertainers
"A Conscientious Objector" (Alfred Lester), 24
Cooper, Gladys, 17
costumes, 50, 51, 122, 136. *See also* female impersonators; improvisation; performance

Courcelette (1916), 15, 51
Courville, Albert de, 11
culture: postwar, 126–28
Cunningham, Private W.I. (Bill), 3, 45, 59
Currie, Sir Arthur, 54, 71

Dale, Alan, 132
Day, Lieutenant R.W. *See* Canadian Corps Training School
death, 1, 76, 105, 106, 144; comedic use of, 79, 101, 108, 109; methods of coping with, 36, 83, 111; taboo use of, 109
Diaghilev Russian Ballet, 66, 100, 195n150
drag, 119–20. *See also* female impersonators
Drummond, Lady. *See* Parker, Grace Julia
The Duchess Entertains, 101–4; accessibility of 103; popularity of, 103
"The Dumbell Rag," 13, 115–17; postwar success of, 117
Dumbells, 2, 33, 106, 127, 134, 147; as all-star group, 58, 67; amalgamation with other groups, 58, 69, 70; cast, 40, 56, 67, 73, 132; command of, 52–53; controversy, 137–38; delivery, 5; end of, 142; estrangement, 140; fame, 2, 4, 57; formation, 6, 53, 56; influenced by, 33; influence of, 82–83, 143, 150; legacy, 7, 149–52; music hall material, 17; official recognition, 151; performance conditions, 4, 134; permanency of, 53, 57; popularity of, 67; professionalism, 69; as sketch comedy pioneers, 2; as soldier entertainment prototype, 143; success, 32, 65, 69, 82, 83. *See also* Jack Ayre; Jerry Brayford; female impersonators; Ross Hamilton; *H.M.S. Pinafore*; Mons; music hall; Al Plunkett; Captain Merton Plunkett; Bill Redpath
Dumbells: performance and repertoire, 19, 22, 101, 106, 114; command performance, 67; first professional revue, 132; first performance, 56, 57; moral ambiguity in, 30; repertoire, 20, 22, 29–31; revues, 31, strong vocalists in, 30; touring, 54, 136. *See also The Duchess Entertains*; female impersonators; *H.M.S. Pinafore*; Marjorie; Gitz Rice
Dumbells, postwar: American success, 136; on Broadway, 124–25; Canadian success, 133–35; cast upheaval, 138, 139; finances, 132–33, 139; in London, 65–70; partying, 134–35; performances, 40, 70–73; on radio, 127–28; reunions, 145, 147–49; success, 131, 132, 138, 140, 141; women, inclusion of, 125, 141–42

Entertainment National Service Association (ENSA), 143
"Everybody Slips a Little" (Al Plunkett), 30

female impersonators, 2, 40, 53, 69, 114, 117–25; British music hall tradition and, 119; on Broadway, 124–25; character creation, 122; in concert parties, 55, 117; as cornerstone of Dumbell revues, 69, 117, 118; costume creation, 50, 122; exceptional portrayals as, 117, 122, 124, 125; Miss Genevieve Few-Close, 102, 103; Gladys, 117; "Miss Skinny," 114; morale and, 125; popularity of, 103; as real women, 120; as risqué element, 118; as surrogate women, 119, 121; training at Mons theatrical school, 125. *See also* drag; *The Duchess Entertains*; Marjorie; Ross Hamilton; Charlie McLean; Alan Murray
Fenwick, Fred, 45, 68, 121, 139
Few-Close, Miss Genevieve. *See* female impersonators
"The Field Postcard," 22, 23
Filson, William, 60, 65, 134
First Nations soldiers, 27
folk songs: Celtic and traditional Scottish, 33
Forde, Florrie, 20, 21, 32
Foster, Kenneth Walter, 57
French-Canadian soldiers, 26
Full O' Pep (Originals revue), 139
"Fun in Flanders" (Gitz Rice and Henry Burr), 111

Gaieties, 40, 143, 190n28
gas, 104–10; fear of, 105; as off-limits material, 104, 107; as weapon of war, 104–5
Gault, Lieutenant Colonel Alexander Hamilton, 41–42, 44, 53; injured, 47; theatre, 60. *See also* PPCLI CC
German Spring Offensive, 63, 67

"Good Luck to the Boys of the Allies" (Morris Manley), 25
The Goon Show, 144, 145
Gouy-Servins: theatre at, 62, 121
Great Depression, 142
Gwatkin, General Willoughby, 27, 199n7
Gwyn, Sandra, 6

Ham, Percy, 59, 148
Hamilton, Ross, 20, 60, 61, 81, 107; background, 123; costumes, 50; as female impersonator, 55, 69, 119, 123–25; gassed, 107; as Marjorie, 20, 120, 123; in Originals, 148; popularity of, 118; post-Dumbells, 138, 141–42; on radio, 128; refusal to be in show with girls, 141–42; songwriting, 138. See also "Hello My Dearie"; Marjorie
"Hello My Dearie," 31–32, 118. See also Ross Hamilton; Marjorie
Henson, Leslie, 40, 143
"Here We Are Again," 18, 20
heroism: satire and mockery of, 75, 83–86
Highland character or Scotch comic, 15, 16. See also Sir Harry Lauder
Hillman, Charles, 68
Hindenburg Line, 67
"Hitchy Koo," 18
H.M.S. Pinafore (Gilbert and Sullivan), 68, 70, 71, 71, 76, 196n7
Hodder-Williams, Lieutenant Ralph, 44, 46, 52, 69, 91; records of concert parties, 154
Holland, Jock, 16, 39, 139. See also Bow Bells; female impersonators; Originals
home–war dichotomy, 80–82
Hughes, Sam, 93, 96
humour, soldier. See soldier humour
Humphries, Jack, 22

If You Were the Only Girl in the World" (Clifford Grey and Nat Ayre), 29–30
"I'll Make a Man of You," 23, 24
immigrants as subjects of parody, 26, 27
improvisation, 50, 58–63; of equipment, 62; as key to survival, 58
"In the Shadows," 18
"It's a Long Way to Tipperary" (Jack Judge and Harry Williams), 18, 20, 23, 33, 81;

lack of popularity with soldiers, 23, 25, 100; parody of, 118
"I Want to Go Home," 24, 131

jingoism, 26
Jolliffe, Lieutenant Norman, 54

"Keep the Home Fires Burning" (Ivor Novello and Lena Ford, 1914), 19
"Keep Your Head Down Fritzie Boy" (Gitz Rice), 106–7
"The Kit Inspection," 86, 87, 87, 198n45
Kreisler, Fritz, 20

Langley, Bertram, 20, 21, 72, 139, 140
LaRue Minstrels, 11
Lauder, Sir Harry, 15, 37, 100. See also "Roamin' in the Gloamin'"
Lee-Enfield rifles, 96–97
The Legend of The Dumbells, 149
Lew Dockstader's Minstrels, 12
Lifebuoy Follies, 142, 198n45
"Life in a Trench in Belgium" (Gitz Rice and Henry Burr), 111
Lilly, Tom J., 45, 64, 68, 114, 115; at Canadian Corps Reunion (1934), 147–48; as "Chinaman," 28
"Lily of Killarney," 20
Lipsett, Major General Louis J., 52, 53, 63, 92, 193n98
London Lady Parties, 50
"The Long Trail" (Stoddard King and Alonzo "Zo" Elliot), 18
Lorraine, Violet, and George Robey, 30
Ludendorff Drive, 63
Ludendorff Offensive, 90

"Mademoiselle from Armentières," 106, 113–14, 118
Maharg, Lieutenant Ivan Clark, 60
Major Beecher Gale's Theatre, 56, 62, 121
Manley, Little Miss Mildred, 25
Maple Leaf Concert Party of the Canadian 4th Division. See Maple Leafs
Maple Leafs, 54–56, 58, 73, 138, 144; Alladin, 54
marching songs, American, 33
Marjorie, 31, 117, 120, 124; development of, 123; photos of, 21, 117, 123;

popularity of, 123, 124, 137; songs
performed, 20, 31, 118. *See also* Ross
Hamilton, "Hello My Dearie"
McCormack, John, 16, 19, 20, 131
McLaren, Jack, 4, 11, 24, 52; as actor, 102,
103, 114; background, 41–43; and Frederick Banting, 127; Canadian material,
98; as comedy sketch writer, 12, 44, 69,
89, 91–92, 114; death, 149; in Dumbells,
68, 69, 91, 119, 127; on female impersonators, 120, 122; Group of Seven and,
127, 149; influences, 12, 75; as influential, 45; inspiration, 125; Lifebuoy Follies, 142; painting, 41, 127, 148–49; on
performing, 121; in PPCLI CC, 12, 40,
44–47, 65, 67; reunions, 147, 148; on
Sam Hughes, 93; as "Scotty," 16; songs,
89, 97–98; 148; photos of, *42, 64, 150*;
postwar life, 135–37, 148, 149; Royal
Command Performance, 63; screen
test offer, 103; wartime observations,
51, 62, 70, 86, 88. *See also* Arts and
Letters Club; *The Duchess Entertains*;
Steenvoorde Nine
McLean, Charlie, *53*, 54, 139. *See also*
female impersonators; Y-Emmas
McLellan, William John, 56–57, 124
McNeil, Bill, 148, 151
"Medals on My Chest" (Waite), 85
military audiences, 82–83; alienation and,
79, 99; disconnection with civilians, 79;
reaction to war myth, 83; taste in music,
25; wartime experience, 34, 69. *See also*
"It's a Long Way to Tipperary"; morale;
philanthropists; Milligan, Spike, 144
mimesis, 120
mimicry, 120
minstrel shows, 11–12, 28, 43, 44; American, 11; blackface in, 11, 12, *12*; concert
parties and, 28
Mons, 23, 67, 68, 70; Armistice concert at,
33, 70; Grand Theatre at, 70; theatre
school at, 37, 54, 125. *See also H.M.S.
Pinafore*
Monty Python and the Holy Grail (1975),
87–88
Monty Python's Flying Circus, 87, 88, 109,
110, 144

moral ambiguity, 30
morale, 1, 67, 83, 91, 126; civilians and, 99;
concert parties and, 35, 47, 54, 89, 144;
contempt, sharing of, 93; Dumbells
and, 67, 71, 91, 143; emotional exhaus-
tion and, 75; female impersonators and,
125; funding for, 37; humour and, 36;
importance of, 1, 35; mandate, 152;
morale-building tools, 110; need to
raise, 2, 15, 142, 149; rum and, 111; of
soldier-entertainers, 62; YMCA and, 47,
48, 50. *See also* alcohol; concert parties;
Captain Merton Plunkett
Morrison, Stanley, 4, 59
Murray, Alan, 63, 69, 102, 107, as female
impersonator, 118, 122–23
music as therapeutic, 23
music hall tradition (British), 2, 9–34,
77; appropriation of, 2; catchphrases,
32; comedic aesthetics, 16; connecting
soldiers and civilians, 34; drag in, 119;
form and content, 13; French revue, 11;
humour in, 75, 76, 104; influence of, 6,
16; as low culture, 100; as melancholy,
32; nonsense in, 113; popular musical
trends in, 16; soldiers' love for, 16, 17;
songs, 32, 84; as sources of material, 16.
See also female impersonators; minstrel
shows; sentimental songs
musical comedy, 29, 31, 121. *See also*
female impersonators
"My Motta," 108
"My Old Dutch" (Charles Ingle), 19

Napier, Jack, 26
nationalism, 7; pan-Canadian, 126
Nettleingham, F.T., 23
Newman, Red, 4, 54, 85, 128–29, 139; as
actor, 101–2; death, 129; at Dumbell
reunion, 147, 148; as gas victim, 106,
107; songs performed, *14*, 19, 20, 85,
113; in Y-Emmas, 56, 107
New York Evening Telegraph, 136

O'Connor, Tommy, 12
officers, 69; as butt of concert-party skits,
69; green officers, 90; postwar derision
for, 93; relationships with performers,
91–92

"Oh, It's a Lovely War" (Long, Scott, and Felman), *14*, 24, 84–85, 126, 145

Oh! What a Lovely War (1969), 24

"The Old Barbed Wire," 111–12

"Old Bill," 22

Old Nick, 91, 92

"On the Staff," 89–90

Originals, 128, 139, *140*, 148, 207n41; cast, 139; reunion, 209n86

The Other, 26–28; French-Canadian soldiers, 26; immigrants as comedic course, 27; non-white soldiers, 27. *See also* minstrel shows; racism

pacifists, 15

"Pack Up Your Troubles in Your Old Kit Bag" (George Asaf and Felix Powell, 1915), 20

Parker, Grace Julia (later Lady Drummond), 99

parody, 10, 32, 86, 98, 111; acceptable, 32; *The Duchess Entertains*, 101; of privileged classes, 92; of songs, 32, 84; tailored, 98; as way to relate to soldiers, 3. *See also* comedy; satire; soldier humour

Passchendaele, 59, 60

The Passing Show of 1915 (revue), 29

patriotism, 25, 79

The Pavilion, 62

peace, 70–73

Pembroke, Captain H.E., 45

performances, 40, 50, 72, 121; admission, 40; conditions, 4, 44, 50; content, 26; cost, 37; first concert party, 44; improvement of, 51; logistical support for, 40; material for, 32; at Mons, 67–70; theatres, 62; transportation, 40; in war zones, 40, 50–52, 62, 63. *See also* civilian audiences; Dumbells; military audiences; PPCLI CC; soldier-entertainers

performers, 78, 81; in active duty, 59, 61; bond with audience, 98; cast make-up, 40; combat readiness of, 45; as fellow soldiers, 4; guilt and thankfulness, 60; injuries and death, 47, 59, 92; made permanent, 47; officers and, 91–92; poaching of, 55, 56, 58; rations,

62; shared experience with audience, 78; special treatment, 61. *See also* soldier-performers

philanthropists, 99–100; parodies of, 101. *See also The Duchess Entertains*

Pike, Ernest, 19

Plunkett, Al, 19, 60, 100, 122, 132; alcoholism, 135; in blackface, 9, 28; as crooner, 54; "Everybody Slips a Little," 30; in Maple Leafs, 54; matinee-idol looks, 33, 54; in new cast, 138; post-Dum bells, 135; on radio, 128; Ross Rifle, 96; wounded, 3, 50, 59; at Y smoker, 50. *See also* Dumbells; Maple Leafs; Captain Merton Plunkett

Plunkett, Captain Merton ("Mert"), 67, 71, 100, 192n74; 192n76, 193n98; background, 49–50; business dealings, 132, 133, 138–40; casting, 67, 68, 125; compositions, 138; definition of permanent concert parties, 50, 52–54; death, 143; Major General Lipsett and, 92; management of Dumbells, 53, 65, 125; most important soldier-entertainer, 44; postwar plans, 68; profits from Dumbells, 206n10; as saviour, 60; scouting, 50, 56, 60; Second World War and, 143; women in Dumbells, 125; with YMCA, 49, 106. *See also* Dumbells; Maple Leafs; *H.M.S. Pinafore*; theatre school at Mons; Y-Emmas

Plunkett, Morley, 54, 138, *139*

popular songs, 18–26, 86, 118; risqué, 29–33; as safety valve, 117. *See also specific titles*

PPCLI CC (Princess Patricia's Canadian Light Infantry Comedy Company), 2, 4, 53, 68, 91, 121; amalgamation with Dumbells, 69, 70; amateur nature of, 69; first official performance, 45–47; independent spirit of, 69; legacy, 149; marching orders of, 51, 67; "Miss Skinny," 114; original cast, 45; origins, 41–44; photos of, *59, 64, 115*; resourcefulness, 51; Royal Performance, 63–65; satire of, 44; sketches, 101; success, 46, 47, 51, 52; Vimy Ridge and, 52, 62. *See*

also Lieutenant Colonel Alexander Hamilton Gault; Jack McLaren
PPCLI Comedy Company. *See* PPCLI CC
Priestley, J.B., 25
Princess Patricia's Canadian Light Infantry's Comedy Company. *See* PPCLI CC
private citizens: failed attempts to entertain troups, 100
professional entertainers, 37–38
prostitution, 121

racism, 11, 27. *See also* minstrel shows; "The Other"
radio, 127–28
ragtime, 13
recording sales, 137
recruiting song, 23
Redheckles, 73
Red Patches, 58
Redpath, Bill, 16, 50, 60, 148, 209n88
repertoires, 20, 26, 76, 95–129; class parody in, 92–93; criticism of superiors, 89–93; effect of war on, 3; fusing high and popular culture, 100; influences on, 13, 15–17; lack of censorship of, 91; musical content, 2, 13, 15–17; risqué material, 118; parody, 98; subversive material, 83; taste of enlisted men, 76; topical material, 98; treatment of standards, 32; uniquely Canadian perspective, 98, 125; writers for, 89. *See also* comedy; female impersonators; music hall; sentimental songs; sketch comedy; soldier humour; themes
revues, 10, 11, 13, 22, 32, 85; concert-party revue, 28; Dumbell, 7; French, 10, 11; influence of, 29; in London, 17; popular revues, 29, 31; popularity with Canadian soldiers, 29; ragtime in, 13; social criticism in, 88. *See also* music hall; *specific revues*
Rice, Sergeant Gitz, 4, 43, 147, 201n58, 201n59; as gas victim, 4, 106; as songwriter, 106, 107, 111, 116
Richardson, Private Charles Douglas, 52
"The Rose of No Man's Land" (Caddigan and Brennan), 18

"Roses of Picardy" (Frederick E. Weatherley and Haydn Wood), 18
Ross Rifle, 95–99; abandonment of, 97; parody of, 32, 98–99; problems with, 96
Royal Canadian Legion, 146

sarcasm, 36, 81–82, 125; playful, 24. *See also* black humour; soldier humour
satire, 10; 32, 44; adaptation as, 84; limits of, 89–90; as mirror, 125; of military system, 86–89; of superior officers, 89–93; topical nature, 44; in vaudeville, 10; of war and heroism, 83–86. See also PPCLI CC
Saturday Night Live, 145
Savage, Charles Henry, 25
Second Battle of Ypres, 104, 105, 106. *See also* gas
Second World War, 142, 143; entertainers in, 143, 144
sentimental songs, 18–26; lack of jingoism, 26; love of home, 25; patriotic and quixotic anthems, 23; persuasive techniques, 19; popular love songs, 20; to soothe audience, 19
sets, 51. *See also* improvisation
sex and soldiers, 120–21
sheet music sales, 13, 117, 137, 138
Sheridan, Mark, 20
"Shirts," 88
silliness, 113–17. *See also* vaudeville; female impersonators
singalongs, 24, 38, 50, 106, 118. *See also* smokers
"Sister Susie's Sewing Shirts for Soldiers," 18
sketch comedy, 2, 34, 51, 56, 110; Dumbells as pioneers, 2; music hall, 10; minstrel show influence, 12; subject matter, 112
Small, Ambrose, 133
smokers, 19, 38, 106. *See also* Captain Merton Plunkett; YMCA
soldier-entertainers, 1–6, 68, 69, 70, 121; active duty for, 63; attuned to audience, 77, 108; closeness to battle, 44; humour of, 83; individual performers, 43;

influences, 12, 32; legacy, 88; military tasks for, 63; morale of, 62; parody of privileged classes, 92; as soldiers, 3, 92; special treatment of, 61. *See also* concert parties; Dumbells; *H.M.S. Pinafore*, PPCLI CC; Captain Merton Plunkett

soldier humour, 2, 3 , 6, 7, 23, 36, 75, 141; catchphrases, 32; civilian reaction to, 118, 141; coded, 78–80, 82; death as fair game, 79; to disable horror, 35, 36, 82; emerging, 76; evolution of, 75, 104; as exclusive, 10, 77, 78, 80, 81, 95; gallows humour, 108 in-jokes as bonding, 80; key to, 77; mechanics of, 6; metamorphosis of, 20; mockery, 75; pacifism and, 24; as safety valve, 81, 83; self-referential, 79; shared experience and, 77; trench humour, 82. *See also* black humour; comedy; mockery; parody; satire

soldier slang, 4–5

"Someday I'll Make You Love Me," 20

Steenvoorde Nine, 46, 52, 59

Stephens, Conrad, 69

Steward, Colonel, 63

subject matter: limits on, 104

subversiveness, 83; taboo subjects, 109; targets of, 75; in trench newspapers, 79; unwritten code, 109. *See also* black humour; concert parties; mockery; morale; satire; trench newspapers

taboo subjects, 2, 109

"Take Me Back to Dear Old Blighty" (Mills, Godfrey, and Scott), 20–22

"Take Me Back to the Land of Promise" (Gitz Rice), 116

Tate, Harry, 32

Tennent, Bill (Dumbell), 16, 20, *21, 31*, 68; in blackface, 28; "The Cobbler's Song," 29; with Dumbells postwar, 134; gassed, 107; "Hello My Dearie," 123; home, 131; in Originals, 139

Thalberg, Irving, 103

theatre, Canadian, 2, 9; development of, 75–76; domination by British music hall, 9; racist traditions in, 11. *See also* music hall; racism

theatre school at Mons, 54, 125. *See also* female impersonators

themes, 95-129; alcohol, 110-12; gas, 104–10; philanthropists, 99–100; Ross rifle, 95-99; silliness, 113–17; women, 117–25. *See also The Duchess Entertains*; female impersonators

"These Wild, Wild Women Are Making a Wild Man of Me," 33

Thiepval (1916), 51

"Three German Soldiers," 118

"Till We Meet Again" (Egan and Whiting), 20

Tin Pan Alley style, 13–15

Toronto Star radio, 128

trench newspapers, 78–79. *See also* soldier humour

troop journals. *See* trench newspapers

Vachon, Séraphin, 11–12

vaudeville, 10, 12, 76, 114, 125; in Canada, 10, 38; and concert-party comedy, 126; in London, 65; military procedure compared to, 89. *See also* minstrel shows; satire; sketch comedy

veterans: peacetime difficulties of, 146. *See also* Canada Corps Reunion

Victoria Palace, 65, 132

Vimy Ridge, 2, 59, 62, 78, 126; gas attack at, 106; Harry Lauder and, 37; troop movement towards, 51, 52; Murray and Hamilton at, 82. *See also* Leonard Young

The Volatiles, 56, 58

Wayne and Shuster, 144, 145

Weartherly, Frederick E., 18

West End (London), 66

"Where Did That One Go To?" 79

The Whizz Bangs, 58

The Wipers Times, 78. *See also* trench newspapers

women: absence of, 95, 103; as performers, 125, 141; as reason for fighting, 119. *See also* Dumbells; female impersonators

The Woodpeckers, 58

The Y-Emmas, *53*, 54, 56, 107, 128. *See also* Red Newman; Captain Merton Plunkett

Yes, Uncle (revue), 31

YMCA, 47–50; singalongs, 38. *See also*
    Captain Merton Plunkett

Young, Leonard, 4, 45, 55, 59, 107

Zig Zag (revue), 31, 123–25